First Edition

HISTORY AND FILM

MOVING PICTURES AND THE STUDY OF THE PAST

Maarten Pereboom
Salisbury University

Routledge
Taylor & Francis Group

LONDON AND NEW YORK

First published 2011 by Pearson Education, Inc.

Published 2016 by Routledge
2 Park Square, Milton Park, Abingdon, Oxon OX14 4RN
711 Third Avenue, New York, NY 10017, USA

Routledge is an imprint of the Taylor & Francis Group, an informa business

Cover Designer: Bruce Kenselaar

ISBN-13: 978-0-13-193846-5 (pbk)

Library of Congress Cataloging-in-Publication Data

Pereboom, Maarten L
    History and film : moving pictures and the study of the past / Maarten Pereboom. — 1st ed.
        p. cm.
    Includes filmography and webliography.
    Includes bibliographical references and index.

    ISBN-13: 978-0-13-193846-5

    1. Historical films—History and criticism.   2. Motion pictures and history.   I. Title.
    PN1995.9.H5P45 2010
    791.43'658—dc22
                                                                            2009025661

CONTENTS

PREFACE

I hope that you are drawn to read this book, as I was drawn to write it, by a love for both history and film. The exploration of the human experience, whether in words or images, can never fully reconstruct the past with absolute accuracy, but it is a vital human endeavor nonetheless. Moving pictures, projected images of real or staged activity, have become an integral part of human life today, as a wonderfully effective means of entertaining and informing. Studying history through film involves much more than simply scrutinizing movies for historical accuracy, though that is an important part of the analysis. Moving pictures also offer a vast trove of historical information and insight, and learning how to work with them will enable you to enjoy and engage moving pictures on multiple levels and to understand the human experience with a greater degree of sophistication.

This book presents different ways of thinking about history in film. For example, in a history course, or maybe just flipping channels one evening, you may see all or part of *War and Peace*, a movie about the Napoleonic wars set in Russia. You could assess its historical accuracy if you had studied the scholarship on the subject, whether it dealt with the wars themselves or with Russian society at the time. You could comment on how accurately it reconstructed that world based on what historians have been able to reconstruct themselves. Fair enough.

However, to appreciate and understand the historical merits of the film fully, you need to consider a number of issues. First of all, as just about everyone knows, *War and Peace* is a famously long novel written by the great Russian novelist Leo Tolstoy, and published serially between 1865 and 1869. Any film—and there are several, actually—called *War and Peace* is probably an adaptation of that novel. Natasha, Andrei, and Pierre are therefore fictional, not historical, characters. Napoleon is in the book, too, obviously a historical character, but also fictionalized to the extent that Tolstoy imagined many of the thoughts and actions portrayed in the book. Tolstoy devoted long passages in the book to his philosophy of history, but the telling of the story itself is in many ways more interesting to the historian, rich as it is with insight into the human condition. So in addition to the accuracy of the battle and drawing room scenes you would also want to discuss how the filmmakers adapted the qualities that made the novel so brilliant.

Then there's the film itself, as a film. The first version of *War and Peace* was a silent film made in Russia in 1915, during the First World War. You probably weren't watching that version. The two best-known versions are the 1956 Hollywood production, directed by King Vidor and starring Audrey Hepburn, and the mammoth 1967 Russian version, directed by Sergei Bondarchuk. As you can imagine, these films were made by very different filmmakers for very different audiences. To be able to comment effectively on either version as history, you need to explore who made the film, where, when, and why. Finally, the impact of the film is another matter of substantial historical interest. Was it or is it considered an artistic success? Did lots of people go to see it? Who has seen it since? Has it stood the test of time to become a classic? How, and to what extent, has it shaped people's perceptions of Russian life and history in the early nineteenth century?

Studying history in moving pictures is a complex undertaking, therefore, and this brief preface does not raise all the issues to be explored in this book. For students of history and students of film, it explores the rich potential of the medium as a historical resource. It is not a history *of* film, though Chapter 2 aims to promote thinking and discussion of the role moving images have played in human society since their invention. Subsequent chapters explore the fundamental categories we use in analyzing film as history, though it will also become clear that most movies do not fit in just one category. Later the book explores ways in which film can serve as an introduction to the diversity of world civilizations and cultures, albeit with limitations we must keep in mind. The last part of the book is aimed at launching you into your own historical research using moving pictures, with the firm warning that moving pictures alone cannot support historical research and analysis. The written work of professional historians remains the most common and reliable source of historical information and insight, but a rich body of film work exists to illuminate the extraordinary potential of film as a means of exploring the past, and one can hope that in the future more professional historians will make it their medium.

I would like to thank those anonymous peer reviewers from across the country who evaluated the manuscript or portions of it during the past few years. Writing a book is often a solitary exercise, but it is not possible without the help, support, and encouragement of family, friends, and colleagues. My own teaching experience and my involvement in the Quality in Undergraduate Education (QUE) project in the early 2000s helped convince me of the need for this book. Charles Cavaliere, my editor at Pearson, has provided invaluable assistance throughout the process. Diane Kunz read several chapters early on, and the following reviewers assisted at various points in the writing process: Eleanor Alexander, Georgia Institute of Technology; Scott Beekman, Ohio State University; Jesse Berrett, University of California, Berkeley; Martin B. Cohen, George Mason University; Andrew Feffer, Union College; Juan R. Garcia, University of Arizona; William B. Hart, Middlebury College; Caryn E. Neumann, Ohio State University; Molly Patterson, University of Wisconsin, Whitewater; S. Mike Pavelec, Ohio State University; Dona Reaser, Columbus State Community College; Dan Smith, University of Kentucky; Rosemary Stanfield-Johnson, University of Minnesota, Duluth; John Matthew Stockhausen, Ohio State University; Carolyn Williams, University of North Florida; Daryle Williams, University of Maryland. A sabbatical from Salisbury University in the spring of 2007 allowed me to get most of the manuscript drafted, and I thank all my

ABOUT THE AUTHOR

Maarten Pereboom is professor of history and dean of the Fulton School of Liberal Arts at Salisbury University. He earned his doctorate at Yale University, and his first book, *Democracies at the Turning Point: Britain, France and the End of the Postwar Order, 1928–1933*, earned *Choice Magazine*'s Outstanding Academic Book Award in 1996. In 1998 he won Salisbury University's Distinguished Faculty Award. He lives in Salisbury, Maryland, with his wife and their two sons.

1

Moving Pictures as a Historical Resource

The other night my twelve-year-old son walked into the room and asked: "*What* are you watching?" To him, it was some old black-and-white movie or maybe a *Twilight Zone* episode. Actually it was *Since You Went Away*, a three-hour sentimental drama from 1944 about a mother, Anne Hilton (Claudette Colbert), raising her two daughters (Jennifer Jones and Shirley Temple) alone while husband Tim is off to war. This was a "women's picture" made by producer David O. Selznick of *Gone with the Wind* (1939) fame, based on a "women's book" by Margaret Buell Wilder. It did well at the box office, earning almost $5 million, roughly double the cost of the production, and it was the third-highest grossing film of the year at a time when people went to the movies much more than they do today.[1] It was nominated for nine Academy Awards, including Best Picture, but won only for Best Musical Score. So, in its day, it was a "major motion picture."

In its day, fine—but how many people today have heard of it? What *was* I watching, and why was I watching it now? This movie is long, mildly entertaining as a classic, but rather offensive as well: making a face, a police officer tells family friend Tony (Joseph Cotten), getting ready to ship out, to "get one of them Japs for me," to everyone's merriment. I was watching the film as a historian: to me the film is a significant portrayal of Second World War American culture, an artifact that I might be able to use with my students to illuminate and discuss attitudes and outlooks from the time. One interesting sequence even leaps out at today's viewer as relevant to the topic of gay men serving in the military: might it be linked to *codes* used in other

---

[1] Susan Sackett, ed. *The Hollywood Reporter Book of Box Office Hits.* New York: Billboard Books, 1996, 51.

Hollywood films over the years to address that taboo subject? The movie's portrayal of African Americans is a topic that can be explored in a little more detail, beginning with one of its major characters, the domestic Fidelia, played by Hattie McDaniel. She does not have a last name, apparently, and her name makes a very obvious point about where an African American woman's virtue apparently lay in those challenging times: in loyal service to decent white folks. McDaniel played a role very similar to the one she had played in *Gone With the Wind*, and for which a stereotype was named: Mammy. While this portrayal may make today's audiences cringe, it is also historical evidence of how white filmmakers and their audiences viewed or idealized the roles of African-Americans in "their" society.

Since You Went Away is most interesting both as a presentation and as a representation of feminine virtue in wartime. Anne is our heroine, but her struggle is to find the best way to serve. Her epiphany comes through her final confrontation with town gossip Emily Hawkins (Agnes Moorehead), and in the end, Anne pushes off from her to become a welder in the local shipyard. Yet for us to use *Since You Went Away* as a historical resource, we need to study the broader context in which the film existed and exists, and that requires, among other things, studying its production to understand what the filmmakers intended the film to be and the reception the film received by critics and audiences. The fact that it did well in its own time suggests that it resonated with audiences, and brings us one step closer to the conclusion that viewers shared its values and attitudes. I would also look at this film as an example of, to quote the subtitle of a book by film scholar Jeanine Basinger, "How Hollywood Spoke to Women."[2]

A very different movie made fifty years later about the same war presents a very different story, but one which historians and film scholars also can study. Indeed, there are many books available on war films, and the Second World War in particular, including another one by Basinger.[3] *Saving Private Ryan* (Steven Spielberg, 1998) presents a fictional story set against the backdrop of the D-Day landings and subsequent push into France. I recently used the opening sequence of that film in my Second World War class, because I think it is an impressively realistic reconstruction of what the landings at Omaha Beach must have been like that morning of June 6, 1944. Afterwards we discussed how Steven Spielberg, working with cinematographer Janusz Kaminski, had used the "language" of film to portray and interpret the D-Day landings. My students pointed out the rapid succession of short takes and close-ups, to show the initial fear, confusion, and horror as the first men came ashore, the arbitrariness of who lived, who died, who got an arm or leg shot off. The brutality is relentless and the viewer is not spared the worst: the takes are short, but we can assume the men seeing these things

[2] Jeanine Basinger, *A Woman's View: How Hollywood Spoke to Women, 1930–1960*. New York: Knopf, 1993.
[3] Jeanine Basinger and Jeremy Arnold, *The World War II Combat Film: Anatomy of a Genre*. Middletown, CT: Wesleyan University Press, 2003.

first hand did not linger or stare either. My students also commented on the absence of music and the cinematographer's choice of a washed-out color palette. One suggested that redder blood might be harder to take, but another commented that the color scheme corresponds to soldiers' descriptions of what they remember. As the men progress toward establishing a beachhead, the camera pulls back to give us a longer view, and the takes are also longer in duration. A student who had been to the Normandy beaches described the differences between what he saw there and what was portrayed in the film. We were all keenly aware that what we were watching was a reenactment and therefore not real, but despite its necessary limitations as such, it gave us insights into a pivotal moment in the history of the Second World War, based on the perspectives of those who experienced it firsthand.[4]

My point in showing the clip was to give students a sense of the Omaha Beach landing that I could not convey in words and an opportunity to focus on a pivotal moment in the Second World War. An outstanding director, working with the best talent in the filmmaking business, supported by a prolific and widely respected historian of the Second World War, Stephen Ambrose, and a big-studio budget had reconstructed the landing in a way that made the past come to life. While I am certain that my in-class PowerPoint presentations have a similarly riveting effect on my students, this scene from *Saving Private Ryan* is brilliant, and it engages students with the realities of combat to the limited extent that one can do that apart from the real thing.

These are two very different films, but both have something to contribute to our understanding of the Second World War and its enormous impact. They have different relationships to the events in question, but once we establish what those relationships are, these films become pieces of evidence and works of interpretation that can enhance our understanding of this massive event in ways that words alone cannot. This book is intended to give you the knowledge and skills necessary to make use of film as a historical resource. To do that, you must be able generally to determine a film's historical context. Once you can identify the relationship of a specific moving picture to a historical problem you wish to address, your research into its content, production, and reception can yield valuable insights into that problem.

MOVING PICTURES, HISTORY, AND CULTURE

The ability to view recorded moving pictures has had a major impact on human culture since the development of the necessary technologies over a century ago. For most of this time, people have gone to the movies to be entertained and perhaps edified, but in the meantime television, the videocassette

---

[4] Thanks to Grant Albertson, Halston Ericson, Brittany Krempel, Philip Portier, Thai Hilton, Matthew Miller, and Andrew Webster for their contributions to this discussion in History 452/552, October 9, 2007.

recorder (VCR), the digital versatile disk (DVD) player, the personal computer (desktop and laptop), the Internet, and other technologies have made watching moving pictures possible at home, in the classroom, and just about anywhere else. Today, moving images are everywhere in our culture. Every day, moving-picture cameras record millions of hours of activity, human and otherwise, all over the world: your cell phone makes a little video of your friends at a party; the surveillance camera at the bank keeps an eye on customers; journalists' shoulder-carried cameras record the latest from the war zone. We call this actuality footage, in that it purports to be recording and presenting real or actual life. At the same time, across the world, film artists work on all kinds of theatrical productions, from low-budget independent projects to the next big-budget Hollywood blockbuster. As we shall see, the lines between actuality footage and theatrical productions on film can blur or be blurred, but it is an important distinction to bear in mind.

Moving pictures have had a great influence on human culture, and this book focuses on using moving images as historical evidence. Studying history means examining evidence from the past to understand, interpret, and present what has happened in different times and places. We talk and write about what we have learned, hoping to establish credibility both for what we have determined to be the facts and for whatever meaning or significance we may attach to our reconstruction of the past. Studying history is a scientific process, involving a fairly set methodology. We tend to favor written sources, and we have tended to favor writing as a means of presenting our views of the past. But historians also use all kinds of other documents and artifacts in their work of interpreting the past, including moving pictures.

Of course, just because something is written down does not make it true: as historians we need to determine—or sometimes just make the best educated guess we can—who wrote the words, why, where, and under what circumstances. Likewise, the appearance of a moving image on a screen *can* provide us with historical evidence, but we need to learn more about moving pictures in general and the circumstances and characteristics of that particular moving picture to be able to use it as legitimate historical evidence. This book focuses on the use of moving pictures as historical evidence, but one point that will become evident quickly is that film and video also offer an alternative to writing as a way of presenting historical interpretation. They are unlikely ever to *replace* writing entirely, but they have become a very important medium for presenting the past. Indeed one could argue that, to understand our collective understanding of the past as a society, one cannot ignore the presentation of the past as we see it presented in documentary and narrative films.

Our culture is the human environment in which we live: while each of us is different, we are also similar in important ways. The anthropologist Karl Heider has defined culture as ideas about behavior that groups of people learn and share. It might also be described as a whole society's way of life, as demonstrated in a wide variety of activities, including, for example, religion, politics, food, sports, art, and music. Probably the best way to understand what culture is, or what distinguishes one culture from another, is to visit a foreign culture, or to explore a subculture within your own society: there are particular qualities we can identify in Anglo-American culture, in African American culture, or in Latino culture that make them unique. We can learn about these through film, but film can just as well take us inside the lives of those whom we might consider to be "other" and show us that, essentially, we are not different at all. On a global scale, film gives us opportunities that real life unlikely will: to learn about cultural similarities and differences in settings we are unlikely to ever experience. Real life also does not permit time travel, so to the extent a film represents and interprets the past, we can see and hear the past as recorded or recreated on film.

Culture shapes who we are and how we think. Our culture, or cultures, will be reflected in the ways we respond to historical evidence, and how we interpret that evidence. It is not the only factor—everyone has his or her own unique character and outlook—but it is an important one. Engaging effectively and meaningfully in the process of reconstructing and interpreting human experience requires an awareness of all the different factors that affect how we look at evidence—what we in the academics business call theory—and while we very much want to get on with the business of *doing* history, we do need to be able to describe and defend what we do and how we do it.

In doing historical research, we distinguish between primary sources—any kind of document or artifact that can be used to reconstruct the past—and secondary sources—interpretations of the past presented in articles and books. John E. O'Connor calls drawing moving pictures into the realm of historical research *moving image artifacts*. These can serve as both primary and secondary sources: they can document aspects of the human experience, or they can present an interpretation of the past. Compared to the written word, moving pictures possess both advantages and disadvantages. While they are unlikely to replace the written word as the main means by which historians practice their craft, they offer an invaluable resource for the study of the human experience, and the twentieth-century experience in particular: they can document the most significant events or the most prosaic details of life; they can present us with the everyday realities of our own culture or those of any other culture in the world; and they can document events as they happen and preserve them forever.

Without dismissing the historical significance of your cell-phone videos (you or your friends may change the world famously one day), the bank surveillance camera, or the nightly television newscast, this book focuses primarily on what we call movies or films, arrangements of moving images into narratives or documentaries that can last just a few minutes or several hours. The analytical skills we develop from studying movies as historical evidence are largely transferable to the study of film fragments available in archival and other sources. They may also guide you one day as you try your own hand at presenting historical insights using film or video. But for now, we will focus on moving pictures in the form we most often see them and in the form in which they most often aspire to "do history."

"Moving pictures" or "moving image artifacts" may sound a little awkward at first, but they represent attempts to refer generically to the body of material we want to study. More commonly we use the terms *movie* and *film*, which can be used interchangeably, to an extent: *movie*, short for *moving picture*, is more colloquial, and it is the word we are more inclined to use when we are talking about entertainment; *film* sounds a little more serious and highbrow, maybe even a bit snooty, but it better encompasses every kind of moving picture, whether feature-length or short subject, documentary or narrative. Its name derives from the physical entity on which the images and sounds are recorded, and from which they are projected, or at least used to be. These days the only place you are likely to see actual film projected is in a movie theater, and even there digital projection is beginning to replace film projection. Most major movies these days are still *film*ed, as opposed to digitally recorded. So while we may keep the term *film* around for old times' sake, *movie* may turn out to be the more enduring term.

We experience movies by going to the theater, watching a television broadcast, popping in a DVD (or maybe still a VHS [video home system] tape), or downloading via the Internet. We make distinctions among the kinds of movies we watch. Crudely, a narrative film is "fiction" to documentary's "nonfiction," but the distinction between "real" and "made up" is much more complicated and requires careful thinking. A biographical film, or "biopic," in which an actor plays a historical figure is not considered a documentary, even though it is, as the cliché goes, "based on a true story"; but some films labeled as documentary use actors to reenact scenes (though this makes some people uncomfortable), and others can be downright untruthful. Narrative movies can be of any duration, but conventionally they run between ninety minutes and two hours. Some of the all-time box office champions run much longer, such as Francis Ford Coppola's *The Godfather* (1972) at 175 minutes, James Cameron's *Titanic* (1997) at 194 minutes, and the already mentioned *Gone with the Wind* at 226 minutes, but longer films are a more costly and risky undertaking. At 219 minutes, Michael Cimino's *Heaven's Gate* (1980) became a legendary flop. Documentaries are less governed by convention, but the potential for commercial theatrical success is greater if a documentary is comparable to a normal narrative movie in length.

Their entertainment value may draw us to movies as a source of historical information and insight, but it can also present a barrier. Movies that are of historical interest may or may not be movies that we enjoy as entertainment. But if you are accustomed to watching movies without really thinking about them, you will have to learn to watch them more actively and analytically. For some, this may take some of the fun out of the experience at first, but education need not come at the expense of entertainment, or vice versa. Thinking, and responding intelligently and articulately to what we see in film or on television, can be fun! But it is also important. The psychologist Sam Wineburg has worked with young people to determine how they shape their views of the past and found that many of their ideas, correct or incorrect, come to them through movies and other electronic media.[5] Their understanding of the world can sometimes be a crazy patchwork of passively received ideas. We share an interest in ensuring that movies do not spread ignorance, and while we can hope that filmmakers seek and promote the truth, we have a responsibility to pursue the truth actively ourselves, and certainly never rely on a single source.

STUDYING HISTORY IN FILM

In 1931, renowned historian of ideas and president of the American Historical Association (AHA) Carl Becker told his fellow academicians that, while they might claim ownership of the study of the past, the understanding and memory of the past belongs to everyone: "Berate him as we will for not reading our books, Mr. Everyman is stronger than we are, and sooner or later we must adapt our knowledge to his necessities."[6]

Movies make that point powerfully: the movie industry is responsible for countless representations of the past, but it is an industry in which professional historians have very limited influence. Historians themselves have been reluctant to embrace film as a source of historical information and insight, for reasons having to do mainly with tradition and training. Historians traditionally have been most comfortable with print sources, and they tend to respect most those works of historical scholarship that are based solidly on archival sources. Most of them would acknowledge the value of still and moving images as documents, but most are still most comfortable with the written word as the means by which they convey their own historical interpretations. The AHA does present an award in recognition of the "outstanding interpretations of history through the medium of film or video," named in honor of John O'Connor, but, effective as these films are, very often the filmmakers honored do not have graduate training in history.

The "fun" factor is another reason why some might view film skeptically as a significant historical resource. Watching films is usually associated with recreation, and recreation is not often associated with serious scholarship. (It should also be noted that academics are not above an occasional bit of snobbery or status consciousness.) This is a problem, but for a different kind of reason. Too many students have been babysat with movies in school, and I have had to train students not to put their heads down and their notebooks away when I use film in class. Using film as a scholarly tool requires some significant reorientation, though it does not mean abandoning the "fun" element altogether. It does mean learning to enjoy engaging your mind and senses to develop your knowledge and insights. It means *studying*

---

[5] See, among other works, Sam Wineburg, *Historical Thinking and Other Unnatural Acts: Charting the Future of Teaching the Past*. Philadelphia, PA: Temple University Press, 2001.
[6] Annual address of the president of the American Historical Association, delivered at Minneapolis. December 29, 1931. *American Historical Review*, 37(2), 221–236.

film as you watch, rather than absorbing content passively and unproductively. Do not disregard a film's entertainment value, though, because that is relevant to the film's reception, an important element in its historical significance. You should be able to weigh your own enjoyment of a film against the experience of others: if this was a popular film, more people will have seen it and its impact will be that much greater.

Indeed, the film theorist and historian Siegfried Kracauer (1889–1966) argued sixty years ago, in a book called *From Caligari to Hitler: A Psychological History of the German Film*, that popular or commercial film more effectively represented the spirit of the times than more esoteric or "high art" films, and he identified in the German movies of the 1920s the stirrings of nationalism that would bring the Nazis to power in the 1930s. One needs to distinguish between movies as a reflection of society and movies as agents of change, and historians have debated his thesis ever since.[7] The lines of the debate are familiar to us in our own time, for example, as we discuss movie violence: does it reflect the violence in our society? Does it stimulate further violence? As historians, we can pose the questions more generally: how do movies reflect the realities of a particular time and place? How do they shape those realities? Any assertions we make, of course, must be carefully reasoned and supported, and they are subject to scrutiny and debate: that is precisely what the historical profession is about.

The study of history in film places us at the intersection of a number of academic fields, including film studies, which at different universities might find itself in the English, communications, or possibly its own department, or of course, the history department. The field of film studies includes the history of film, or the development of the medium over time, which is not what this book is about. It also includes film theory, or the ideas that scholars have developed about the nature and significance of the medium. Film theory is closely related to literary theory, and literary theory makes reference to history. Within the discipline of history, however, some scholars are more inclined toward empiricism, or interpreting the sources or evidence as he or she understands them in an effort to reconstruct an aspect of the human experience. Other historians are more theoretically oriented, interpreting the sources in light of what scholars argue or assert to be true of human nature in general or of a particular culture at a particular time. The study of theory suggests that academic study is not purely objective, but affected by our precepts and biases; it also suggests that those who consider themselves to be empiricists may be deluded about their own objectivity and the scientific nature of their work.

Theory can be very interesting, and it can be a lot of fun to argue about. Unlike theory in the hard sciences, this kind of theory can come and go and it can be debated endlessly. That does not discredit the importance of reflecting

---

[7] Robert Sklar, Film: *An International History of the Medium*. Englewood Cliffs, NJ: Prentice Hall and H.N. Abrams, 2001, 126–127. Kracauer's book is available from Princeton University Press' Classic Editions (2004).

on human behavior and positing ideas about how people and cultures operate, how they think, and how they know. In this book, we will examine the work of scholars who have thought about how to study film as a historical resource, and we will also discuss some of the ideas that have shaped literary and film theory in recent decades, because they may help to shape your analytical abilities.

Theory may help shape your general outlook, but specifically this book is about using film as a historical resource. It should prepare you to

1. analyze film critically, particularly for historical content, using it to gather information about the past, paying attention to the kinds of material and information it uses;
2. distinguish between a film's historical and fictional elements, and identify ways in which even the fictional elements may be a source of historical insight;
3. examine film as a historical or cultural artifact, answering questions about the production, content, reception, and historical context of a film;
4. use print and electronic sources effectively in the study of history in film;
5. use film effectively as a primary and/or secondary source in the study of historical topics; and
6. communicate insights effectively in writing that meets the standards of the discipline of history.

In general, this book is intended to guide you toward becoming a person who can contribute to discussions about history using film as a resource. It does not push a particular theory or assert any orthodoxy on the subject. Instead, it should prepare you to think openly, knowledgeably, and creatively about film and to write effectively about it. It should encourage you to read, and it should encourage you to watch lots of different kinds of films, conventional and unconventional, in a thoughtful and engaged manner, looking for evidence and patterns. As Robert A. Rosenstone writes, film itself is going to teach you things about history in film that this or any other book cannot.[8] While this book and others will lay out the issues to consider, the point is that you consider these issues as you watch and study films for clues about and insights into the past.

For an active and curious mind, film is an extraordinary resource that can, with limitations, transport you through time and space to situations you could otherwise visit only in your dreams or nightmares. Film enables us to experience vicariously (more inexpensively and with a greatly reduced carbon footprint) sights and sounds that otherwise would be accessible only to the most well-heeled and intrepid world traveler. It also enables us to gain a sense of that which we would never want to experience directly—the horrors and atrocities of warfare, for example—but which can help us to remember

---

[8] Robert A. Rosenstone, *History on Film/Film on History*. Harlow, England: Pearson/Longman, 2006, 1.

that which should not be forgotten and which can make us more sensitive to the suffering of our fellow human beings, past and present. It is *not* real—having seen *Saving Private Ryan* does not mean that you now have experienced what the soldiers who landed at Normandy experienced—but it aids the imagination powerfully in attempting to reconstruct and understand experience.

Finally, this book should prepare you to develop a set of skills that will help you personally and professionally throughout your life. Skills in research, analysis, and writing are of great value in today's workplace whether or not you choose to be a historian. But, like literature, music, and the visual arts, film is an important part of our shared culture and heritage. As a popular medium, it has both captured and become an important part of our experience as human beings. It can capture the specifics of a particular people, time, and place; it can capture basic truths about human nature common to us all; it can also capture ideals and fantasies that do not reflect everyday reality: but once we get to know the medium, including its strengths and limitations, the doors open wide.

My goal is to take as broad-minded an approach to the subject as possible, beginning with the notion that just about any film, whether it deals with the past or not, is a document that can be used to explain or understand some aspect of the human experience. Some documents are richer than others, however; if, for example, you were to conduct research on the *American Pie* (1999–) series as an indicator of the spirit, or *zeitgeist*, of turn of the millennium America, you might find something significant to say. However, you would really need to extract yourself from your personal enjoyment of the film to determine whether, with some objectivity, you can discuss its historical relevance. You need to ask yourself basic questions about the purpose, content, and response to the film, essentially whether the film can be taken seriously on any level as an exploration of the human experience. Persuading your audience that the *American Pie* series should be taken seriously might be an additional challenge. The filmmakers themselves might be more surprised than anyone to see articles about the films in scholarly journals. But *Fast Times at Ridgemont High* (1982) and *Dazed and Confused* (1993) do show up in scholarly studies, and in time *American Pie* might as well. Another danger of using very recent films set in the present is that your analysis may not really be historical, at least not yet. You can use film as a resource in the study of philosophy, or sociology, or any other academic subject, but this book is focused on history. Check with your professor, to be sure, but I would expect that any scholarship you do using this book as a guide will be expected to take up the concerns of the discipline of history, broad as they may be.

A course that explores history through film, or a research paper that does the same, should draw on films that do a particularly good job of exploring the past, or documenting the times in which they were made. Your favorite films and mine may not necessarily work well for a historical study. Good scholarship involves studying topics that interest and engage us personally, but there is also an important social dimension as well: will your topic interest and engage the broader community of scholars? Will your analysis be both de-tached and persuasive enough to pass review by your scholarly peers? That essentially is what we aim for when we write history. You may not aim to pub-lish your work, but you should aim to make it good enough to publish.

Watching films is time-consuming, especially in class, where your pro-fessor has to weigh the time spent viewing against time for discussion and analysis. Showing excerpts, or clips, or works to illustrate a point saves a lot of time, but a strong argument can be made for viewing a film in its entirety, and therefore choosing carefully those films that are rich in material we can identify as historical. Likewise, depending on the time that is available for your own research, you may want to identify films that show significant promise as historical documents or resources.

THE ALLURE AND PERIL OF THE "GRAND NARRATIVE"

A familiar tension between history and film is the notion that, in order to entertain, movies inevitably distort the historical record, diminishing the ability of film to educate people about the past. Another challenge for film-makers is the inclination to pronounce the last word in a "grand narrative" on a historical subject. It might be a little like the naïve assumption a college student might make that he or she could write a paper on the Vietnam War in ten pages. One certainly *can* summarize the history of the Vietnam War in ten pages, but it is certainly not going to present any original insights or advance our knowledge of that experience. A film in its standard two-hour format likewise cannot teach us comprehensively about major events. Because of the way we watch and experience movies, even historical movies usually have to focus on a few individuals, and they must, almost out of necessity, fictionalize aspects of the experience.

A film that makes this point, and which I like to use in my History and Film class because it is a rare exploration of the subject of history in film, is Atom Egoyan's *Ararat* (2002), a film about the making of a film about the Armenian genocide that took place within the Ottoman Empire during the First World War. The film links several stories set in contemporary Toronto with the history being presented in the film and with the story of the Armenian-American artist Arshile Gorky (1904–1948). The structure of the film is quite complicated, and those who might have hoped for a film that would simply "raise awareness" of the Armenian genocide—in the way *Hotel Rwanda* (2004) portrayed the 1994 genocide there or *Blood Diamond* (2006) portrayed the dark side of the diamond trade—got a little more than they bar-gained for. The art historian Ani (Arsinée Khanjian), who has written a biog-raphy of Gorky, becomes involved in the film project as a historical consultant. Her son Raffi (David Alpay), meanwhile, is detained by an airport customs officer (Christopher Plummer) who suspects that the film canisters he has taken back from Turkey contain contraband. The customs officer has a trou-bled relationship with his son Philip (Brent Carver), a security guard at the museum where the famous Gorky painting, "The Artist and His Mother," is being exhibited. His partner Ali (Elias Koteas) is an actor who plays a Turkish military official in the film. Raffi's girlfriend Celia (Marie-Josée Croze) blames Raffi's mother for the death of her father, heckles her at a public lecture, and attacks the Gorky painting at the museum. Ani had been married to Celia's father after the death of her first husband, Raffi's father, an Armenian who had carried out a terrorist attack against Turkish officials in Canada.

All in all, the intertwining of the stories may seem improbable and melodramatic to some, but the question we must ask is: where is the history in all this? Most obviously, it is in the film that Edward Saroyan (Charles Aznavour) is making, focusing on the experiences of Clarence Usscher (Martin Harcourt, a fictional actor played by a real actor, Bruce Greenwood), the U.S. doctor who bore witness to the events and wrote about them. However, the filmmakers allow certain factual distortions, including the looming presence of mystical Mount Ararat in an area where it would not have been visible. They also want to weave in the story of Gorky, who lived through these events prior to moving to the United States in 1920. His mother starved to death in 1918, and one of his most famous paintings, "The Artist and His Mother" (later 1920s), quietly expresses his enduring sorrow. Though Gorky is a historical person who did suffer through these events, the filmmakers do not have a verifiable account of his actual experiences at the time. But including him adds something to the film, they feel. Ani, incensed at what she sees as distortions, comes off as the purist scholar, storming through the set while the cast and crew are filming, prompting Harcourt to shout: "Who the f*** are you?"

In the midst of all the plotlines and melodramatic elements, the film suggests that people should not look to films to tell them everything they need to know on any particular historical subject. However, while Egoyan rejects the idea of a "grand narrative," the choice of the Armenian genocide as a topic is hardly incidental or accidental. Clearly this film does raise awareness about the Armenian genocide. But it cannot stand alone as an account of what happened, simply because the film does not intend to, nor does it provide a full explanation of what happened.

Also of interest to the historian is the film's portrayal of memory: the way events are remembered, and the role they play in people's lives. Raffi lives with the fact that his father was branded a terrorist; his father, in turn, presumably did what he did to settle a historical score. Raffi gets into an argument with Ali over his role as a brutal Turkish officer and issues of guilt. To the extent that the film focuses on any one character, it follows Raffi on a voyage of discovery of his own past and the past of the Armenian people.

My purpose here is not to tell you everything you need to know about this film, but rather to suggest that you see for yourself how it treats the past and what it has to say about the role that the past plays in people's lives. It certainly is a more complicated film than many you will see, and some viewers may fault it for that, but as a study of history in film it is very interesting and worthwhile viewing. The film was Canadian-made and got limited theatrical exposure in the United States, but it took several of Canada's top film awards (Genies), including best picture, and a variety of international awards, including one from the Yerevan Film Festival in Armenia itself. Needless to say, it has had its detractors as well. Some may simply dislike the film on artistic grounds, or they simply do not enjoy it. But politics play a role as well. The film itself acknowledges the ongoing dispute over the nature and significance of the events themselves, in the sense that, unlike the Holocaust during the Second World War, the perpetrators have never acknowledged responsibility for these mass deaths. By contrast, the Germans have acknowledged their guilt and in fact made a crime of Holocaust denial. It also makes a difference when denial is the stance of isolated individuals versus the position of a government. Additionally, however, at least one scholar has suggested that the reception of the film also was not positive among many Armenian-Americans. One is tempted to think that the film within the film would have provided the "grand narrative" that, despite its weaknesses as history, would have given audiences what it wanted, a compelling story that encompasses the principal realities of the genocide.

Ararat should stimulate viewers to learn more about the terrible fate of over 1 million Armenians in the Ottoman Empire during the First World War. But it also sets forth—in a film, obviously but significantly—many of the challenges of dealing with history in film. Most films you see will not be so self-conscious in their exploration of history, but that may not be a bad thing.

The chapters that follow explore the different ways in which you can study history through film. Differentiation and categorization of films is not an end in itself, but it should help you to determine precisely the relationship of the film material to the history in question and establish the analytical framework that you will need. You also need to know a little about film itself: how it is put together, how we analyze it generally, and how we examine its historical content specifically. This text also assumes that, in addition to preparation for and participation in class sessions, you will be doing your own research and historical analysis. But it also should help you if your plans are only to view film in a more leisurely but engaged manner.

In our pursuit of historical understanding, we should not overlook the fact that film is also an art form, no matter how commercialized it may have become. There is no reason why we should not be training our artistic sensibilities at the same time: to appreciate the "look" the cinematographers, set designers and costume designers have achieved, and how these work with sound design and music. Indeed, what we can say about the film's esthetics may well be related to its historic significance.

A final question is one that historians frequently ask themselves about their work: so what? Your goal in pursuing this study, and all your other studies, should be to advance your knowledge and to make you a better thinker and problem solver. The pursuit of knowledge, which your professors do because they enjoy it, also has real practical value. But before we proceed, we should think about why studying film as a historical resource matters. Robert A. Rosenstone has written about looking at film as history in a "postliterate age" and has encouraged his fellow scholars to increase their comfort level with film as a vehicle for "doing" history.

In the past that I have studied, leaders often referred to "public opinion" as a test for their policies and actions. Somewhat in that spirit, I suggest that, while many people in our world, and even in our own country, know very little about the past—they make for amusing contestants on *Are You Smarter Than a Fifth Grader?*—most people understand that the past has shaped who we are today, and the past also can contribute to our sense of who we are. Ignorance of specific facts is not as fatal as it would be for a surgeon, but we do have a collective need and a collective interest in understanding the past.

Portrayals of the past do matter. For example, even the recent film *300* (2007), which historians and film critics largely dismissed as a cartoonish distortion of a real historical battle between the Spartans and Persians at Thermopylae, was a big hit, especially with younger audiences. Some Iranians and others of Iranian origin took exception to the portrayal of the Persians as the "bad guys," particularly in a time when Iran was under fire, figuratively, in the international community generally and in the United States particularly as a member of the "axis of evil." It should be noted that other people of Iranian origin dismiss the film, or at least dismiss the film as serious history. I suppose we should be pleased if a significant number of viewers would even make the connection between ancient Persia and modern Iran, but to the extent that they do, a negative characterization does not pass unnoticed, particularly in sensitive times. It helps the filmmaker, and all of us, therefore, if the film aims for some level of historical accuracy if it is going to portray any aspect of the past at all.

History is our story and the story of all humanity. Studying it helps us to know ourselves better and the people with whom we live and interact in a diverse society and world. Movies provide us with a multisensory source of information for which we must develop analytical skills as well as a less tangible *feel* for the medium. It can be an enormously interesting and rewarding pursuit, if you put the time and effort into making yourself a bit of an expert on the subject and developing the research, analytical, and writing skills necessary to achieve and share your insights. As we pursue greater understanding of the human experience through film, I think you will find it to be richly rewarding for yourself, not just as a scholar, but as a person: you will have developed an ability to think and appreciate an art form on many different levels, an ability that you can use and enjoy throughout life.

Questions for Discussion:

1. How is studying movies for historical insight both similar to and different from watching movies purely for entertainment?

2. Why are so few professional historians filmmakers?

3. How does the film *Ararat* serve as both an introduction to and an example of the portrayal of history in film?

2

■ ■ ■

The Interaction of Moving Pictures and History

The ability to record visual information has transformed the human experience over the past century, as the multisensory appeal of moving images accompanied by sound has served as a means of entertainment, education, and even indoctrination. In the twentieth century, film and television have had a major impact on both private and public life, shaping the politics that affect the welfare of whole societies and affecting the experience of every individual living in technologically advanced societies. The influence of the electronic media on individuals, their thinking, and their behavior is a subject of much speculation, study, and controversy. But while individuals may disagree as to the precise effects, they would agree that the moving image has had a profound impact on the way we live our lives and the way we behave. The movies are one form of media, but the culture of motion pictures is a broader phenomenon, affecting us as we watch TV, listen to the radio, surf the Internet, or play video games.

In this chapter, we will explore the impact of moving images on the human experience. We will examine

- the role of moving pictures in twentieth-century history and
- movies' portrayal of the role of moving pictures in twentieth-century history.

There are many angles to this discussion, but one of the most interesting questions to consider is the *difference* that moving pictures have made. Life has changed so much with the revolutions in transportation and communications in the past century that this particular change is difficult to isolate, and yet no one would deny that their impact has been profound.

The influence of the electronic media on public life is a matter of ongoing debate as well. While, in the earliest days, thinkers embraced new technologies as instruments of progress, disillusionment set in as commercial media "pandered" to public tastes and humanity itself showed little sign of overall improvement as it plunged itself into ever more destructive conflicts. In the 1960s, the Canadian scholar Marshall McLuhan was hailed as "the spokesman of the electronic age," if not an oracle or prophet. His famous argument, "the medium is the message," suggested that, rather than simply functioning as a means of communication, television in particular (at that time) was a force in its own right, and he expressed a more common anxiety over the power of technology to overwhelm human civilization. More broadly, he believed that technology was the driving force in human history. McLuhan himself became a cultural phenomenon, and while he had his followers as well as his detractors, he played an important role in the history of thought about the electronic age. The emergence and growth of the Internet have renewed interest in McLuhan's thought on the influence of technology and media on human life.

Since the 1960s, we have become more comfortable with, or at least resigned to, the power of the media to shape both public and private life, with new technologies adding ever greater complexity to the picture. As scholars, we tend to focus on more specific questions: the impact of televised debating on the 1960 presidential election, for example, or more recently the effect of the Internet on election campaigns. Rather than view "the media" as a monolithic and menacing force, we should look at its various manifestations as human enterprises in which individuals and groups participate with varying degrees of influence.

Radio, film, and television have been powerful tools for the spread of ideas and issues. Compared to the more recent advent of the Internet, the older media appear to be one-way forms of communication, with the viewer passively receiving the information sent out by whoever controls the medium. During the twentieth century, and still today, regimes try to control the media. The Nazis used film to cultivate among the German people the illusion that they had restored stability and unity to a society threatened by chaos and Bolshevism. Communist states such as the Soviet Union did not permit private radio or television networks, hoping to "educate" the public in the virtues of socialism and eliminate subversive dissent. These are extreme examples, but the control of expression, or censorship, in the media was and is an issue for every society, including our own.

What history has shown is that the all-powerful, seemingly inhuman, state is an all-too-human creation. Likewise, even in our own society, "the media" have been vilified as a monolithic source of whatever is "wrong" with society. But, in fact, radio, television, film, and now the Internet are human activities carried out by all kinds of people, and the technology itself is becoming ever more difficult for any one person or group of people to control. As the printing press did five hundred years ago, the audiovisual media have dramatically affected the way human beings communicate with one another. The moving picture has recorded, preserved, and interpreted the human experience in ways that force us to think carefully about what history is and the role it plays in our lives. Assessing the historical significance of a moving image, a film, or a television program requires significant research and analysis, and even then the full impact of the moving image remains immeasurable in important ways.

This chapter explores the intertwined history of moving pictures and the broader social and political developments of the twentieth century. This is not a history *of* film: there are already many good books on film history. Nor is it an examination of the movies as a historical cultural phenomenon, though that comes closer to describing it: Robert Sklar's *Movie-Made America: A Cultural History of the American Movies* (1994) is one excellent place to look for a history of the movie's place in American culture. The impact of moving pictures on everything from the human psyche to human society to international politics is a complicated subject straddling many academic disciplines. This chapter describes the effects of moving pictures in twentieth-century history and how movies themselves have portrayed that impact.

Recognizing and understanding the innovations and techniques that characterize the history of film are important to understanding how films are put together today, and the presentation of time and events in film is of particular interest to the historian. Just as we, as writers of history, must decide how to present the past to readers, the filmmaker also has options. The filmmaker has to find ways of presenting events that make sense to audiences and entertain them as well. Though writing presents comparable challenges, film is a more expensive and more collaborative endeavor where financial stakes often have a decisive impact on what gets made and how it gets made.

FIN DE SIÈCLE AND THE EARLY TWENTIETH CENTURY

To understand fully the impact of the moving image both on daily and public life over the past century, imagine life in the late nineteenth century. Of course, for many people worldwide, the Industrial Revolution meant little or nothing: peasants still farmed the land as they had for centuries earlier, and in some remote places, people still lived as hunters and gatherers, never having met a European or an American. But for that part of the world developed through industrialization, the mass production of goods had made societies affluent and changed the look of cities over the course of the nineteenth century so that by its end, cities had electricity, "horseless" public transportation, and affluent citizens with time and money to spend in leisurely pursuits.

Two recent films that help us to imagine the world into which film would be introduced are Neil Burger's *The Illusionist* and Christopher Nolan's *The Prestige*, two movies about magic released in the United States within a month of one another in the fall of 2006. Neither movie dominated the box office or the awards ceremonies for 2006, but they both integrated interesting historical content into films of artistic merit that made money.

The Illusionist is set in and near Vienna, the capital of the Austro-Hungarian Empire, near the turn of the twentieth century. *The Prestige* is set in London, and partly in Colorado, at around the same time. Both are thriving and exciting places where we could imagine living quite comfortably. Advances in technology are broadly accepted as evidence of progress. Both cities have lively musical and theatrical offerings, and audiences are also eager to be thrilled with magic tricks that blur the distinction between illusion and reality. Prestidigitation is a precarious living, however: in *The Prestige*, Alfred Borden (Christian Bale) faces a fierce and deadly rivalry with another magician, Robert Angier (Hugh Jackman). In *The Illusionist*, Eisenheim (Edward Norton) uses his magic to win the beautiful, upper-class Sophie (Jessica Biel) away from the brutish Crown Prince Leopold (Rufus Sewell).

While historians love an authentic location shoot, these movies both rely on illusion—sets and believable locations—to simulate London and Vienna: *The Prestige* was shot entirely in the United States and *The Illusionist* was filmed in the Czech Republic. Both films portray audiences fascinated with magic, eager for innovation, and ever greater thrills, and specifically the tricks that can be played on our eyes and our sense of time, elements key to the "magic" of motion pictures. Nolan, who gained prominence with his inventive reversed narrative in *Memento* (2000), carries out his own sleight-of-hand in telling the story of *The Prestige*, underscoring the point that film itself is a form of illusion. *The Illusionist* likewise has its audience identifying with the audiences in the film, drawing parallels between our experience and theirs.

Part of *The Prestige* plays out in the United States, specifically near the laboratories of Nikola Tesla, the Serb-born electrical engineer and inventor who was a pioneer in bringing electricity to American cities. His work on such projects as a death ray for military use earned him a reputation as a mad scientist, a notion carried over into the film as Tesla (played by David Bowie) works on an invention that will help Angier defeat Borden. The invention is fictional, but corresponds generally to the sort of far-reaching inventive imagination Tesla, in fact, had. Though the destruction of his Colorado Springs facility by agents of rival Thomas Alva Edison is also a fiction, the rivalry itself was real. While we can trace the history of cinema in terms of developing technologies and evolving economies, these films remind us of significant aspects of the culture into which film was born: the surprise, wonder, and delight of the invention itself; the fierce struggle to shape and dominate the new industry; and the artistic and commercial imperative to keep the medium fresh and innovative.

An older film that captures the realities of American life in early days of film effectively is Milos Forman's *Ragtime* (1981), based upon the acclaimed and bestselling novel by E. L. Doctorow. One of the characters, Tateh (Mandy Patinkin), a Jewish immigrant from Eastern Europe, turns from silhouette drawing to filmmaking, an element that resonates with Robert Sklar's point that the pioneers of filmmaking often hailed from impoverished immigrant circumstances, and that poor urban dwellers were also among the first moviegoers.

These movies all portray life in the developed world before there were movies as we know them. The technological, artistic, and commercial roots of film are many, but historians of film can trace the first movie screening to a day in Paris in 1895. It is difficult for us to imagine paying to see women leaving a factory at the end of the day, but when the first moving pictures, more or less as we know them, appeared over a century ago, the thrill indeed derived from just seeing the picture move: it did not matter what it was that moved. Before long, however, filmmakers added new dimensions to the simple moving picture, driven forward both by artistic creativity and the desire to make money. Using their hand-cranked *cinématographe*, Auguste and Louis Lumière showed ten short films, each less than one minute long, to the first paying audience, at Paris' Salon Indien du Grand Café on December 28, 1895. The program included their first film, *Workers Leaving the Lumière Factory*. Albeit in primitive form, all the elements were in place for a commercial movie industry. The Lumière brothers, unlike many inventors, also knew how to make money, and they aimed to take their new invention across Europe and indeed throughout the world. The British and the Germans were making strides as well. But the Americans, keeping pace technologically but even more savvy about doing business, would soon dominate the young industry. One of the consequences of Europeans marching off to war in 1914 would be that America would consolidate that trend and assume a predominance that has lasted to this day.

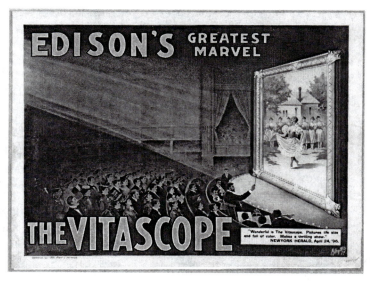

Images such as this 1896 poster advertising Edison's Vitascope help document the early days of motion pictures, when fierce rivalries and rapidly changing technology characterized an industry in its infancy. Note also how the picture frame around the screen and the conductor represent an attempt to market moving pictures as high art, not cheap amusement. *Source:* Courtesy of the Library of Congress.

The French were not done yet, however. Filmmaking pioneer Georges Meliès was also a magician, and it was perhaps that sensibility that led him to innovate in his film *A Trip to the Moon* (1903). Obviously he could not film an actual trip to the moon, and thus his film relied on special effects to create the illusion of a trip to the moon. He also showed that movies did not have to unfold in real time; one could go back in time and present the story from another point of view. Though an American film, Edwin S. Porter's *Life of an American Fireman* (1902), appeared to introduce the notion that one could go back and forth showing different points of view of the same events, that was a slightly later invention. In other words, his film originally first showed events outside the house from beginning to end, then inside the house from beginning to end. In 1903, his twelve-minute film *The Great Train Robbery* used multiple shots from different locations, edited to tell a thrilling story, rescuing a medium whose novelty had begun to wear off. This discussion reminds us that, in addition to making pictures move and presenting them in a commercially viable way, every technique of filmmaking that we take for granted today had to be invented.[1]

As has been the case with many other technologies, the inventor often did not reap the extraordinary financial rewards that moving pictures had to offer. In a new and largely unregulated environment, the competition was fierce and often unscrupulous. Similarly, the creative minds that produced the very first commercial films would soon be replaced by those that could build on the innovations to ever greater effect. D.W. Griffith (1875–1948) may not have precisely invented, as he claimed, some of the techniques he used in his films, but he certainly was able to take filmmaking to the next level: longer films, more visually exciting films, films that told ever more complicated stories. From 1908 to 1913, he worked for the American Mutoscope and Biograph Company, which had been founded as the American Mutoscope Company in 1895 and from 1909 was called just the Biograph Company. This company made and showed moving pictures, using their own invention, the Biograph, to project the films. Griffith was an extremely prolific filmmaker, and in 1910, he traveled west for the company to explore the possibility of establishing a studio in southern California, where varied topography and fine weather year-round offered ideal conditions for filmmaking. His movie *In Old California* (1910), notably a drama set in the days when California belonged to Mexico, made in a little town near Los Angeles, became the first Hollywood movie, and Biograph opened a studio in Los Angeles itself.

Griffith split with Biograph in 1913 when the studio would not support his production of the film *Judith of Bethulia*, deeming it too long for audiences. But Griffith was right that audiences would pay to see longer films, and in 1915, he achieved great commercial success with *The Birth of a Nation*,

---

[1] Robert Sklar, *Film: An International History of the Medium*. Englewood Cliffs, NJ: Prentice Hall, 1993, 32–42. Lavishly illustrated, and as the name indicates, this book provides a detailed international history of the origins of cinema.

a controversial film about the Civil War and Reconstruction. The full version of the film ran over three hours, and though banned in some cities for fear of incitement, became America's top-grossing movie until *Gone with the Wind* (1939). The version people commonly see now is about two hours, which has become the standard length for narrative feature films. Though its racism leaps out at viewers today and makes the movie painful to watch, at the time it demonstrated the extent to which filmmakers had created a cinematic experience for which people would be willing to sit for extended periods in a theater: a dramatic story told across a sweep of space and time, with scenes that could not be reproduced in a theater, including battle scenes that are still quite impressive today. Biograph also miscalculated on the phenomenon of the film star, and indeed one of Griffith's own complaints had been about the company's reluctance to credit him onscreen for his work. Vanity and celebrity were emerging as key elements of Hollywood culture. But Griffith himself would be eclipsed by the rapidly changing industry. His career declined in the 1920s, and he made only two more movies after the advent of sound.[2] Though the racism so blatant in this film became less virulent in future mainstream films, the presence or absence of African Americans and other minorities would continue to reflect the state of relations among different ethnic groups in American society. These divisions appeared also in the production of films and in their reception by audiences and critics.

From its earliest days, movies served multiple purposes: information, education, indoctrination, but above all entertainment. The movie-going experience evolved into a program that included newsreels and animated shorts. Newsreels date from the 1910s, and have their roots in the actual events filmed by the earliest filmmakers. In 1896, the Lumière brothers filmed the coronation of Russia's new czar, perhaps the first example of film being used politically, to solidify the new alliance between France and Russia. In presenting several news events in one film, as the newsreels did, Britain was first, with the Pathe Animated Gazette in 1910, followed by the United States, where William Randolph Hearst saw newsreels as a way to boost newspaper sales.

By the First World War, many industrialized countries had established film industries, and the fact that films were not accompanied by sound made it relatively easy for countries to compete internationally. With much of the world under colonial rule, European countries and the United States also dominated the film industry; even countries as small as Denmark and Sweden had strong industries. In the Americas, Brazil had a brief period in which it produced many of its own films, but Italian and French productions dominated there by 1914. The outbreak of war in 1914 severely disrupted Europe's global reach through film, however, and paved the way for U.S. predominance in the market.

---

[2] See Sklar, *Film*, 54–66. For a biography of Griffith, see Richard Schickel's *D.W. Griffith: An American Life*. New York: Limelight Editions, 2004.

THE ERA OF THE WORLD WARS, 1914–1945

The First World War had a profound impact on the world motion picture industry, but moving pictures, still relatively new, did not have a major impact on the conduct or course of the war itself. British and French forces had film units that recorded combat in a limited way, but rigid censorship ensured that whatever audiences might see of the war would be carefully controlled. A good deal of the footage was faked. Still, as the work of Roger Smither at the Imperial War Museum demonstrates, camera crews captured some remarkable moving images, and the story of the production and reception of these images reveals significant aspects of the conflict itself. The United States did not enter the war until 1917, however, and in the meantime American newsreels included footage that British or French censors would not have allowed. William Randolph Hearst, an Anglophobe, used film of the sinking of the British ship *SS Audacious* in 1914 in his newsreels, prompting boycotts from Britain and Canada. The Hearst-Selig News Pictorial also filmed the destruction of Louvain, Belgium, by German forces in the early months of the war.[3]

After the war, however, a kind of stunned silence ensued that would last until the late 1920s, when a rush of books, plays, and films began to appear, most highly critical of a war that appeared to have resolved few problems and indeed created a great many more. Most of these avoided entirely the political aspect of the war, and those that did not condemn war itself as senseless focused on the bravery of the soldiers rather than the righteousness of the cause. With its strong current of extreme nationalism, Germany was not as prolific as Britain or France in the output of antiwar works, but Erich Maria Remarque's *All Quiet on the Western Front* (1929) became the most famous one of all. This German antiwar novel, widely translated and a phenomenal bestseller that is still widely read today, became the basis for a largely faithful film adaptation by Lewis Milestone in 1930. It won the Best Picture Academy Award for that year, and like the novel it has become a classic.

Three years earlier, William A. Wellman's movie *Wings* (1927) became the first movie to win the Academy Award for Best Picture. In its quest for respectability for motion pictures in general, the Academy of Motion Pictures Arts and Sciences (AMPAS) instituted the Academy Awards ceremony to promote and highlight quality films. *Wings*, still quite interesting and enjoyable to watch today, tells the story of two friends who go off to war, longing for home and the girl next door as they engage in heroics in the skies over France. Clara Bow, who became known as the "it" girl because she had that difficult-to-describe quality that made someone a star, is not that girl

---

[3] See Louis Pizzitola's *Hearst over Hollywood: Power, Passion and Propaganda in the Movies*. New York: Columbia University Press, 2002. University of San Diego Professor of History Steven Schoenherr includes this incident in his timeline "History of the Newsreel" at http://history .sandiego.edu/gen/filmnotes/newsreel.html (accessed March 29, 2007).

The "Oscar" got its name in the 1930s, but the first Academy Awards ceremony took place in 1929 to honor films made in 1927 and 1928. The Oscar is not the ultimate arbiter of a film's quality or significance, but it is one significant indicator of a film's reception by the industry itself in the short term.   FABRICE COFFRINI / Staff

next door, but she brings energy to the film and, one world war before Rosie the Riveter said "We Can Do It," showed that women could do it then, too.

Though the "Great War" was not fondly remembered in the America of the 1920s, *Wings* achieved success by focusing on individual heroics rather than the merits of the cause itself. Viewers today may be surprised at its more risqué aspects, as the film was made before the Production Code aimed to restore "decency" in the 1930s. Viewers today may also be a little surprised at the portrayal of the strong relationship between the two men, not a romantic love but an intense bond nevertheless. The "buddy" film would become a popular and enduring genre, but it would also develop conventions aimed at assuring audiences that the characters were indeed "just friends," to ward off discomfort with or fear of homosexuality.

In America where a cultural divide existed between religious conservatives and those of a more secular orientation, the 1920s were a time of particular conflict. In 1925, a Tennessee high school teacher, John Scopes, was arrested and put on trial for allegedly violating the state's Butler Act, which forbade the teaching of any theory that denied the story of creation as presented in the Bible or asserted that humans evolved from a "lower order of animals." The trial itself almost literally became a media circus—trained monkeys performed on the lawn outside the courthouse in Dayton—but its historical significance grew when, in 1955, it became the subject of a successful play by Jerome Lawrence and Robert Edwin Lee, *Inherit the Wind*, which Stanley Kramer adapted for the screen in 1960. The play and film revived the nation's memory of an event that drew out powerful figures on either side of a growing cultural divide. If the 1950s and 1960s appeared to be a time when everyone would see the folly of such a conflict, that same conflict remains a part of public life today.

Though politically conservative, the 1920s also produced a more socially permissive climate as men and women alike enjoyed the "world's highest standard of living," including drinking (though made illegal by Prohibition) and smoking, and the movies. For conservative Christians, movies were added to a list of vices including card-playing, gambling, and activities such as bicycle riding on Sunday. To build up the respectability of the movies, and to forestall possible external censorship of their work, producers embraced what became known as the Production Code, with its three general principles:

1. No picture shall be produced that will lower the moral standards of those who see it. Hence the sympathy of the audience should never be thrown to the side of crime, wrongdoing, evil, or sin.
2. Correct standards of life, subject only to the requirements of drama and entertainment, shall be presented.
3. Law, natural or human, shall not be ridiculed, nor shall sympathy be created for its violation.

Enforced from 1934, they remained in place until the Motion Picture Association of America established its ratings system in 1967, aimed similarly at self-policing the content of Hollywood productions and placating those with an impulse to judge movies as subversive, decadent, or immoral.

The prospect of eternal damnation did not appear to be bad for business, however, and the movies were now a prominent feature of American cultural life. Movie audiences had grown during the first third of the century to the point where 65 percent of Americans went to the movies weekly by 1930, the high point for the century. That percentage dropped during the Great Depression to about 40 percent in 1934, but rose again to about 60 percent ten years later, during the Second World War. But after that, especially because of television, the percentage would decline steadily—with a brief up tick in the mid-1950s as movies fought back with big-screen epics and drive-in theaters—to about 10 percent in the late 1960s, where it has stayed ever since. But while that was bad news for the theaters, the movies themselves would find their way into homes through television broadcasts and later through videotape and DVD.[4]

---

[4] Michelle Pautz, The Decline in Average Weekly Cinema Attendance, 1930–2000, *Issues in Political Economy* 11 (2002), http://org.elon.edu/ipe/pautz2.pdf (accessed February 19, 2008).

The 1930s brought the World Depression and severe economic hardship to much of the developed world. Though for many Americans, poverty was so great that movies were simply not a part of their lives, the movies offered inexpensive entertainment for millions and the film industry continued to do well. Historical dramas and other "prestige pictures" garnered awards, but comedies and musicals, such as the Fred Astaire-Ginger Rogers movies, have proven to be the more popular classics from the era, offering audiences escape and lighthearted entertainment then and now. Backstage musicals such as *42nd Street* (1933) and *Gold Diggers of 1933* (1933) showed that entertainers had to struggle against the Depression like everyone else. Adventure movies such as *King Kong* (1933) and *Gunga Din* (1939) were popular as well, while material directed specifically at younger audiences, such as the comic book–based *Flash Gordon* series (beginning in 1936), proved formative in the lives of millions, including future filmmakers.

Woody Allen's 1985 film *The Purple Rose of Cairo* evokes this era, in which studios cranked out enough pictures for people to go to the movies several times per week. Films could be seen more than once, of course, but once they were gone from the theater, in most cases, that was it. A New Jersey housewife, Cecilia (Mia Farrow), escapes the unhappiness of her life with an abusive husband by going to the movies whenever she can. The man of her dreams, Tom Baxter, is a character in the film *The Purple Rose of Cairo*, played by Gil Shepherd (played by Jeff Daniels). The film's magical element appears when Cecilia's feelings, instead of reaching helplessly at the screen, evoke a response: Tom speaks to Cecilia and steps from the screen. The two start a romance that is both touching and comic, given the layers of reality through which the viewer must sort. Cecilia relates to a friend that she is in love, conceding that "he's fictional, but you can't have everything." Viewers are more than willing to accept the ruse, because, more than being merely clever, it shows precisely how the movies play out our fantasies, in part because of the way they can appear to break the laws of nature.

The emergence of the movies as a form of mass entertainment also raised the possibility that "the masses" could be swayed in their opinions. The term "propaganda" is often associated with political extremism, and indeed one can identify examples of it from Nazi Germany and Soviet Russia, in particular Leni Riefenstahl's *Triumph of the Will* (1935), which portrayed Germany's National Socialists as they wished to be portrayed: strong, orderly, restoring glory to Germany. The impact of such a film is difficult to assess, given that "the masses" already supported the regime and in any case had little choice in the matter once the dictatorship was in place. It won some acclaim outside Germany, at the 1936 Venice Bienniale and the 1937 Paris World Exhibition, but in its own time, it was principally a film for German audiences. Unlikely to win over converts, it excited the already excited and intimidated those who were less so.

In the democracies, governments stepped into filmmaking primarily during wartime. In the United States, Pare Lorentz' films promoting New Deal programs, *The Plow That Broke the Plains* (1936) and *The River* (1938), were greeted with suspicion, especially from conservatives; both are very

Throughout the world, movie houses serve as cultural artifacts that illuminate the historical significance and universality of the film medium. The Ciné Afrique in Stone Town, Tanzania, bears some resemblance to the 1930s Art Deco palaces one might find elsewhere, but shows some indigenous influence as well.   *Sources:* © Remi Benali/ CORBIS All Rights Reserved.

interesting films to view and to study today as unusual forays into peacetime propaganda. During the Second World War, however, many films promoted the war effort; even if the government did not foot the bill for the production, Washington's Office of War Information "guidelines" ensured that the movies would support the cause. But Hollywood needed no convincing: in addition to outright propaganda such as Frank Capra's *Why We Fight* series (see Chapter 6), feature films across the board promoted the Allied cause. The Hollywood studios were happy to wave the flag for a highly popular cause, from the grim dramas such as Mark Sandrich's *So Proudly We Hail!* (1943), about the nurses in the Philippines at the time of the Japanese invasion, to William Wyler's sentimental *Mrs. Miniver* (1942), in which Greer Garson portrays a solid English housewife dealing stoically with the challenges of war, to musical variety shows that drew out the studio's stars to salute the troops: for example, Michael Curtiz's *This Is the Army* for Warner Brothers, the top box office draw of 1943, and Frank Borzage's *Stage Door Canteen* for United Artists, the fifth biggest draw that same year. The movie industry also played a key role in promoting the effort to sell the war bonds that to a large extent financed the war effort. Clint Eastwood's recent film *Flags of Our Fathers* (2006) show how soldiers were drawn into this marketing effort. A vast trove of movies from the war and about the war provides a rich source of information and insight into this pivotal era in American and world history.

Over the years, filmmakers have turned the camera on themselves to provide viewers with a glimpse "behind the scenes." Occasionally, these films offer insight into the filmmaker's craft and the industry itself. One of the best films to do this comes from a brilliant time in Hollywood history, Preston Sturges' *Sullivan's Travels* (1941), in which a film director, tired of making escapist comedies such as *Hey Hey in the Hayloft* and *Ants in Your Pants of 1939*, wants to make a serious film, *O Brother, Where Art Thou?* But when the producers point out that Sullivan's own life has been too pampered for him truly to understand suffering, he decides to go undercover as a hobo. The vanity of this move is not lost on the movie, and his entourage follows Sullivan on his travels in a decked-out bus. What follows is fairly slapstick, and the film passes through several genres as Sullivan finds himself back where he started, in Hollywood, several times before he lands himself in jail and undergoes some involuntary suffering. Veronica Lake plays "the girl," and her anonymity is another point of self-reference for the film: aware of the charade she and Sullivan are enacting, she remarks at one point about how the story is going to end. During the course of this episode, he and his work detail are invited to a film screening at a rural African American church, where Sullivan learns that the oppressed do not want to see serious films about their condition, but rather movies that make them laugh. Along the way, there is plenty of satire on Hollywood culture and a number of references to the war in Europe and enduring hardship in America. *Sullivan's Travels* does hold the mirror up to society, but concludes that maybe mindless entertainment is not such a bad thing. In many ways,

Sullivan's Travels itself is the social problem movie Sullivan wants to make: the problem of making "social problem" movies is that the film industry, revolving around wealth and glamor, needs to understand itself; without condemning the efforts of serious filmmakers, Sturges admonishes them not to take themselves too seriously.

THE COLD WAR AND CIVIL RIGHTS

The victory of Allied Forces in the Second World War, in which U.S. industrial might and military campaigns in Western Europe and the Pacific played a pivotal role, made the United States a superpower. Unlike after the First World War, the United States retained a global political and military presence to ensure that its economic interests would not be harmed by another challenge: communism, particularly as manifested in the power of the Soviet Union. In this effort, culture played an important role in winning "hearts and minds" to the American way of life. The global popularity of American culture generated some concern and resentment abroad, but the appeal of that culture was strong. Antipathy for American culture found expression among cultural and intellectual elites, but "the masses" consumed it eagerly.

The film industry continued to evolve, and its support of the war effort carried over into postwar projects that took on significant challenges to postwar society. Though comedies and musicals did well commercially, the most acclaimed films of the later 1940s included: Billy Wilder's *The Lost Weekend* (1945), which examined alcoholism; William Wyler's *The Best Years of Our Lives* (1946), exploring the lives of veterans returning to civilian life; and Elia Kazan's *Gentleman's Agreement* (1947), a film about anti-Semitism in American "polite" society. Not all these films were as "cutting edge" or courageous as they might have been: though Kazan's *Pinky* (1949) took on segregation, 20th Century Fox declined to cast Lena Horne in the title role. Though Horne's skin was "light enough" to "pass for white," the studio instead cast Jeanne Crain, who was white, lest the film run afoul of the Production Code and audiences become uncomfortable with the love scenes involving William Lundigan, who also was white.

A new genre of crime and suspense dramas, often set in somber or seedy settings, became known as "film noir." Exploring the grimmer aspects of human nature, these films were not necessarily commercially successful, but in retrospect reflect the experience of a more cosmopolitan American changed by the experience of the war and postwar occupation roles. The character of Holly Martins (Joseph Cotten) in Carol Reed's *The Third Man* (1949), written by Graham Greene, can be seen as representing a somewhat naïve America entering the sinister world of old Europe. The British and American versions of this film (mostly a U.K. production) portrayed the complicity of the American in different ways, but the viewer follows Martins as he learns the harsh realities of life in Vienna, an occupied city full of intrigue.

One of the ingredients necessary for history to exist in people's minds is an awareness that a past exits. That sounds very broad and obvious, but it is an important point. Doing history, whether in writing, on film, or by oral tradition, involves breaking off an aspect of the human experience and describing and analyzing it separately from the jumble of experiences that we carry around with us as we live our lives. After 1910, Hollywood had a record of filmmaking events associated with it, but it would require a special effort to tell its own story, as opposed to telling the stories, fictional and real, of others. Billy Wilder's *Sunset Boulevard* (1950) does not reconstruct a "Golden Age" Hollywood, but it draws a clear line between the past and the present in telling the story of fictional reclusive screen legend Norma Desmond (played by the legendary Gloria Swanson), who employs an unsuccessful writer, Joe Gillis (William Holden), to attempt a comeback. Gillis falls into the role of a gigolo in the gothic atmosphere of Norma Desmond's mansion, but he also falls for Betty Schaefer (Nancy Olson), a bright and perky young woman also trying to make it in "the business" as a writer. The film is an incisive and funny look at the way Hollywood works, circa 1950, but it also looks back with some affection and reverence at a great period in filmmaking now obviously over, namely the silent era. There were those who felt that film was a purer art form without sound, and while Wilder did not go that far, the silent era was now clearly a discrete era in Hollywood's history.

   Sunset Boulevard also marked a crisis point in Hollywood's history. Television was keeping more and more people home. Television was certainly seen as competition for the movie industry, but the relationship between the two was not a zero-sum game. Watching television was not like going to the movies, but even with snowy reception and a small black-and-white image, it boomed as a new form of entertainment that kept people home from the movies. But television also could promote movies, and Hollywood aimed to address the challenge of television by developing ever more spectacular films that people would want to see on the big screen. While the television networks began broadcasting some programs in color in the 1950s, the hours were limited, the technology of the receivers was imperfect, and the consumer demand for black-and-white sets remained high, so that in 1965 still only 10 percent of U.S. homes had color TV. From the late 1960s, however, color TV sales took off.[5] Television had become a fixture of American cultural life and would have an impact on politics, for example, such as the movies had never had.

   While many Americans hoped and expected that life would resume its comfortable patterns after the Second World War, the war itself had empowered many people who previously had been kept in subservient roles, notably African Americans and women. After the war, the contradictions became too great, particularly for those African Americans and other visible minorities who had fought for their country in the name of a freedom they

[5] David F. Donnelly, "Color Television" in the Museum of Broadcast Communications' *Encyclopedia of Television* at www.museum.tv.

did not possess back home. Segregation and Jim Crow laws that denied voting rights remained in force, and white supremacist terrorists fought to preserve a wretched status quo. But as news of renewed injustice drew broad attention and assaulted many American's own sense of fairness, the moving image would assist in publicizing the most blatant forms of discrimination in a country that claimed to lead the "free world." Film and television ensured that the ensuing drama played on a world stage.

Segregation was most visible in the South, where laws written after the Civil War demanded that white- and dark-skinned people would not share public facilities. Southern segregation could be documented easily, as in photographs of drinking fountains labeled "whites only." Photographs of lynchings, often with "ordinary" looking white people looking on, also seared their way into the public consciousness. As African Americans took the lead in agitating for civil rights, whether through the Montgomery bus boycott, the sit-ins at the lunch counters of the South or attempts to gain access to its educational institutions, these dramatic events drew world attention to a glaring anomaly in America's claim to lead the free world. Attempts to quell the movement with violence merely amplified the brutality of segregation and pushed the nation, however slowly, toward equal justice.

Television played a more important role in the civil rights movement than did the movies, which tended not to push too hard. As mentioned earlier, *Pinky* took the safe route of casting a white woman in the title role. Edgier films came later, though: Otto Preminger's *Carmen Jones* (1954) adapted Georges Bizet's opera *Carmen*, using an all-African American cast, including Dorothy Dandridge in the lead and Harry Belafonte as Joe; and Stanley Kramer's *The Defiant Ones* (1958), with Sidney Poitier and Tony Curtis, has escaped convicts chained together, despising each other but learning through their ordeal to respect and like one another. Robert Wise's *Odds Against Tomorrow* (1959) was the first film noir featuring a black protagonist, Johnny Ingram (Harry Belafonte). The film industry for the most part continued to produce separate movies for black and white audiences; though these gradually would merge, the making and marketing of movies today suggests that there is still a cultural divide.[6]

The presence of television in people's homes positioned it to exercise an influence far beyond that of the movie screen. It provided escapist entertainment. It also carried news of events that would change the way Americans thought of themselves, embracing a greater sense of equality and justice through the nonviolent agitation led by Martin Luther King, Jr. Television also shaped American political life as networks covered campaigns and candidates used advertising to try to persuade voters. Televised debates could help voters make more informed choices, but ads could diminish the quality

---

[6] Allison Graham's *Framing the South: Hollywood, Television and Race during the Civil Rights Struggle* Baltimore, MD: The Johns Hopkins University Press, 2003 is an excellent study of the impact of moving pictures on the civil rights movement and vice versa.

of election campaigns by appealing to less rational considerations. Though one could think of TV as just a medium with a channel changer and an on/off switch, it dramatically changed American lifestyles and American culture.

VIETNAM AND MALAISE

The later 1960s brought great distress to American public life as the civil rights movement took on more intractable issues and the Vietnam War dragged on inconclusively, with ever higher casualties. New York Senator Robert F. Kennedy entered the presidential race on March 16, 1968, seeking the Democratic nomination in opposition to President Lyndon B. Johnson, who withdrew two weeks later. With the assassination of Martin Luther King, Jr., in April, the sense increased that America was a deeply divided country badly in need of national reconciliation, and for many Kennedy offered the greatest hope. However, the evening of his California primary victory on June 5, a young Palestinian, Sirhan Sirhan, shot Kennedy as he was leaving a victory celebration at the Ambassador Hotel in Los Angeles.

As a professor of history, I sometimes ask students their earliest memory of a news story from public life. For me, it was the funeral of Martin Luther King, which my family watched on television. For Emilio Estevez, also born in 1962, it may well have been the assassination of Robert Kennedy, whose death made an indelible impression on the young boy. In his 2006 film *Bobby*, Estevez reconstructs the day of the assassination. Kennedy appears in the film only in archival footage, showing him making campaign appearances and giving speeches. The film focuses on a day in the life of the hotel and develops the characters of more than twenty people: hotel workers, guests, and campaign workers. An astonishing cast of stars took small roles, willing to work in an ensemble cast rather than in showy starring roles, in support of the film.

The Ambassador Hotel was a luxury establishment, perhaps best-known to film viewers as the hotel featured in *The Graduate*. Though it catered to an affluent, almost exclusively white clientele, the hotel staff is more representative of the diversity of American society. While Estevez included specific historical details in his film, much of the narrative is intended not to reconstruct precisely, but to represent the realities of American society at that time: the kitchen staff has an interesting discussion about race among its black and Latino personnel, with Laurence Fishburne's sous-chef character Edward offering an eloquent soliloquy to the kind soul, José (Freddy Rodriguez), who gives him tickets to the Dodgers baseball game at which Don Drysdale pitches his sixth consecutive no-hitter; Ashton Kutcher plays the hippie drug dealer Fisher; Elijah Wood plays draftee William who faces deployment to Vietnam unless he marries Diane (Lindsay Lohan), whose story Estevez based on the testimony of a woman who was actually at the Ambassador that evening. These diverse lives come together at a tragic moment in the late hours after the primary.

Throughout the film, little dramas play out, with references to the voting process that is going on in the state that day. The hotel is preparing for the arrival of the senator that evening, but the atmosphere is surprisingly calm, with a few exceptions. Through the campaign workers, the viewer gains a sense of the hope people placed in Kennedy, so that the full import of the tragedy is felt when the shooting takes place.

Bobby is an excellent example of the interaction between moving pictures and history. The Kennedys owed some of their political success to the medium of television, which had showcased the charisma of John F. Kennedy, in contrast to Richard Nixon's relative lack thereof, in 1960. Rather than reconstructing all of the events, Estevez uses archival footage to show Walter Cronkite calling the primary for Kennedy, and Kennedy himself giving a victory speech at the Ambassador. The film's characters meet Kennedy, but viewers see Kennedy only from behind. The representation of iconic figures in film is always a challenge: in this case, the filmmaker wants to preserve a kind of reverence, and the moment of meeting the man himself should not be marred by distraction, caused either by a poor resemblance to the real person or an impressively good one.

Bobby in a sense merges a documentary with a narrative film. No doubt his technique helped keep the budget relatively low, but it also raises some interesting cinematic issues. Most, but not all, of the characters in the hotel are fictional; some were created around specific incidents remembered about that evening, such as a distraught campaign worker throwing a chair in frustration and despair. Viewers who remember the famous photograph of the kitchen worker cradling the wounded Kennedy in his arms will identify José as that person. Estevez built characters around historical events that would help to present the hotel, its workers, and its guests, as a microcosm of American society one day in 1968. For the writer/director, it was a heartfelt project, in which Kennedy figures as the last great hope, and whose death was catastrophic.

The reception of *Bobby* was a little odd. It certainly is an interesting and effective film, with excellent production design and an astonishing cast and a script that is at times eloquent and moving. Made on a limited budget, it grossed about $20 million worldwide. It probably did not lose money but it made very little for a film with such a stellar cast. It was nominated for a Best Drama Golden Globe by the Hollywood Foreign Press Association, and the Screen Actors Guild nominated it for Best Cast (its closest thing to best picture), but the Academy Awards overlooked it entirely. One can only speculate as to the reasons, but one thought worth investigating is whether such an earnest and heartfelt film can do well in times as cynical and divided as our own. *Bobby* is perhaps not as seamless as more expensive productions, but the interaction of fiction and reality makes it fruitful for historical study.

Historians have called the Vietnam War the "television war," and indeed the fullest documentary treatment of the U.S. involvement, focusing on the period from the 1965 escalation to the 1973 withdrawal, is called just that. Because of television, Americans developed a visual sense of what the war was like, and they could mark its seeming lack of progress on a daily basis as newscasts tracked the growing toll of dead and wounded. The communists' Tet Offensive early in 1968 ultimately failed, but in the meantime television audiences had been shocked to see reporters on the U.S. embassy compound in Saigon take cover as insurgents attacked. Though movies from that period reflect the turmoil within society—one can see war coverage on TV as the characters go about their sad lives in Richard Lester's *Petulia* (1968)—movies did not focus on the subject until the later 1970s, when Hal Ashby's *Coming Home* (1978), Michael Cimino's *The Deer Hunter* (1978), and Francis Ford Coppola's *Apocalypse Now* (1979) began the process of sorting out the Vietnam experience cinematically.

Television, however, reached far larger numbers, and alone among the media was capable of providing a national experience. That could be a Sunday night movie: even blockbusters from the 1950s such as *The Ten Commandments* (1956) and *Ben-Hur* (1959) could get strong ratings in the 1970s, when more people had color television sets. The NBC broadcast of *Gone with the Wind* in November 1976, thirty-seven years after its initial release, drew phenomenal ratings and still ranks among the Nielsen ratings' largest viewing audiences ever. More than 33 million households watched, so it is possible that during those two evenings, 100 million people saw *Gone with the Wind* either again or for the first time. In the late 1970s and early 1980s, television miniseries such as ABC's *Roots* (1977), NBC's *Holocaust* (1978), and ABC's *The Thorn Birds* (1983) also drew huge audiences. All were historical family sagas, with the first two able to claim a redeeming social purpose as well: *Roots* had about half the population of the United States following the stories of captured slave Kunta Kinte (LeVar Burton), Kizzy (Leslie Uggams), and Chicken George (Ben Vereen), and the eighth and final episode had over 36 million households tuned in. With a smaller but still large audience, *Holocaust* had millions of Americans following the perils of a Jewish family in Nazi Germany before and during the Second World War. In both cases, we can safely assume that a majority of viewers were not watching because this was "their own" history, but because these were compelling and significant chapters in history, period. Historical purists could object on issues of accuracy, but these dramatizations played a significant role in expanding the scope of popular history.

With the advent and spread of cable television, with regular and premium movie channels, audiences dispersed considerably to watch new channels that catered to specific tastes. Beginning in the 1980s, consumers could buy or rent movies on videotape and watch them whenever they wanted on their videocassette players. DVD began to replace videotape in the 1990s, and the readily mailable format, combined with efficient postal service and the Internet, has made movie watching extremely convenient, and the variety of offerings almost unlimited, today. There is always anxiety over the profitability of movie theaters, but experience has shown that there is an enduring demand for movies.

MOVIES AND CULTURE WARS

Movies today remain a very significant part of our culture, whether audiences have seen them or not. Throughout the past one hundred years, "the movies" as a whole have been a flashpoint in the culture wars that have pitted the film industry against those who see film as a purveyor of immoral ideas and behaviors. This conflict has been especially bitter in the United States, in which Christian fundamentalism has been especially pervasive and influential, but which also boasts the world's greatest concentration of filmmaking money and talent. In the early days, churches equated moviegoing with dancing, gambling, and alcohol consumption as sinful activities. In the 1920s, studio bosses founded the Academy of Motion Pictures Arts and Sciences, whose Academy Awards were intended to lend artistic and moral respectability to Hollywood productions. In the 1930s, the Production Code aimed to curb what was shown onscreen by way of violence and, especially, sex. Hollywood rallied strongly to the patriotic cause in the Second World War, but budding Cold Warriors in the later 1940s vilified it once again, now as a hotbed of subversive ideas. Part of Hollywood's response to this challenge, and that of television as a rival for audiences, was the sprawling biblical epic of the 1950s, though films like *Samson and Delilah* (1949) presumably did not owe all of their great box office success to an insatiable public demand for Bible study.

Another avenue to greater commercial success was to get rid of the old Production Code and simply to warn audiences about sex, violence, and other potentially offensive content with a label. Directors such as Otto Preminger had chipped away at it from the artistic side, but declining profitability also created a commercial push for "edgier" material. In 1968, the Motion Picture Association of America introduced the ratings system. This organization, both run by and accountable to the studios, would hire a panel of viewers to rate a film according to content viewers might deem offensive or inappropriate for younger viewers. Essentially the system served as a sop to Hollywood's critics by alerting audiences to problems with language, drug use, nudity, and violence. While one might imagine such a system to be somewhat scientific, ratings based on instances of certain "bad" words or degree of sexual explicitness, in fact the ratings system has proven to be quite subjective, yet at the same time reflective of the society it aims to protect. Lest one think that the ratings system protects young people from depictions of "bad" behavior, in fact it is remarkably tolerant of violence while taking a relatively hard line on sexuality, with a particular bias against homosexuality. Over the years, the system has been modified, but it has many critics. In the meantime, it has a considerable impact on the production, content, and reception of movies.

The ratings system, meanwhile, has not ended the cultural battle over the movies, given the inclination of some to condemn the movies as a monolithic a purveyor of immorality or promoter of violence. That is not a helpful or realistic position. Movies are not inherently evil. As Robert Sklar has argued, movies from their earliest days offered affordable entertainment to the poorer classes, and from the earliest days those who wanted to control the behavior of those people feared the influence of this new medium over which they themselves had no control. However, immorality predates the movies and would certainly exist without them: movies portray immorality, but most often do not promote it. We live in a world where information comes at us from many different sources, including depictions of "bad" behavior that are shown for different reasons, perhaps intertwined. Violence can teach us not to be violent, but violence also excites and entertains, perhaps all at the same time.

While movies are often dismissed as entertainment, and entertainment is often dismissed as diversion, the way we entertain ourselves, and what we find entertaining tells us a great deal about who we are. How do movies entertain? They make us laugh, cry, cringe, but how do they do it? Answering those questions tells us lot about who we are, and history is very much concerned with questions of identity. We love the stories that movies tell us, but why do we love them? Because they end the way we think they should, with any luck with a surprise. We also very much want to see justice in the end, whether it is a matter of a criminal being punished or the nice guy getting together with the nice girl.

Many churches condemned moviegoing as immoral, perhaps superficially because of the behaviors they depicted, but more significantly because the movies might compete with the church in reflecting or shaping the moral outlook of society: hence the blanket condemnation of moviegoing rather than educating the faithful to choose wisely. That position has not survived, but religious and other conservatives still attack "Hollywood" and "the movies" as a monolithic purveyor of evil. Even if the argument inside is a little more subtle, Michael Medved's 1993 book *Hollywood vs. America: Popular Culture and the War on Traditional Values* contains in its title an inflammatory accusation that "Hollywood" is not only out of step with "true" American values but also waging a concerted, militant campaign against them.

This simply is not true. The filmmaking industry has a distinctive culture, just as a rural, predominantly Baptist community in North Carolina has a distinctive culture. Upon close observation, neither is monolithic: both communities have people we would like and people we might dislike. Even allowing for a more cutthroat and competitive environment in Hollywood, the studios want people to like their movies and pay money to see or purchase them. Movies reflect society, and we actually should hope that they do so in ways that are varied, interesting, and challenging. Tracing the artistic ancestry of the movies would take us back to theater, which has significant roots in religion. While it is perfectly possible to see a film that promotes immorality—even in ways more subtle than Leni Riefenstahl's Nazi-loving *Triumph of the Will*—I believe that most movies play out according to our sense of what is right and wrong. The Production Code aimed to ensure that movies play out as morality plays, but its demise has not really led to a wholesale demise of film morality. Earlier, Michael Corleone (Al Pacino) would have had to die in *The Godfather: Part II* (1974); instead he finds him-self isolated and lonely as a result of his homicidal ruthlessness. This out-come may not be as cathartic as a sound and unambiguous punishment for his many misdeeds, but it is a more realistic treatment of the subject. Breaking away from the artistic limitations of the Production Code, *Bonnie and Clyde* (1967) focused on the bad guys instead of the good without pro-moting bank robbery as a way of life, and William Friedkin's *The French Connection* (1971) presented viewers with a drug-fighting cop (Gene Hackman) who was as ruthless and miserable as the criminals he pursued, though he happened to be on the right side of the law. These films ask us to think in a more nuanced way about the morality of a particular situation than would a "B"cowboy movie with bad guys and good guys clearly iden-tified, respectively, in black and white hats. A satisfying film is one that pro-vokes thought and challenges its audiences. The ratings system that replaced the Production Code identified elements that viewers might consider objec-tionable—language, violence, sexuality—and established age limits to keep younger viewers away from movies containing that material. The system is far from perfect, but it does put the burden on the individual—and the par-ents of children—to make their own choices, which is most appropriate for a free society.

Yet some continue to yearn, or clamor, for movies that reflect what they like, for material that is comfortable. We often want our history that way, too. We plumb the past for tales of inspiration and hope. If things end badly, we hope at least for some sense of catharsis, that the death was not in vain or that the cause eventually was won. Movie history presents special chal-lenges: we may not see the past as it really was because if it offends our present-day sensibilities. An interesting example is the treatment of animals. In Ermanno Olmi's *The Tree of Wooden Clogs* (1978), we see and feel the pace of peasant life in Italy more than a century ago. This includes significant vio-lence to animals, which is portrayed onscreen, and in filming life as it was the filmmaker aimed for a level of authenticity that meant that, in real life, the animals really died.

Those of us who are nonvegan cannot complain about the killing of animals per se, but the *portrayal* of the treatment of animals raises issues for filmmakers. Of course (and now more than ever), films can use special effects to portray the treatment or mistreatment of animals, with assurances to the audience in the credits that what *appears* to be happening is not actu-ally harming the creatures being filmed. Historians can appreciate Olmi's methodology and his quest for authenticity. Nonvegans have no real ethical right to complain about the destruction of animal life in the film, and these particular animals probably had a better life on the movie set than do most of the animals we consume today. But this example illustrates that filmmak-ing is a human activity subject to moral considerations. Makers of narrative films *dramatize* life and, in doing so, they assume moral responsibility for what happens "on the set." However, moving pictures can also *document* what is happening in real life: in 2008, the Humane Society released footage of cattle being horribly abused, helping lead to the recall of tons of meat from a California meatpacking plant. The Humane Society was not responsible for the mistreatment, but saw that in the portrayal of that mistreatment lay the power to address the problem.

In recent years, most movies have lain low as the culture wars raged between, to a large extent, opponents and supporters of the administration of George W. Bush. The bitterness engendered by the election itself—more so than the campaign itself, which was marked by significant complacency as to who occupied the White House—and the partisanship that followed, had the country divided into "red states" (conservative) and "blue states" (liberal), though in reality, the divide was more urban and rural across the country. In any case, the sense that a conservative administration would promote a conservative social agenda had many Americans up in arms. The ascendancy of Christian conservatives had many wondering whether the separation of church and state was at stake, and the appointment of conservative justices to the U.S. Supreme Court and other courts threatened some of the key earlier rulings affecting the lives of women in particular. But what appeared to be hardening into historical trend dissolved as economic turmoil and an increasingly unpopular Bush presidency led to Republican collapse and the election of Barack Obama as President in 2008.

The culture wars played out on television and talk radio, as networks found that, for a time at least, people shouting at each other made for good ratings. Fox News challenged the Cable News Network (CNN) from the right, while MSNBC, though generally more mainstream, also brought in conservatives to host shows. By and large, people did not want to pay $8 to see these battles play out in movie theaters, but a couple of films in 2004 became important cultural and political events, even if their influence in the end was muted. Interestingly, neither film found distributors among the major studios, true to their aversion to controversy.

At a time when conservative critics chided Hollywood for its liberal views and lax moral values (hardly a new phenomenon, as we have seen), Mel Gibson's *The Passion of the Christ* (2004) became an unusual box office smash and a major cultural event. Shrouded in controversy from before its release, it drew huge audiences and grossed over $600 million worldwide, about 60 percent of that in the United States and Canada, a relatively high proportion for a movie that makes that kind of money. The fact that it was subtitled makes its commercial success that much more remarkable. The film essentially told the story of the death of Jesus Christ, a historical event, though it drew more on the Roman Catholic tradition than on the accounts that appear in the Bible itself. Unfortunately, the legacy of anti-Semitism in the Roman Catholic Church, an acknowledged fact by the church itself, manifested itself in the film in the portrayal of the Jewish people as associated with evil forces.

That same year, Michael Moore's *Fahrenheit 9/11* presented a scathing indictment of the Bush Administration's path to war in Iraq, and the timing of the film's release, in the summer before the election, seemed clearly intended to influence the campaign. But in a highly polarized environment, Moore spoke in his unapologetically opinionated way to an audience already largely receptive to his views. Certainly conservatives, still united behind the Bush/Cheney administration only one year into the Iraq war, were not going to pay to see the movie, a fact that illuminated the problem: though arguably well-intentioned, Moore was not the person to bridge the great gap in American society; even if the film itself in parts might have been persuasive. Movies can and should be part of the national debate on important issues, but in the end, the medium is *not* the message. History's verdict on the Bush administration may include *Fahrenheit 9/11* in the discussion, but the real evidence will come from the administration's own acts and the consequences of those acts.

More than a century after their introduction, moving pictures have gone from being a technological curiosity to becoming integral to the way we communicate, educate, and entertain ourselves. As cultural historians, we are interested in how they have shaped people's lives. Political historians cannot ignore the role of moving pictures in shaping political culture and major events. All historians can use moving pictures as documents in their work of reconstructing and interpreting the whole range of human experience. The rationale for studying film is beyond dispute. But might we dare also to try our hands at conveying historical meaning by using moving images? Exploring, understanding, and enjoying the full range of movies' potential as a historical resource might inspire a few of you to make it your medium.

Questions:

1. What do you think of the idea that technology is the driving force in history? Can you think of a force that might be more fundamental?

2. Think about the place of movies in twentieth century American culture: as popular entertainment, as an art form, even as moral challenge in conservative circles. What are the tensions among these ways of looking at movies, and how have they shaped the movie industry?

3. While motion pictures are sometimes identified as a universal language, your discussion of question 2 considers specifically the role of movies in American society, and perhaps even specific sectors of that society. How might the cultural history of movies be different in other countries and parts of the world?

3

■ ■ ■

The Sum of Its Parts: Understanding the Medium

From a very young age, we experience moving pictures as entertainment. How does a film or a show make us feel: happy, sad, romantic, frightened? Were we bored or did we enjoy it? Those feelings are very important to our experience of the film. But to make use of film as a historical resource, we have to watch and study films critically as well. While you may wish to view Stanley Kubrick's *The Shining* (1980) at least once just as entertainment—for the sheer thrill and horror of it—it is also interesting to explore and think about why it has the effect that it does: how does this combination of moving images and sounds, obviously not happening in physical reality, neverthe-less have you scared out of your mind? The ability to analyze what you see and hear on film is essential to studying history through film. To do that, you need to understand the elements that make up a film as well as the choices available to filmmakers as they do their work. In this chapter we will dis-cuss, in particular,

● the practical and theoretical basis for analyzing film;

● the elements of film and the filmmaking process; and

● the "Hollywood Style" and the challenges of historical representation.

Besides learning some of the basic terminology, we will also begin to get a sense of the *culture* of filmmaking. As historian Lary May has said, Hollywood—and this would be equally true of filmmaking centers around the world—is a specific community with its own unique identity. Movies are products of that subculture as well as the products of our broader culture.

In carrying out their work, filmmakers try to imagine and anticipate how the viewer will respond to what they have created. In exploring the basic terminology of filmmaking, its essentials, and its conventions, it is helpful to bear in mind the three aspects of film that John E. O'Connor has identified as keys to its historical significance: the story of its **production**, the story of its **reception** by critics and general audiences, and the **content** of the film itself. Practical and user-friendly as O'Connor's approach may be, it represents a **theory** of how to approach history through film that is rooted in scholarship both in history and in film.

Of course many scholars outside the field of history study film, and the field of film studies is a natural place to go to learn about studying film. As an undergraduate, I took a film course in which the textbook was James Monaco's *How to Read a Film*, a title that suggests that the study of film is closely related to the study of literature, though of course, with film we are interested in far more than just the "text" that the script would represent. The most challenging chapter in that book was the one on theory, and I remember struggling to get a handle on **semiotics**, or the study of signs and symbols in film. What was difficult about that was the notion that there were these set "codes" in film that a scholar had to be able to identify: basic precepts about humanity and society conveyed through language, symbols, and conventions that appear again and again in movies. Semiotics has been closely associated with **structuralism**, which emphasizes the study of texts to discover the writer's intent through reasoned analysis. This approach assumed that there was an objective reality, or structure, at the heart of every artistic or literary work. Structuralism was big in the 1950s and 1960s, and an abundance of scholarship on literary theory produced a vast body of literature. In fact, one of the classic texts of structuralism is the analysis of John Ford's historical film *Young Mr. Lincoln* (1939) by the editors of the *Cahiers du cinéma (Cinema Notebooks)*, a French film magazine (founded 1951) that was very influential in the field of film theory and criticism. As Geoffrey O'Brien writes in his own essay on *Young Mr. Lincoln*, the *Cahiers* editors did a dense, scene-by-scene analysis of the film "as if here the secret mechanisms of the American ideology itself might be decoded and exposed." O'Brien notes that the film itself has a much freer feel to it than this analysis would suggest. As for history, it is clear that Ford took considerable liberties with the facts, and yet managed to convey an interpretation of Lincoln's life that historians and others find compelling.[1]

Since then, **poststructuralism** has rejected some of the key assumptions of structuralism, based on the notion that language and symbols represent not objective reality but constructions of what the "signifier" thinks is true or would like to be true. Poststructuralism is less interested in the artist's intent

---

[1] O'Brien's assay appears on the website for the Criterion Collection, an exceptional collection of cinema classics from all over the world. http://www.criterion.com/asp/release.asp?id=320&eid=464&section=essay&page=1 (accessed February 22, 2008). These DVDs are of exceptional quality. John Ford's *Young Mr. Lincoln* was presented as "a collective text" by the editors of the *Cahiers du cinema*, 223 (1970).

than it is in the ways a work and its meaning can be perceived by different individuals or audiences. All of this thought has had an impact on the study of history, where there is much discussion today of "constructed identities." Indeed, the idea that we use language to express who we *think* we are or want to be may owe a lot to moving pictures, where so often we have seen idealized representations of life: was there ever really a wife, mother, and homemaker so perfect as June Cleaver in television's *Leave It to Beaver*? We should be interested in the identity that the show's writers and actor Barbara Billingsley constructed for this woman, but the fact that June Cleaver is an **icon** or symbol of American life circa 1957 to 1963 has much more to do with how audiences responded to the show and that character, both at the time and later, when the show was still broadcast as reruns in syndication. In 1959, no one watching the show would have guessed that the series or its characters would become icons of American life; June Cleaver's iconic status owes everything to the response of audiences who had witnessed or experienced the changes of the late 1960s and 1970s, including the women's liberation movement, and the stark contrast that she represented to the emancipated woman of, say, 1975, whose identity was also constructed, of course. That tension established her as an icon, but responses to her would continue to change. Every assessment is subject to revision as times and views change.

Theory can be very helpful, therefore, in developing the critical thinking skills we need to carry out scholarship and solve other life problems, challenging us to think creatively about specific topics, explore every possible angle, and communicate our ideas effectively with others engaged in the study of the same or similar issues. Unfortunately, theory itself has often been discussed in very esoteric terms, making it difficult for younger scholars, if not the rest of humanity, to understand. Structuralism and poststructuralism deal very broadly with literature and film, but other kinds of theory may be helpful in dealing with more specific issues. Depending on the specific theme or topic of the course or the research project for which film is to be used as a source, theory may play a greater or lesser role. The movies contain abundant materials for the study of how we construct masculinity and femininity in our culture, for example, and a course focusing on the portrayal of masculinity in film would include reading and discussion of theory on the topic. Those readings and discussions can furnish the necessary and desirable theoretical underpinnings for individual research projects; however, those projects should focus on a specific historical topic, not only on the discussion of theory.

Just as theory should not be intimidating or distracting, scholars of history should not feel overwhelmed by the basic elements and the conventions of filmmaking, which this chapter aims to explain. We can begin with the term "film" itself. In one sense, film is a physical entity: reels of celluloid, usually thirty-five millimeters wide (the industry "standard," though many different widths have been in use over the years), stored in cans, and mounted on projectors for viewing. But when we talk about seeing a film, we do not mean looking at a reel of celluloid; we mean the experience of seeing moving images stored on film projected on a screen and (usually) hearing sounds amplified through speakers, arranged by filmmakers into a complete work meant to entertain or educate, or to be experienced as art. Today, people of modest means can collect their favorite films, but very few would own that collection *on* film, but rather in different **formats** that have made it possible for people to watch films at home, at will: first VHS tape and then DVD.

We can use the words *film* and *movie* interchangeably, even though we are reaching the point where the word *film* no longer describes the physical entity responsible for the sights and sounds we experience when we watch a movie. Formerly, movies were recorded on film and we had to watch them projected from reels of film as well. Television eliminated the need to go to the theater, creating a home video "projector" for movies broadcast by networks. Videotape and the home video cassette player liberated humanity both from the limited choice of movies playing at local theaters and from having to see movies chosen by networks to broadcast. So at home we would say we watched a tape, or more recently a DVD, of a movie or a film. As long as movies are recorded on film, we can cling to the use of that term, and it may live on as a souvenir or vestige of older technology. But some films already are shot using digital video equipment, and increasingly, movie theaters will be projecting not big reels of film, but movies stored as data on hard drives, which are cheaper to produce, lighter to transport, easier to manage, and cleaner to watch. Film prints deteriorate with each run through the projector; digital prints can be damaged in different ways, but with good care they should last much longer. So, while we have tended to use the term *movie* for the fun stuff and *film* for the more serious stuff, technology is challenging the accuracy of the word *film* to describe moving pictures. People may, however, keep it around for old times' sake.

PRODUCTION AND COMPOSITION OF A FILM

In discussing film, we can distinguish between the essential elements present, without which the film would not exist, and the *style* of the film, those aspects of the production over which the filmmakers can exercise artistic control and technical skill. In describing the basic elements of film, the following discussion covers some of the most common terms with which you should become familiar, though there are far more: the Internet Movie Database has a glossary that is extensive and helpful (http://us.imdb.com/ Glossary).

While we will focus primarily on the artistic elements of a film, we can never forget that major films are the products of the film industry, in which **producers** are very powerful figures who, to a large extent, determine what gets made and what does not. While the director heads the creative team and deservedly gets much of the credit (or the rotten tomatoes), producers raise the funds to make and promote the movie, hire the director and other key personnel, and secure the **distributor,** companies that distribute prints of the movie to **exhibitors** (companies that represent movie theaters), and DVD copies of the movie to retailers. Looking at a finished film as it relates to the production process, the planned sequences, scenes, and shots require logistics that can spread across the world, involving separate production units working on different parts of the film. Advances in transportation and communication, not to mention huge amounts of money available to make films and the potential for even larger profits, can make the production of a film a global enterprise.

Movies are big business. According to *The Hollywood Reporter* (June 15, 2007), a Motion Picture Association (MPA) study showed that the U.S. film industry made $42.6 billion in sales in 2006: $24.3 billion (57 percent) in the United States and 18.3 billion abroad. DVDs accounted for 44 percent of the total market share, while box office revenues accounted for only 19 percent. "Major motion pictures" are often produced by the major studios, which include Disney, Paramount, Universal, Warner Brothers, 20th Century Fox, and Sony, which owns Columbia, one of the oldest Hollywood studios, and the combination of the historic Metro-Goldwyn Mayer and United Artists (MGM/UA) studios. Each of these studios is part of a corporate empire. An **independent film** is a film not produced by one of the major studios, though in recent years many of the major studios have developed specialty film divisions to produce and distribute movies with an independent look or feel. For example, Miramax was acquired by Disney for this purpose, Paramount developed Paramount Vantage, and Fox developed Fox Searchlight. While the major studios crank out the blockbusters that keep the studios profitable and the corporate parents happy, the specialty film divisions produce the material that wins Academy Awards.

Typically, the production of a film begins with an idea. It could be a great new idea—a vision of a compelling work of film innovation, creativity, and genius—or it could be a less exciting idea—a marketable film product to keep movie stars out there in front of their fans and movie companies in business. No idea can reach the screen, however, without being developed into a script or screenplay. Throughout the filmmaking process, the **script** or **screenplay** will undergo revision and expansion into different forms that track what has been shot or changed. The script includes the dialogue and tells the story to be filmed, but it also becomes the blueprint of the film. The screenwriter therefore plays a vitally important role, and good writing lays the foundation for a good film. Not coincidentally, the word we use for a filmmaker with an esteemed body of work and identifiable style is *auteur,* French for author. A screenplay can be an original work, or it can be an adaptation of an existing work of literature .

Each film has its own unique production history, and historians have an obvious interest in that story. It enhances our understanding of the film's content and production, but it also can reflect a great deal about filmmaking culture and culture in general. The story of the making of a film can itself become the subject of articles, books, and films. The making of *Gone with the*

Wind (1939) for example, is itself a fascinating piece of 1930s culture. Though making *Casablanca* (1942) several years later involved no hyperpublicized search for lead actors or burning massive studio sets, its story too reveals a lot about the studio system and how some of the greatest films did not set out to become great films.[2]

Getting a story onto film involves breaking it down into something filmable as a series of shots, scenes, and sequences. Where the film derives from an existing work of literature, critics and viewers who know the literature will inevitably judge the film against the book. Even though they are separate media, with different strengths and weaknesses, experienced differently, what made the book good is expected to make the film good too, unless the filmmakers can come up with something even better. The nature of the media is very different, and one key factor is the fact that a novel usually is the work of one person, whereas any film you are likely to see is the work of many people. The **director** leads the production team and gets most of the criticism, good or bad, for the final product, but writers, cinematographers, sound, set and costume designers, editors, and actors can make or break a film. The first Harry Potter films, for example, skillfully adapted J. K. Rowling's phenomenally popular books for the screen, illustrating impressively the power of digital technology to create special effects and portray fantasy in ways that were not possible before. They represent an extraordinary pooling of talents to convey visually and sonically what Rowling rendered with the written word alone. Yet as films they do not surpass the books, in the sense that the books have been a much greater publishing phenomenon than the movies have been a cinematic one. Movies that are adaptations of popular or well-regarded literary works face the same challenge that historical films do: the people who see them because they "read the book" or know the history from the scholarly sources expect the movies to retain all the subtlety, detail, and power of the words they have read. Movies, however, communicate not just with words— and as a rule, they should not have too many of them—but through images and other forms of sound, not to mention silence.

In the transformation of a script into a movie, **scenes** are the most significant unit, involving decisions about location, set design, costuming, lighting, and sound. Several cameras will be present on the set, and the scene in the movie will be composed from the footage of many cameras. An action unfolds in the scene the way we might see it live on stage, but the recording of that action is not usually the continual working of one camera, but rather a combination of individual shots capturing the dialogue and action, often repeated in the course of a filming session (creating potential problems of continuity, or inconsistencies in the final edited work, discussed below).

---

[2] As the title indicates, Herb Bridges and Terryl C. Boodman, *Gone with the Wind: The Definitive Illustrated History of the Book, the Movie and the Legend* (New York: Simon and Schuster, 1989) takes up the whole phenomenon, including production and reception. Aljean Harmetz, who has also written about *Gone with the Wind* and *The Wizard of Oz* (1939), provides a production history of *Casablanca* in *The Making of Casablanca: Bogart, Bergman and World War Two* (New York: Hyperion, 2002).

The basic unit of a film, both as it is made and as we watch it, is the **shot** or **take**—the result of running a camera to record a particular moment or action. The terms *shot* and *take* can be used interchangeably, though in some cases one word works better than the other: a **long shot**, for example, refers to a shot in which the camera is relatively far away from the subject, giving the viewer an image of the subject in its surroundings. A shot of long duration might also be considered a long shot, but to avoid confusion, we call that a *long take* instead. Movies can and do exist without sound, but by definition, a movie cannot exist without a shot or take of perceptible duration.

Generally speaking, shots that belong together make up a **scene**, and scenes that belong together make up **sequence**. Discussing a shot, however, refers most commonly to what the camera has in view and how it is filming it (angle and distance), whereas we discuss scenes as parts of the film's overall **narrative**: we can discuss sets, costumes, lighting, color in this or that scene, but we also begin to understand the story that the movie is telling, and how it is telling it. Shots might be considered "sentences," and scenes and sequences can be discussed as "paragraphs" and "chapters." A sequence is a group of scenes that can be set apart in one way or another within the film: for example, older movie musicals often contained a "dream sequence" in which one of the main characters dreams or fantasizes about someone or something. The dream sequence became a common element, or **convention**, in musicals not because they were necessary to advance the narrative of each of these films, but because, from a production standpoint, they allowed many of the artists involved in the production of the film to show off a more extravagant flair: these sequences stand apart almost as separate films within the film. The definitions of shot, scene, and sequence can be fluid: Alfonso Cuarón's *Children of Men* (2006), for example, contains a single shot, lasting over six minutes, in which the camera moves through the streets of a warring coastal town in England, from one scene to another; even more remarkable is Aleksandr Sokurov's *Russian Ark* (2002), an entire film shot in a single take.

The individual shots that make up the scene are carefully planned and executed, and require both technical competence and artistic ability. The camera films its subject from a particular **angle**, a factor which alone can establish a mood or relationship with the subject: from a low angle, we look up at the subject; from a high angle, we might gain a greater sense of perspective or context on a scene or character. The camera also can move: it can **tilt** up or down or **pan** from side to side; it can **track** alongside an action or toward or away from it. The camera also can circle the action; indeed there are many possibilities, limited only by a sense of convention and the fact that viewers can become nauseous from too much camera movement.

Of course, the camera work should not just be interesting. It should also help to tell the story clearly. A shot of an action may be followed by a **reaction shot**, recording a character's response. A conversation scene might feature alternating **close-up** shots of the conversation's participants, as well as **medium** or **long** shots of all the actors and their surroundings. The **point of view** shot also is common, in which the camera "sees" what one of the characters is seeing, helping the viewer to identify with that character and to see events from his or her perspective. While that may be an effective technique, it would be highly unconventional to film an entire movie from one character's perspective. Julian Schnabel's *Le Scaphandre et le papillon* (*The Diving Bell and the Butterfly*, 2007) starts out this way to get viewers inside the mind of Jean-Dominique Bauby (Mathieu Amalric), a prominent fashion editor left almost completely paralyzed by a stroke. However, Schnabel and his cinematographer Janusz Kaminski, after effectively establishing a connection between the viewer and the central character, wisely chose not to limit themselves visually to what Bauby would have seen. The 1947 film *Lady in the Lake* did do that: the camera essentially became the eyes and ears of detective Phillip Marlowe. The film, based on a Raymond Chandler novel, is in other respects an interesting example of **film noir** (dark film) popular at the time with its stylish portrayal of the criminal, seedy side of life. What is weird about the film is precisely the way it deviates from the way camera work normally is done and the way that shots and scenes normally are composed and edited into movies.

The **cinematographer** is the person in charge of the film's camera work. Technical skill—ensuring that what appears on film is what the director wants—is a prerequisite, but some cinematographers become famous for a distinctive visual style. Lighting and focus are two elements at every cinematographer's disposal, but Gregg Toland became celebrated in the 1940s, using deep focus photography in films such as *Citizen Kane* (1941) and *The Best Years of Our Lives* (1946). With **deep focus**, everything in the frame is in focus, whether near or far from the camera. That may not sound especially remarkable, but for audiences accustomed to shots in which only the central subject is in focus the visual effect is one of crispness and clarity. It is also closer to the way people actually see. In contrast, cinematographers conventionally used soft focus to film love scenes, especially for close-ups of the lead actresses, to create a dreamy, romantic effect. To the extent that this convention also portrayed women as weak and submissive, not to mention the fact that it became a screen cliché, helps to account for its passing.

Lighting plays a major role in establishing the mood of a scene or film, and the cinematographer also uses it to direct the viewer's attention. Low lighting can create a somber or intimate effect; bright lighting generally yields the opposite effect, though again the variables allow for a wide range of expression, and the creative cinematographer can defy convention. Sven Nykvist, regarded in his lifetime as the world's greatest cinematographer, worked on a number of American movies, including *Sleepless in Seattle* (1993). But he earned one of his three Academy Awards for *Fanny and Alexander*, a 1982 Ingmar Bergman film that begins with an all-night extended family Christmas celebration. Obviously the **production designer** and **costume designer** also played vital roles in making that part of the film a true visual feast, but Nykvist worked with candle light to give the scenes a warm intimacy and atmosphere that demonstrate beautifully what outstanding camera work does for a film.

Color also is a major component of a film's look. Color alone has emotional associations. Warm colors like red and yellow associated with warm emotions such as love, passion, and anger. Blue and gray, by contrast, are cool. Production and costume design are concerned with color, but cinematographers also can do a great deal with color, including defy convention. Until the 1960s, many films were made in black and white, even though color dated back to the teens, when film stock could be tinted, and became more common for major productions in the 1930s. The **esthetics**, or standards for assessing beauty and artistic merit, are different for black and white film. Even though color represented a technological advance, black and white held its own, and not just because it was less expensive. Occasionally, films today still use black and white, primarily because of its historical and nostalgic associations. Occasionally you may see a film in which the color is so washed out as to appear almost black and white. This may create a vintage effect short of going entirely to black and white, as in the case of *Sky Captain and the World of Tomorrow*, a 2004 film largely computer generated but celebrating a look of 1930s and 1940s–style futurism. Or it can contribute to an atmosphere of bleakness in a film dealing with subjects such as poverty and other forms of hardship, such as *Norma Rae*, a 1979 film that portrayed a struggle to form a labor union in a Southern textile mill town.

Though we take color for granted today, it did not become the norm as quickly as sound did. **Technicolor** refers to the color process used commonly in Hollywood from the 1920s to the 1950s, in which the color was turned up loud and used to dazzling effect and advantage in major productions, especially musicals. Sets and costumes showed off color to a degree that would seem garish in everyday life, and seemed garish to those purists at the time who believed that black and white allowed for greater artistic expression, and black and white movies remained common until the 1960s. As in painting, however, color is an essential component of artistic expression in film. Some films from the 1940s and 1950s, such as Michael Powell's *The Red Shoes* (1948, with cinematography by Jack Cardiff) and Jean Renoir's *The River* (1951, with cinematography by his nephew Claude Renoir; the impressionist painter Pierre-Auguste Renoir was Jean Renoir's father), demonstrated that color could be manipulated to great artistic effect.

Film stock refers to the actual material on which the film is recorded. Depending on the speed of the film being used, the image appears finer or grainier. Whereas earlier one might associate grainy with cheaper film stock, low budget, and lower quality, over time the grainy film stock acquired a certain artistic cachet that film artists with the means to buy the best would actually seek out. The "B" films, lower-budget movies made to sate the demand for films in the days when people went to the movies several times a week, had their own look that later directors, nostalgic for the films of their youth, would emulate. A good example of using different film stock to different effect is *JFK* (1991), in which Oliver Stone and cinematographer Robert Richardson pulled out all the stops to stunning visual effect, but one of the more unusual techniques was to use different kinds of film stock to differentiate among kinds of scenes and experiences being portrayed. Film stock may become entirely obsolete as digital cinematography advances, but film artists will continue to work with resolution as an artistic variable. Even as resolution improves with technology, as with color versus black and white, some artists will continue to opt for the effect of the less advanced technology. In Andrew Dominik's *The Assassination of Jesse James by the Coward Robert Ford* (2007), the cinematography stands out for its evocations of 1880s America, from the blurring out of the image at the sides of the screen, reminiscent of the stereoscope through which people would have paid to see the death photos of Jesse James, to the distorted images seen through windows paned with glass of uneven surface.

An obvious though crucial part of a film's look is reflected in a decision we make when viewing a film on DVD: that is whether to choose the full screen or widescreen version of a movie. Technically speaking, this relates to the film's **aspect ratio**, or the ratio of the width to the height of the image. Until the 1950s, the ratio was a fairly standard 1.33:1, but the introduction of Cinemascope (2.35:1) and other more panoramic looks increased the aspect ratio in an effort to press the advantage of the big screen and get audiences back into the theaters. Presenting these images on the small screen presented a problem, however. Whereas the older movies pretty much fit the dimensions of the standard television screen (before high-definition), widescreen movies (between 1.66:1 and 1.85:1) would either lose some image on the left and right to fill the screen and keep the image in the center of the screen as large as possible, or the entire image would be shrunk down and "letterboxed" to fit the television screen, leaving empty black bands on the top and bottom of the screen. Broadcasters often chose to go "fullscreen" (losing the sides), but others insisted that content and proportions of the image not be compromised in any way. Consumers have the choice: "full screen" or "widescreen" versions of movies are available on DVD, sometimes on either side of one disk. Esthetically, the case for choosing widescreen, and the whole image, is strong. With the aspect ratio of high definition television (HDTV), it is a less obvious issue.

We think of film as a visual medium, but **sound design** equally requires both technological competence and artistic interpretation. The common elements are dialogue, music, and sound effects. As important as actors' facial expressions and body movements are the ways that they use their voices. The screenwriters also affect the sound of the film through the kind of dialogue they write. Short, snappy sentences have a different effect from slower, longer sentences. In addition to human voices, a scene also normally includes sound effects: from birds singing, a telephone ringing, foghorns blowing, etc. Throughout the film, the sound has to be what the audience needs to hear at that moment: unlike the human ear and brain, which can "sort" and interpret the sounds that surround us, the sound designers and engineers need to do that sorting for us.

From the visual cues, the viewer expects sounds such as words when an actor opens his or her mouth to speak, the sound of a door closing when a door closes, and music when someone turns on a radio. We refer to the "world of the film" as **diegesis**, and the sounds that the characters in the movie would hear (provided they can) as **diegetic**. **Nondiegetic sound** is any kind of sound that is not occurring in the scene itself, but which can help with the storytelling or shape the mood of the film, such as voice-over narration or a musical soundtrack. Soundtrack music in many ways is a curious addition to films, especially films that attempt to portray life realistically; but, however artificial, it is a very popular convention present in most films, regardless of topic or theme. The aim of the music soundtrack is to enhance without overwhelming the rest of the content or drawing too much attention to itself (the television series *30 Rock* does this, but presumably for obnoxious comic effect). Bernard Herrmann was one of the great movie music composers, most famous for his work with Alfred Hitchcock that effectively captured the suspense, adventure, and horror of such films as *Vertigo* (1958), *North by Northwest* (1959), and *Psycho* (1960).

In all of these elements, we have noted the importance both of technical skill and artistic ability. Bringing all the elements together into a coherent, esthetically pleasing (and we care about that whether we know it or not) and, yes, enjoyable film, is primarily the responsibility of the **director**. Like the conductor of an orchestra, the director has to bring his or her own artistic vision to filmmaking, harmonizing the artistic work of others. The financial stakes and the potential for fireworks among talented artistic egos make directing a very high-pressure job. Critics rightfully attribute a film's artistic success to its director; more often than not, for example, Academy Award nominations and wins for Best Director and Best Picture are closely aligned.

A director who demonstrates a distinctive style to an acclaimed body of work becomes known as an *auteur*. It just means "author" in French, but film theorist André Bazin and editors at the *Cahiers du cinéma* put forth an *auteur* theory that asserts the primacy of the director as the "author" of the film, and emphasizes the film itself as a realization of the director's artistic vision. This notion in turn fit with their emphasis, as structuralists, on decoding the filmmaker's intent. Regardless of our theoretical orientations, we can use the term *auteur* to describe a director who has made a mark on the medium and whose work merits global acclaim and study: a partial list includes Sergei Eisenstein, Carl Theodor Dreyer, Jean Renoir, Akira Kurosawa, Satyajit Ray, Vittorio De Sica and other Italian neorealists, François Truffaut and other directors of the French New Wave, Ingmar Bergman, Rainer Werner Fassbinder, John Ford, Oscar Micheaux, and Alfred Hitchcock. Among contemporary filmmakers, another very incomplete list would include Steven Spielberg, Oliver Stone, Jane Campion, Spike Lee, Margarethe von Trotta, Ang Lee, and Yimou Zhang. The list of "greats," or, in our own country, those directors who have been nominated for Academy Awards, is short on women and visible minorities, because movie directing has long been a male-dominated profession and the movie industry has reflected the ethnic divisions of the broader culture.

It was not always so for women, as film historian and theorist Jane Gaines has described in her work on the silent era, when women figured prominently in moviemaking, more so than in other businesses. She asks both "what happened?" and "why did we forget about these women?" In mapping out an approach to answering these questions, she notes that, despite the fact that since the 1970s, **feminist film theory** has examined the portrayal of women in movies, looking especially for patterns and stereotypes, feminist scholars made assumptions about the history of film that allowed significant chapters to be lost or forgotten. Likewise, the fact that the name Oscar Micheaux, the most prominent of the early African American filmmakers, is unfamiliar to most people today points out not only that our collective memory is faulty and shaped by a legacy of racism but also that we as scholars have been remiss in recognizing and examining significant bodies of work. In our own time, movie directing in the United States and elsewhere is beginning to reflect more the diversity of society. Many of these *auteurs* made films on historical subjects, but their "auteurism" alone makes their whole body of work culturally, and therefore also historically, significant.[3]

In an industry where success depends on the skill and artistry of so many different people, and perhaps the director most of all, the **actors** are the most famous and best-paid members of the entire production team, cast and crew. Actors do the most visible work on the screen, and the appeal of the film therefore has a great deal to do with the appeal of the actors. The fact that actors are among the most prominent celebrities in society, that their fitness or lack thereof, their graceful aging or lack thereof, make headline news is one of the more curious elements of film culture, and one that says a lot about our general culture. The English scholar Richard Dyer theorized in his book *Stars* (1979) that perceptions about film stars greatly influence audience's perceptions and experience of movies. Certainly that factor affects our ability to be transported back in time, figuratively speaking, as we watch historical movies. In Wolfgang Peterson's *Troy* (2004), an adaptation of Homer's epic poem *The Iliad*, Brad Pitt plays the warrior Achilles. Every tabloid and gossip magazine in 2004 featured the comings and goings of Brad Pitt and then-wife Jennifer Aniston, making it difficult for Pitt to disappear into the character. One wonders also what Dyer, who also is a leading theorist of gay culture, would have said about the film's representation of Achilles' relationship with his cousin Patroclus. In the original story, it is clear that Achilles has deep feelings for Patroclus, and it would not have been out of the ordinary in ancient Greece for that relationship to be sexual. It quickly becomes clear in watching the film that Hollywood was not going there, but it is somewhat amusing to note that Patroclus, played by Garrett Hedlund, looks a little like Jennifer Aniston and even sported a similar hairdo. But because celebrity is thought to draw people to movies, those of us who went to see the film because we liked *The Iliad* have to deal with Brad Pitt the movie star because more people went to the movie to see Brad Pitt than went to assess the historical merits of Peterson's work. A major motion picture needs

---

[3] Jane M. Gaines, "Film History and the Two Presents of Feminist Film Theory," *Cinema Journal* 44:1 (Fall 2004), 113–119. Accessed through Jstor (http://www.stor.org; February 23, 2008).

its bankable stars. But occasionally, good sense prevails where a star clearly would not work: the producer and director of *The Day the Earth Stood Still* (1951) were able to ward off the interest of a major star as they cast their film about a wise and noble visitor, Klaatu, from another planet. Imagine the effect on audiences of having Spencer Tracy—a celebrated and very recognizable actor who actually wanted the role—emerging from a flying saucer that has just landed on the Washington Mall.

The shooting of a film requires careful organization and management. The work of many people has to be coordinated, and the shooting itself has to be carefully planned both to avoid costly errors, to ensure that all the necessary material is filmed and will come together in the end. The director is responsible for all the artistic work on the set, but coordination occurs at other levels as well. The script supervisor ensures that **continuity** is maintained from shot to shot, so that within a scene no changes take place without explanation, such as objects appearing or disappearing from the set. Given that shooting a film takes place over a period of weeks or months, the script supervisor's job of minding the details and ensuring that no errors are made is a very important one. The Internet Movie Database (imdb.com) includes a category of "goofs" for each film. At the beginning of Michael Bay's *Pearl Harbor* (2001), for example, fighter pilots are seen training over the ocean near what the film calls Long Island. While it is not uncommon for films to be shot on locations different from the purported setting of the film—the Cuba scenes in *The Godfather: Part Two* (1974) were shot in the Dominican Republic, for example—many of *Pearl Harbor's* viewers would know that there are no mountains on Long Island.

For students of history, continuity has an added dimension. Films set in the past should avoid **anachronisms**, or anything that does not fit the time period, as a rule. Though the artist enjoys the freedom to play with time as with any other element, one would not want that to appear accidental. And if films normally are supposed to be absorbing and convincing in their portrayals, historical continuity matters. One of the most famous film anachronisms, ironically, is the appearance of a timepiece, a watch, on one of the charioteers in the 1959 film *Ben-Hur*. No doubt it was a mistake, but as a flaw it arguably adds to what is otherwise still a spectacular scene in a widely acclaimed classic Hollywood film.

The **film editor** cuts and splices shots to create scenes and assembles the movie from all of the footage shot. Much more material is shot than will appear in the actual movie, which means that the editor has to eliminate material that is not vital to the development of the narrative and would make the movie too long. The editor plays a critical role in determining the pacing and duration of the film, aiming for an arrangement of shots, scenes, and sequences that is coherent and pleasing to viewers. The **final cut**, the version which the filmmakers agree with the studio to put into release, is not *always* the end of the story, however. Though the director and editor have every interest in getting along to create an artistic and commercial success, there have been some famous clashes: in 1942, the RKO film studio cut fifty minutes from Orson Welles' *The Magnificent Ambersons* while he was in South America and gave it a happier ending, hoping it would play better that way with audiences in an America that had just gone to war. The cut footage was lost, apparently destroyed. More commonly today, a successful film may be reedited and reissued as a (usually) longer "director's cut," in some cases theatrically, but more often on DVD.

Editing provides opportunities both for creativity and instruction, particularly in the arrangements of the shots: **juxtaposition** of certain shots can suggest meaning. Sergei Eisenstein's films, made in the early decades of the Soviet Union, created a cinematic analogue to the Marxist dialectic—the theory that revolutionary clashes between dominant and ascendant social classes, fueled by economic disparities, drove history forward. Eisenstein's films about revolutionary activity in Russia, such as *Strike* (1924) and *The Battleship Potemkin* (1925), were edited in such a way as to teach these historical lessons. Eisenstein's editing style became known as "Russian Montage." It should not be confused another meaning of the term **montage**, referring to the editing of a group of brief shots into a sequence that expedites the narrative from one part of the film to another: one very common example of a montage is shots of newspapers coming off the press intercut with different headlines chronicling a person's rise to prominence. Pages flipping on a calendar is another visual cliché that punctuates an accelerated part of the narrative.

Viewers have many different tastes in film, but the critical viewer must be able to say something about the overall **look** (and sound) of the film. Two key factors affect that look and feel: the design of shots and scenes, which we refer to as **mise-en-scene**; and the effects of the editing, which we refer to once again as **montage**. Viewers of Oliver Stone's *JFK* (1991) may have steeled themselves as they bought their tickets not to be swayed by the conspiracy theories and controversy, but the look and feel of the film were distinctive and powerful, agitating audiences to open their minds to what Stone was saying. While editors typically aim for smooth transitions and overall clarity, Joe Hutshing and Pietro Scalia opted successfully for a more jarring and exciting effect; Robert Richardson's work with different film stocks and color tones—which actually helped the viewer to keep the many different threads of the narrative straight—was one of the factors that made his work on the film so exceptional. While the Academy voters chose not to name *JFK* Best Picture that year, they did like the look: with eight nominations, the film won for Best Film Editing and Best Cinematography.

Esthetics is the branch of philosophy that deals with the study of theory of beauty and the human response to it. Classic major Hollywood films usually display excellent **production values**, meaning that, while the studio certainly wanted its production crews to stay within budget, it ensured that the quality of the finished project on a technical level was outstanding. Production values certainly contribute to a film's esthetic appeal, but esthetics is also concerned with the appropriateness of a film's look to what it is all about. So while the first part of Ingmar Bergman's *Fanny and Alexander* is an extraordinarily beautiful rendering of a turn-of-the-twentieth century Christmas celebration in Sweden, the predominantly austere look of the second half of the film has its own visual appeal, and it is certainly appropriate to what happens in that part of the film.

Taste is a subjective matter, however, and while some viewers may have very refined notions of film esthetics, there are no real fixed principles or dogmas when it comes to judging a film's artistic merit. While at any given time in history, we can identify rules that existed to define beauty in art, rules can and will be broken, and they change over time. Some artists successfully flout notions of beauty in creating their original works of art. The films of John Waters demonstrate a great love for the **schlock** he enjoyed as a youth: the cheesy, cheaply made B-movies that were never intended to be viewed as art or prestige pictures, but which kept undiscriminating audiences coming to drive-ins and other theaters week after week. Where esthetics is concerned with good taste, schlock is all about bad taste. Its appeal of schlock is somewhat mysterious, but undeniable, because while we have individual and cultural ideals of beauty, we can also see the fun in tweaking those ideas to humorous effect.

The "Hollywood" Style

We know it when we see it, but can we define a "Hollywood style"? Often we use the term negatively, as I just did in suggesting that the blockbuster *Troy* dared not "offend" mainstream audiences by suggesting a sexual bond, which would have been historically defensible, between Achilles and Patroclus. The Hollywood style amounts to the sum total of recognizable attributes we can identify in commercial filmmaking: the ways of telling a story cinematically that the movie industry has settled into and which audiences seem to prefer. Watching a bunch of trailers before a movie is one very good way to see filmmaking clichés lined up back to back: does the world really need *another* cute romantic comedy, or spy thriller, or action blockbuster?

The important distinction to make here is between the nature and purpose of high art versus the popular arts. Some analogies may be useful. Though few of us have ever attended a high fashion show, we have seen enough pictures to know that we would never see on the street the really wacky stuff that comes down the runway. High fashion shows are about the **avant garde,** or the "advance guard," those designers who have the creative ability to push fashion forward with new ideas (ideas which certainly draw from the past often enough). These exciting new elements eventually find their way to clothes real people would want to buy and wear. Likewise, avant garde music appeals to the highly trained ear as creative and innovative but does not cater to public tastes. However, the musician looking to sell records, or to continue to sell records, is simultaneously looking for something new and something familiar, and the avant garde may therefore eventually find its way, much changed, onto the pop charts.

The prevailing mode of commercial filmmaking has changed over the years, responding to all kinds of changes in society, changes in technology, and changes in the arts themselves. Different groups of people may want different things from a movie, but commercial success is almost always on the list. Most people never see avant garde films, or films made for purely artistic purposes. Their purpose is to explore the nature of the medium itself, experimenting with camera work, editing, lighting, sound, and so on with no worries about distribution and box office. For example, Andy Warhol's film *Empire* (1964) "consists of one stationary shot of the Empire State Building taken from the forty-fourth floor of the Time-Life Building.... filmed from 8:06 p.m. to 2:42 a.m. on July 25–26, 1964." According to the Museum of Modern Art (MoMA), which includes this film in its collection, "Warhol conceived a new relationship of the viewer to film in *Empire* and other early works, which are silent, explore perception, and establish a new sense of cinematic time. With their disengagement, lack of editing, and lengthy nonevents, these films were intended to be part of a larger environment. They also parody the goals of his avant-garde contemporaries who sought to convey the human psyche through film or used the medium as metaphor."[4] This may well sound like the world's most boring film, but Warhol knew what he was doing, and the MoMA catalogue suggests that he may have been poking a little fun at some of his fellow film artists in making this film.

The MoMA collection also includes such popular films as Vincente Minnelli's *Meet Me in St. Louis* (1944), Alfred Hitchcock's *Vertigo* (1958), and Martin Scorsese's *Raging Bull* (1980), demonstrating that the tension between commercial imperative and artistic value is not a zero-sum game. "The masses" are certainly capable of appreciating good film, even if many viewers cannot articulate specifically what makes it good. Making a film that will be commercially viable, let alone a blockbuster, requires enormous talent and skill. Drawing talent from all over the world, and fueled from within by competition among the studios, Hollywood dominates the world film industry by plowing enormous resources into making movies audiences will flock to see, not just in the United States but all over the world. Most countries cannot compete with the major Hollywood studios in the global marketplace, but when a foreign film breaks through commercially in the world market, it does so by essentially speaking the same language as the films coming from Hollywood. Some may see American dominance in the world film market as American cultural imperialism, but considering that the American film industry draws talent from all over the world, and the fact that audiences all over the world enjoy Hollywood movies, suggests that they speak a cosmopolitan and international language to which world audiences respond.

---

[4] The Museum of Modern Art, *MoMA Highlights*. New York: The Museum of Modern Art, 1999, 2004, 240. From the Web site http://www.moma.org/collection/object.php?object_id=89507, accessed June 5, 2009.

GENRE, CONVENTION, THE "GRAND NARRATIVE" AND THE COMMERCIAL IMPERATIVE

Taken as a whole, movies tend to fall into categories or kinds of films. Given the prominence of French theorists in film studies, we have a French term for movie types, **genre**. Not every movie fits into a genre, and some can fit more than one. Among the common genres, such as the musical, the horror, and the Western, we find typical themes and patterns of storytelling. In the musical, for example, a dream sequence later in the film allows the choreographers, costumers, set designers, and dancers to portray the psychological preoccupations of the central character in a creative fantasy. In the Western, the theme of bringing order and civility to an untamed West is played out among, and often within, the characters. Genre can be applied more loosely as well, to categories of comedy and drama: among the comedies, we can identify the screwball comedies of the 1930s, buddy films, and the ever-popular romantic comedies. Genre is important to the study of history in film because as audiences we gravitate toward patterns in storytelling, and the pressure to conform to these patterns has often led to distortion of historical fact. But genre itself can be very interesting historically: *why* do particular themes and patterns resonate with audiences? Was *film noir*, discussed earlier, popular in the 1940s and early 1950s because Americans saw the world in a darker light given their experiences of the Second World War and the Cold War? Was science fiction popular in the 1950s because it enabled Americans to explore their Cold War fears safely? How did Westerns reflect the preoccupations and concerns of the times in which they were made?

Wittingly or unwittingly, filmmakers, working in a commercial environment, cater to popular tastes. In most cases, historical accuracy submits to the **conventions**, or common and expected patterns, of storytelling, and even most historians will put up with some distortion in the interest of reaching a wider audience with a cleaner plot and simplified characterization. Historians, after all, should be more interested in the kinds of deeper historical insights that can be conveyed through the medium of film, using all of the tools the historical writer does *not* have, to best advantage. So argues Robert Rosenstone, one of the leading thinkers about history in film. As a historical consultant for Warren Beatty's 1981 film *Reds*, Rosenstone put up with the fact that the romance between Jack Reed and Louise Brooks became a central part of the movie story, even if it was largely made up, because he understood that a film that focused solely on left-wing politics in the era of the First World War would not draw much of an audience. So *Reds* became a love story, and the task of assessing its historical significance has to include sorting out the intentionally fictional elements, and also determining whether those fictional elements contribute to or detract from the film as a source of historical insight.[5]

---

[5] Robert Rosentstone, *Visions of the Past: The Challenge of Film to Our Idea of History* (Cambridge, MA: Harvard University Press, 1995), 83–108.

Audiences are not entirely enslaved to convention, after all; in Jean-Jacques Annaud's *Enemy at the Gates* (2001), critics found the love triangle improbable and strange, detracting from what could have been a much better movie about the Battle of Stalingrad during the Second World War.

Historians become most agitated—and perhaps a bit territorial—when filmmakers aspire toward what French thinker Jean-François Lyotard has called the "grand narrative," which historian Allan Megill has defined as "the story that the world would tell if the world itself could tell its story." As Megill explains, historians themselves are divided as to whether the "whole story" on any subject can be told, or whether we can really only know the truth in the fragments of the past that we study. The realities of the moviemaking industry and the potential of the medium itself lend themselves to the creation of films that, at least, appear to aspire toward this "grand narrative" quality: *the* film about the Second World War is certainly more marketable than *just another* film about the Second World War. While Steven Spielberg might reject the notion that his films *Schindler's List* (1993) and *Amistad* (1997) were intended to represent the "whole story" of the Holocaust and American slavery, big budgets and public expectations pushed these films in that direction. Both films provide good illustrations of some of the issues and dilemmas associated with this notion of the grand narrative as it applies to historical film.[6]

To begin with, the Holocaust is a challenging subject to deal with in any medium. Some even argue that respect for the victims of this crime requires that the subject be left alone. But most people believe that this same respect should motivate study and reflection. The issue becomes one of finding the right esthetic and language: a look, sound, tone, and feel that is appropriate to the subject. The premise of *The Producers*—in which two con artists conspire to bilk investors of their money by producing a musical about the Nazis, which they assume will fail—is that the frothy language of musical shows is utterly unsuited to this brutal chapter in history. While audiences could and did laugh at the ridiculous notion of a musical about Hitler, perhaps with some reassurance from the fact that writer-director Mel Brooks was Jewish, many of the genres and conventions of Hollywood filmmaking were not well-suited to such a solemn topic.

Schindler's List was by no means the first film about the Holocaust, but it may be the first film that many took to be *the* film about the Holocaust. Hollywood had made only very oblique references to the subject before George Stevens made a film version of the play version of *The Diary of Anne Frank* in 1959. Though that film certainly found its audience and critical favor, in retrospect its choice of Frank's words "I believe that, in spite of everything, people really are good at heart" to end the film gave it an inappropriately upbeat conclusion, and the film likewise catered to audience

---

[6] Megill, "Fragmentation and the Future of Historiography," *American Historical Review*, June 1991, 696.

expectations by overemphasizing the romance between Anne and Peter, which in reality was short-lived. Yet it is equally inappropriate to condemn the makers of this film: George Stevens had led the army crew that filmed the liberation of Dachau, in color, in the spring of 1945, creating a powerful and enduringly shocking film document of the event. A fairer or more generous observation to make is that the conventions of Hollywood film-making had not yet provided an appropriate language to take on this terrible subject in a way that mass audiences would accept.

Many European and American films took on the subject before 1993. The 1978 NBC television miniseries *Holocaust* became a major event in North America and had an enormous impact in Europe, especially Germany, as well. Though again some critics were uncomfortable with the handling of this subject in a somewhat standard format using the conventions of film drama, one cannot escape the reality that those conventions and formulas helped the series to reach an audience that it would not otherwise have reached.

So when Steven Spielberg completed *Schindler's List* in 1993, on a budget of $25 million, critical and public expectations were high and the release of the film was going to be a major event. Certainly, some of the criticism assumed that this was to be a grand narrative on the Holocaust, a significant but ultimately unwarranted assumption. Undoubtedly, Steven Spielberg wanted to make a great film about the Holocaust, in the sense that it would be a powerful and moving film that motivated discussion and further study of the Holocaust. Film scholar Annette Insdorf, in her book *Indelible Shadows* (2003), discusses the problems of reconciling the truth of the Holocaust with the conventions of Hollywood filmmaking, particularly the urge to sentimen-talize material. There is some of that in *Schindler's List*: near the end, Oskar Schindler parts from the people he has rescued, making a long speech lamenting that he did not do more, as the violins soar. But that bit of Hollywood excess—after three hours we can grasp the power of the moment without the artifice of violins—is more the exception than the rule in this film, in which Spielberg did find an appropriate film language to tell the story of the Nazi businessman's transformation from exploiter of Jewish slave labor-ers to rescuer from mass murder in a way that was direct, honest, and brutal. Some critics did not like that most of the film was done in black and white, suggesting an attempt to give the film the feel of an older narrative or docu-mentary film, neither of which it actually was. But the choice of black and white could also be seen as an attempt to present the story in stark terms or a certain light. I often think of this film when I talk about the Holocaust as showing humanity at its absolute worst, but also, among those who carried out courageous acts of rescue, humanity at its best (though there is a lot of gray, or ambiguity, as well). Others faulted the film for placing a German, and a Nazi party member to boot, at the center of the story. But the chief reason why this film does not work as a grand narrative is not that Schindler is the all-too-rare "good German" but that the experience of the Jews portrayed in the film was not the experience of the majority of Europe's Jews. What gives this story its power as literature and as film is precisely its quality of exception: the goodness that survived amidst all that brutality. Spielberg does not spare us from seeing that brutality, so the story of the rescue is shown within its broader context. In the end, whether or not *Schindler's List* works as grand narrative may depend on Spielberg's intentions—whether he wanted to assert the power of good amidst unspeakable evil as the principle historical significance of the Holocaust—as well as the perceptions of the viewer, some of whom may be overwhelmed by this story of humanity at its worst, others of whom look for hope amidst all that brutality. In any case, it is a question that gets at some very important issues.

Four years after *Schindler's List*, Spielberg completed *Amistad*, based on the true story of a revolt aboard a Spanish slave ship in 1839. The ship ended up in U.S. waters and the struggle over the fate of the Africans on board ended up in U.S. courts, and ultimately came before the U.S. Supreme Court in early 1841. Choreographer Debbie Allen (of *Fame* fame) had come upon two volumes of documents and essays on the case in the 1980s, and became one of the producers of the film version, which Spielberg agreed to direct. Again, with a big-name director (now with *Schindler's List* to his credit and acclaim) and a budget of $36 million, expectations ran high. This story apparently had the power to demonstrate the evils of slavery and the heroism of those who fought against it. But there were some significant potential pitfalls as well: the most dramatic part of the story took place at the beginning, and much of the rest of the drama revolved around the deliberations of white men, not exactly an empowering spectacle. The film deals only tangentially with the African American experience, and it does so by sketching in a fictional character, Theodore Joadson, played by Morgan Freeman. Streamlining, consolidating, and even creating characters to suit the dramatic agenda of a historical film is not uncommon, but in this case, it underscores the fact that this film is anything but a grand narrative of the African American experience of slavery. By dramatizing the story of Sengbe, called Cinque (played by Djimon Hounsou), Spielberg skillfully places the story of the revolt leader in the middle, or at the heart, of the film, in a sequence that shows the horrifying "middle passage" that captured Africans endured across the Atlantic. These scenes provide jarring contrast in what would otherwise have been a conventional courtroom drama, with erudite speeches (rather unlike the real thing) and the suspense of awaiting the outcome on which so much depends. Yet the fact is that, even as a courtroom drama, the outcome is hardly a triumph of justice. Though many courtroom dramas involve the travesties of justice carried out by all-white juries in the segregated South, in this particular case, one would only hope that, despite the inappropriate interference of President Martin van Buren, the courts would find as they did in a case that was really not very complicated. The international slave trade was already illegal under U.S., British, and Spanish law, so once the fact was established that the Africans were in fact Africans who had been abducted by Portuguese slave traders, the courts merely had to follow through to uphold the law, despite the interference of politicians.

Ultimately the story and the film proved to be much less compelling for audiences than *Schindler's List* had been. The former film, which cost $25 million to make, grossed $93 million in the United States and Canada, and another $221 million overseas, ending up with a total of $317 million.[7] *Amistad* cost $36 million to make, grossed $44 million in the United States and Canada, and perhaps another $16 million abroad, ending up with a total of about $60 million (from imdb.com). Though Academy Awards are not the ultimate arbiter of quality by any means, *Schindler's List* was nominated for twelve and won seven, including Best Picture, Director, and Adapted Screenplay; *Amistad* received four nominations and won none. *Schindler's List* was a major cultural event, generating widespread attention and comment; four years later, the story of another boat, the *Titanic*, overshadowed that of the *Amistad*. Both films demonstrate the challenges of taking on major historical topics in a medium that is expensive and difficult to work with, but which can certainly be very powerful when it succeeds.

This chapter underscores the importance of approaching film analytically: understanding the filmmaking process, aspects of the film itself, and the context in which the film is made, including the specific culture of the film industry itself and characteristics of the broader society. To be proficient at analyzing film and using it as a historical resource requires facility with the terminology of the medium. In time, film should become a source that you can use as comfortably as written sources to understand, describe, and explain all facets of the human experience. Furthermore, being a good scholar requires the kind of curiosity, desire for knowledge and high level of engagement that prompts you to follow current events, to read, and learn as much as you can about people, places, and events, and of course to expand your interest in film as broadly as you can. The more you know and want to know, the more creative, interesting and insightful work you will do.

Questions for Discussion:

1. Other than through the obvious means of script, costumes, and sets, how can filmmakers convey historical meaning?

2. How can historians work with or around conventions of filmmaking that would tend to render the past not as it actually was but as myth?

3. Identify some movies that might be considered "grand narratives" of a particular historical era or event. Discuss what makes them "grand" as well as what makes them fall short of such a distinction.

---

[7] Spielberg used his own earnings to establish the Survivors of the Shoah Visual History Foundation, an ambitious project to record interviews with as many living survivors of the Holocaust as possible, all over the world. The material has appeared in a number of documentary films, including the 1998 Academy Award winning film *The Last Days*, about the Holocaust in Hungary and featuring Congressman Tom Lantos (D-California).

4

■ ■ ■

Assessing a Film's Historical Content

Using film as a historical resource requires the ability to analyze film in terms that make sense both to the film scholar and the historian. From Chapter 3 you have a basic grasp of film terminology. This chapter focuses on the process of determining, describing, and analyzing a film's historical significance. From reading the chapter, you should

* become familiar with some of the theoretical underpinnings of and practical approaches to our approach to history in film;
* place a particular film's content, production, and reception into a historical context; and
* begin to distinguish among different kinds of history in film.

John E. O'Connor, in his book *Image as Artifact: The Historical Analysis of Film and Television*, describes an approach that has been very influential and remains highly useful. A film's historical significance lies in the story of its production, the content of the finished product, and the reception of the film both upon its release and in later years. The content of this chapter certainly owes a great deal to O'Connor, other scholars who contributed to his work, and to the general discussion of history in film that has unfolded over the past twenty-five years. Inherent in O'Connor's approach, but worth highlighting as a separate consideration, is the concept of *context*: considering the time, place, and circumstances in which a film is both produced and experienced. A movie itself may seem to us a fixed thing—celluloid in a canister, a DVD on the shelf—but many external factors shape our experience of viewing a movie, and these must be considered as part of your analysis. To that end, I propose a model for mapping the content, production, and reception with in a time frame that in turn can shape your analysis of a particular film.

The purpose of this chapter is to help open your mind to the different ways films can serve as historical evidence, using specific examples to illuminate different approaches.

Scholars are not immune to the biases and prejudices that exist in our society at large, and their values and priorities shape the work that they do, but academic scholarship nevertheless values reason above all as a tool for the advancement of knowledge. Assertiveness and showmanship certainly have advanced a few academic careers, but in the end, reason alone advances knowledge, whether through scholarship or teaching. Objectivity is an elusive goal, since we all approach life and work with certain beliefs and convictions, but it is a goal nevertheless. Indisputable fact makes an argument stronger than rumor or allegation. The word *indisputable* carries with it a social dimension, suggesting not that the fact is hard, objective reality so much as that we agree that it is fact.

Reason also provides common ground for our communications. Each of us may hold religious beliefs or political views that incline us to look at the world a certain way, but we live in a diverse society in which decent, intelligent people can differ on challenging issues. Academics certainly can find themselves on opposite sides of an ideological divide, but they must support their scholarly opinions with substantive evidence incorporated into a persuasive argument. Scholarship invites us to view evidence from every possible angle, our best defense against bias. Conversely, if we observe the world determined to cling to a particularly set of views and allow evidence to be ignored or twisted to suit those beliefs, we are unlikely to be useful participants in the business of advancing knowledge. If anything, the study of history teaches us to appreciate the ambiguities of life and the complexities and contradictions of human society.

IN THEORY

The theories of structuralism and poststructuralism discussed in Chapter 3 have already challenged us to think creatively about film and its importance to the study of history. Scholars also have addressed specifically the epistemological challenges of using film as a historical resource. John O'Connor, Robert Rosenstone, and Robert Brent Toplin are three of the leading scholars of history in film. Of the three, Toplin, a professor at the University of North Carolina at Wilmington and editor of the film review section of the *Journal of American History*, may strike the reader as least theoretical in focus and approach, but his books, such as *History by Hollywood: The Use and Abuse of the American Past* (1996) and *Reel History: In Defense of Hollywood* (2002) do articulate theoretical precepts about the way films portray the past and shape public perceptions about the past. As I have done in this book, Toplin distinguishes between films that document a time and place and movies that interpret the past. He suggests that scholars have tended to take the former more seriously as evidence of what film theorist

Siegfried Kracauer called the "collective cultural consciousness"; and certainly scholars in the field of film studies have gone over every frame of celluloid, applying every theoretical approach. Toplin himself focuses on the historical film: not the films that historians applaud necessarily, but those "major motion pictures" that, for good or ill, take up significant historical topics and give them the "Hollywood treatment." Like it or not, he argues, these films shape our collective understanding of the past. While as consumers we might watch these movies like anyone else, as scholars we must understand the medium, the industry, and our own culture to understand the relationship between film as a big-bucks entertainment medium and film as portrayer of the past.

Robert Rosenstone, whose credentials include serving as a historical consultant on the film *Reds* (1981) and editing the film review section of the *American Historical Review*, is a professor at the California Institute of Technology. His book *Visions of the Past: The Challenge of Film to Our Idea of History* (1995) is a collection of essays that together push the reader to think about filmmaking as a way of doing history that should not be assessed using exactly the same criteria we use to discuss written scholarship. More recently, his *History on Film/Film on History* (2006) continues his highly creative discussion of film as a way of doing history and pushes toward an understanding of history in film that has its own sensibility, independent of the criteria we use to assess written history. He argues that the rub between history as a discipline and film as an art is the fact that movies do not "do" history as history scholars do, basing an argument on empirical evidence cited in the work. Narrative films about the past generally involve more imagination and invention than would be acceptable in written scholarship or a documentary film. But if we can see through the illusory qualities of movies, we realize that they are not "a window onto the past" but, like written history, a "construction of a simulated past" (161). He encourages us to embrace the tools of filmmaking, either as viewers or practitioners, as means of conveying insights about the past.

Inherent in Rosenstone's argument is the notion that doing history is not the sole province of professional historians (indeed historians can ruefully note that some of the most commercially successful works of history have been written quite competently by people without doctorates in history). Pierre Sorlin, a French scholar who began writing about history in film before the video revolution, discusses how audiovisual history can liberate the past from its "official" versions. While he notes that the study of film as a historical resource can be expensive—a notion that has been largely but not entirely swept away by the availability of vast resources on VHS, DVD, and the Internet—he also makes the point that the motion picture record of human events cannot easily be controlled. He uses the example of Nazi Germany in the 1930s, where the film record largely presents a positive picture of Nazis restoring order and dignity to the German people, in contrast with more recent times, in which film captured the abuses of the internment camps in Chile after the coup that overthrew President Salvador Allende in 1973.[1] The notion of controlling the media today is all but dead with the arrival of the Internet and its powerful search engines. While television networks may be vulnerable to control by powerful moneyed interests, or by regulatory bodies controlled by conservative interests, anything can be posted on the Internet. So while the Fox Network censored Sally Field's antiwar statement as she accepted an Emmy in September 2007, YouTube had the uncensored clip from Canada's CTV network almost immediately.

O'Connor, though still active as a scholar, is another pioneering figure in the study of history in film. *His Image as Artifact: The Historical Analysis of Film and Television* (1990) is an edited volume that includes theoretical essays by such scholars as Pierre Sorlin and Robert Sklar, but it also sets forth O'Connor's own methodology for studying history in film that remains very influential. Whereas Rosenstone gives us a great deal to think about in our study of history in film, O'Connor provides an indispensable methodology that focuses on content, production, and reception as the three key dimensions of a film's historical significance. As a work of cinematic art, the film must stand on its own, and in that respect the content is the central element. But each film has its own history: the story of its production, which ideally reveals the filmmakers' intentions; and the story of its reception, including the commentary of critics, awards, and box office information indicating the film's popularity. We can bring these three elements together as we discuss how each of these elements fits into a historical context. In other words, we consider what the film *depicts* as historical evidence of one kind or another. But we also consider the film itself as a cultural artifact. We reconstruct the story of the film's production as a historical event, and how audiences receive the film over time. Our chronological analytical framework will help us to clarify how all of these historical aspects relate to one another by mapping how they relate to one another in time.

In discussing John O'Connor, one should mention also the extraordinary body of work done by his colleague and longtime editor of *Film and History*, Peter C. Rollins. Like Toplin, Rollins is not so much a theoretician as a historian who makes exemplary use of film as a historical resource. In addition to his own scholarship, Rollins has supported the production of countless articles on history in film as editor of *Film and History*, and his book, *The Columbia Companion to American History on Film: How the Movies Have Portrayed the American Past* (2003), discussed further in Chapter 11, is an indispensable reference work for anyone looking to identify both films and scholarly books and articles relevant to any number of topics in U.S. history.

---

[1] Pierre Sorlin, How to Look at an "Historical" Film, in Marcia Landy, ed., *The Historical Film: History and Memory in Media.* New Brunswick, NJ: Rutgers University Press, 2001, 25–49.

MAPPING IT OUT: A CONTEXTUAL MODEL FOR RELATING MOVIES TO HISTORY

To analyze the historical content of a film, you need to identify the relationship of the film to the history it portrays. The film can be a portrayal of the past, but it may also be seen a product of the time in which it was made. That may seem a bit complicated, but don't worry: categorization of the film as history is an initial step in your analysis, not an end in itself. Take, for example, the 1941 Alexander Korda film, *That Hamilton Woman*, about the affair between the Napoleonic war hero Lord Nelson (Laurence Olivier) and Emma Hamilton (Vivien Leigh). As the film deals with an important chapter in British history, it is certainly worth exploring for historical accuracy, given what historians knew then and have learned since. But the fact that it is said to have been Winston Churchill's favorite film, and one which he watched repeatedly during the war as he led his beleaguered country through a war effort that, if anything, surpassed the Napoleonic wars in scale and significance, makes the film perhaps more significant as a document of British wartime culture. Some reviewers found it distasteful that it portrayed an iconic figure in British history through the eyes of a "trollop," though clearly Churchill did not share that sentiment. One can therefore categorize the film as history, but one must also engage the historical imagination to experience the film as people would have experienced it during the Second World War, and to see what it contributes today to the discussion of Britain's national identity then and now. As a secondary source, it depicts events from the conflict that propelled Britain to global power and the *Pax Britannica*; but it is a primary source from the Second World War, which required a Herculean effort from Britain but also marked its eclipse by the United States and the Soviet Union.

The analysis of a film for its historical content is best organized according to the kinds of resources one would use to explore the different historical questions it poses. In the case of *That Hamilton Woman*, research into the production of the film would reveal the historical sources used in making the film and the degree to which the writers and other members of the filmmaking team sought historical fidelity. Exploration of more recent scholarly sources might shed further light on the film's historical accuracy. But the film's reception in Britain during the war would require research into film reviews and evidence that documents Churchill's own responses to the film (John Colville's *Fringes of Power* would be one good source, along with Martin Gilbert's massive, multivolume biography of Churchill). And the film itself would serve as a primary source, furnishing evidence of the filmmaker's own connection of the past to the present. In other words, what might be a stale exercise in measuring the accuracy of the past presented in the film versus what the best written scholarship tells us, becomes much more, a nuanced picture of how we remember the past, choose our heroes, and like to think of ourselves.

The relationship of this film to history is both complex and interesting, and it may help us to clarify our thinking if we try to plot these points on a chronological continuum that includes the following key elements: the events portrayed in the film; the period in which the film was produced and released; the reception of the film over time; and major events or relevant developments taking place throughout the period under consideration. So for *That Hamilton Woman*, we begin with the Napoleonic Wars of the early nineteenth century:

A Contextual Model for *That Hamilton Woman* (1941)

Date/Event	
1758–1805	Life of Vice Admiral Horatio Nelson, 1st Viscount Nelson • greatest naval hero in British history • died at Battle of Trafalgar, decisive naval victory over France
1765–1815	Life of Emma, Lady Hamilton
1792–1815	French Revolutionary Wars/Napoleonic Wars **CONTENT of film: relationship of Nelson and Hamilton against backdrop of above events, late 1700s to early 1800s, as interpreted in 1940–41 (original screenplay by Walter Reisch and R.C. Sherriff)**
1815–1914	"Pax Britannica" • Relative peace in Europe • British industrial and imperial expansion • British dominance in world affairs
1874–1965	Life of Winston Churchill, British statesman, Prime Minister 1940–45
1914–1918	First World War
1939–1945	The Second World War in Europe • June 1940 French defeat and British evacuation at Dunkirk • Summer 1940 Battle of Britain • Aerial bombardment of London and other British cities (the Blitz) **PRODUCTION of film, 1940–41** Oct.–Nov. 1940 Filming in Denham, Buckinghamshire, England **RECEPTION of film, 1941–present** April 1941 U.S. release August 1941 U.K. release 　　　　　　　　Critical and popular reception 　　　　　　　　Special case of Churchill's response 　　　　　　　　　Statesman, historian, imperialist, war leader 　　　　　　　　　Frequent screenings Later Releases in other countries 　　　　　　　　Television broadcasts and other screenings 　　　　　　　　VHS, DVD releases
1945–present	British decline and renewal • Cold War dominated by U.S.–Soviet rivalry • British decolonization, imperialism in disrepute • British economic decline and renewal • Diversification of British culture and society • Postcolonialism in art, literature

Present	How do we view the film today?
	• Events from 200 years ago, movie from more than 65 years ago
	• How have views changed?
	• What does film suggest about British identity, history, culture, change?

The goal of mapping the production, content, and reception of a film into a timeline that includes other relevant development is to get you thinking about the relationships among all these elements and to begin your analysis. It helps you to see the historical context not just of the events portrayed in the film but also for the film itself as a cultural artifact or historical document. Finally, it helps you to see yourself as a scholar studying a film or topic from your own vantage point in the present, influenced by historical events and contemporary circumstances that have intervened between the events portrayed, the production of the film, and now.

PRIMARY OR SECONDARY SOURCE? FILM AS EVIDENCE VERSUS FILM AS HISTORICAL ARGUMENT

As historians, we can use film as a primary or a secondary source, depending on the nature of the film and the topic under study. Film and video have captured innumerable moving images, many of real-life activity, and many of staged activity. All of this activity is real, however, and all can serve as primary evidence for study. Film also can be used to present history, reconstructions, and interpretations of the past, and this too can be real-life or actuality, as in documentary film, or staged, as in narrative film or "the movies."

Possibly the most famous segment of actuality film in history is the one shot unassumingly by Dallas resident Abraham Zapruder on November 22, 1963, as President John F. Kennedy's motorcade passed through Dealey Plaza. Consider the enormous gulf between the filmmaker's intent and what this piece of film came to signify. What was to have become a personal record and souvenir instead captured President Kennedy's death in a twenty-six-second segment of film that served as important evidence in the Warren Commission's investigation, subsequent analyses of the assassination, and endless speculation as to possible conspiracies and cover-ups. Of course, it did not capture the entire event, only the victim, providing evidence for but not answering important questions about the assassin or assassins. Nevertheless, the Library of Congress has included this "home movie" in the National Film Registry as "culturally significant." It shows how moving pictures can capture history in the making and in turn shape history itself. But it also shows how much more evidence is necessary to reconstruct and understand historical events. And it shows that film as a recorder of human events has great limitations. For obvious reasons, no one thought to film the activities of Lee Harvey Oswald that day, or any number of other obscure people who may or may not have been involved in the assassination. Even though someone was much more likely to film the president's visit, the Zapruder film was not the professional work of television journalists, but rather the consequence of a private citizen deciding to take his film camera along and turning it on to record an event that turned out to be something horribly different from what he had expected it to be.

Today, such an event would likely have been more thoroughly documented on video, both by news cameras and amateurs. Unanticipated events, such as the attack on the World Trade Center on September 11, 2001, were recorded by amateurs simply because in a highly populated area, a famous landmark is likely being filmed by someone at any given moment, certainly during the day. The news, on any given day, is supported by film footage. But think about what film does not capture: discussions leading to important decisions; the planning and perpetration of crimes; and acts of war. Moving images, therefore, provide evidence of some historical events, but the record is far from complete. Though it provided important evidence, the Zapruder film did not answer nearly all the questions, including some of the most important ones, about the Kennedy assassination.

Nevertheless film and video document plenty of human activity, significant and insignificant, and any historian studying a twentieth-century subject should examine whatever archival footage may exist on his/her topic. One cannot discuss the life and work of Martin Luther King, Jr., for example, without studying film of him giving speeches, to observe the rhetorical style and presence that helped make him the leader of the civil rights movement.

History examines far more than just the public activities of prominent political figures and other leaders. Film also provides abundant evidence about everyday life, the behaviors, priorities, and preoccupations of ordinary people. While archival film footage—raw footage recording "real life"—exists and can support the making of documentary film, a more readily available source of evidence is the movie: moving images packaged into a story and consumed as entertainment. The movies' obvious and intended fictions make their assessment as primary evidence more challenging, but movies nevertheless document attitudes, values, priorities, styles, preoccupations, and fantasies in ways that are perhaps more refutable than the evidence presented in the Zapruder film, but which are nevertheless worth exploring. The nineteenth-century French novelist Stendhal described the novel as a mirror bumping down a road on a cart reflecting, however imperfectly, that which comes into view; the same can be said of movies.

If, for example, you wanted to study the 1960s and the emergence of the counterculture, you would want to see as many films about contemporary life from that time period as you could. Again, archival footage might be available to assist you, but that would be a different kind of study, and rather difficult to carry out for most undergraduates. You would need to narrow your focus as you developed your research, but you would look for movies that have had a considerable impact. The year 1967 brought us the "Summer of Love," but films such as *Guess Who's Coming to Dinner*, a stagy comedy drama set in a rich part of San Francisco, and *The Graduate*, part of which takes place in Berkeley, show little of the "hippie" culture emerging in the Bay Area. Both were nominated for the Best Picture Academy Award, and Mark Harris compares them to their competitors in his book *Pictures at a Revolution* (2008). They would lose to *In the Heat of the Night*, in which an African American cop from Philadelphia, Virgil Tubbs (Sidney Poitier, who also starred in *Guess Who's Coming to Dinner* as the man who was coming to dinner), investigates a murder in a sleepy Mississippi town. *Dr. Doolittle*, which followed the great musical successes of *Mary Poppins* (1964), *My Fair Lady* (1964), and *The Sound of Music* (1965), had been a critical and commercial flop, and its nomination stands as testament to the Academy's fallibility and the interference of Hollywood studio politics. The production history of these films shows that they were in the works well before most people had heard of hippies or LSD, but they do provide a benchmark against which subsequent films, such as *Petulia* (1968) and *Easy Rider* (1969), could be compared. *The Graduate* is about restless youth, but Benjamin Braddock (Dustin Hoffman) keeps his rebellion private and personal. The most overtly rebellious of the five nominees was Arthur Penn's *Bonnie and Clyde*, a movie about the infamous 1930s gangsters, which, as Robert Brent Toplin writes, tells us more about the 1960s than it does about the 1930s. Its subject matter, outlaws in desperate need of therapy, and its look, strongly influenced by the French New Wave, made it the movie with the most revolutionary potential.[2] However, lest we think the revolution was merely delayed, we should note that Carol Reed's *Oliver!* (1968), the musical based on Charles Dickens' *Oliver Twist* took Best Picture the following year.

For purposes of original scholarly research, you may want to focus on using film as a primary source, but film also can function as a secondary source, as an interpreter of the past in its own right. Certainly, documentary filmmakers can aspire to take their place among scholarly writers in interpreting the past, though more often than not they synthesize the work of scholars, incorporating different relevant scholarly opinions into their work. Ken Burns, for example, is not a trained historian, but he is America's most prominent maker of documentary films that portray important chapters in American history, from the Civil War to baseball to jazz and, most recently, the Second World War. The film production process is challenging enough without the filmmaker him- or herself carrying out original archival research into the topic. But it is certainly not impossible to do so.

If, for example, you wished to examine popular perceptions about significant events in history, you could survey the ways in which different films present the Civil War. D.W. Griffith's *The Birth of a Nation* (1915) presents a view of the Civil War that no serious scholar today could find compelling,

---

[2] See Robert Brent Toplin's chapter on *Bonnie and Clyde* in *History by Hollywood: The Use and Abuse of the American Past.* (Urbana: University of Illinois Press, 1996), 128–153. See also Mark Harris, *Pictures at a Revolution: Five Movies and the Birth of the New Hollywood* (New York: Penguin, 2008).

but it was a view that many people shared in 1915 and which some people today may still hold. If you were to study the film, you would want to explore the historiography of the Civil War and Reconstruction, to see how Griffith's views of those events compare to those of scholars, now and then. Certainly his views on miscegenation had adherents in academia, particularly among those who studied eugenics, and who, perhaps more importantly, served in government and on the courts. The interaction between the world of entertainment and the world of academia is well worth exploring. The tremendous commercial success of that film helped to ensure that the Civil War would remain a popular film topic, much more so, say, than the War of Independence or the War of 1812. Among the fixtures of these films for many years would be a romanticized view of the "Old South" as a genteel civilization (including the slaves) that after the war would be "gone with the wind." More recent films, such as Anthony Minghella's *Cold Mountain* (2003), help to dispel those myths with a more realistic portrayal of the brutality and bitterness of the South as it faced defeat.

IDENTIFYING AND CATEGORIZING HISTORY IN FILM

Bearing all these things in mind, you should now be able to approach any film with a set of questions that will enable you to determine exactly how it relates to the human experience and begin to identify the qualities that make the film historically interesting or significant. The following questions function as a kind of flow chart that will enable you to identify where a particular film fits among the different categories we find useful.

1. Is the film a documentary or a narrative film?

Documentary is "nonfiction" or "actuality" film that explores or documents aspects of real life. Fiction explores real life and the human condition as well, but we expect and accept the artifice of novels and narrative films. In a documentary, the people you see should be themselves, not actors playing roles, and the events you see should be unfolding in real time in the real world. Andrew Dominik's *The Assassination of Jesse James by the Coward Robert Ford* (2007) is *not* a documentary: it is rather a narrative film in which the events of Jesse James' life have served as a basis for a *dramatization*, not *documentation*, of his last days. Actors Brad Pitt (as James) and Casey Affleck (as Ford) may have studied the historical record to understand their characters, and we can look at their performances as acts of historical interpretation, but the filmmakers would not claim to be documenting the past. By contrast, Mark Zwonitzer's *Jesse James*, aired on PBS' (Public Broadcasting System) *American Experience* in 2006, *is* a documentary. A narrator (Michel Murphy) reads a script, but this is a biography of James based on primary and secondary sources. Within the film, historians discuss the life and significance of Jesse James as the viewers see photographs, newspapers, and other archival materials that document his life and his crimes. These are good examples, because in fact both films have elements that blur the distinctions a little. *The Assassination of Jesse James by the Coward Robert Ford* has a narrator who provides historical information such as one would hear in a documentary film; and the documentary film *Jesse James* does have actors playing Jesse James and others, though they do not speak. Because the life of Jesse James predated moving pictures, making a moving picture about his life does mean that there is no archival film footage available. Still photographs and talking historians, no matter how alluring they may be, may not create the visual interest one might seek in a documentary. We should never be entirely comfortable with actors in a documentary, and it becomes even more problematic when they speak, as they did in parts of the BBC (British Broadcasting Corporation) series *Auschwitz*: can we verify that these words were really spoken? If not, are we dramatizing instead of documenting the past? The BBC can get away with it because of its global reputation for quality, though no organization is immune to error or mis-judgment. Reenactments that are based on careful historical study can help viewers to understand the history better, and as we gain experience in film and history we will develop the ability to see each of a film's elements for what it is. For now, however, the line between documentary and narrative film should remain as distinct and clear as possible.

2. If it is a documentary, will you examine it as a primary or secondary source?

A documentary film on a historical topic is most likely to work as a secondary source if it advances an argument and uses archival evidence and the opinions of other historians to support that argument. The *Jesse James* documentary just discussed would be a secondary source if you used it to gather evidence about Jesse James and the opinions of scholars and others. But if you were to examine the role of Jesse James in America's culture and historical memory over time, you might use that documentary as evidence of contemporary views, in which case it would really function as a primary source. In other words, whether a film is a primary or secondary source depends on where and how it fits into your research and analysis.

A documentary film should never be assumed to be objective, simply because it portrays real-life events as they occur or occurred. The act of documentation requires choices: choices of subject, choices of evidence, development of an argument shaped not just by the evidence but by a whole range of values and beliefs, both individual and cultural. Though we would quickly add the term propaganda to describe it, Leni Riefenstahl's 1935 film *Triumph of the Will* is a documentary film that made the Nazis look impressive at their 1934 party rally in Nuremberg. With its impressive angles and camera movements, *Triumph of the Will* accomplished cinematically what the Nazis wanted to accomplish with the real event: an image of unity, solidarity and order, a triumph of propaganda that masked the truth, which was that they would actually bring destruction and chaos on Europe and Germany itself. To place *Triumph of the Will* in the contextual model described above would help to illuminate the importance of context in analyzing this film historically. Consider the vast difference between the film's reception by German audiences in the 1930s and how students of history would view the film today. What may have instilled awe or even fear at the time would now be seen as a skillful and chilling example of propaganda, helping to cultivate an image of the National Socialists as orderly and patriotic. *Triumph of the Will* can only be seen as a cultural and political artifact of Nazi Germany and for scholarly purposes would therefore work exclusively as a primary source.

Using a documentary film as a secondary source can be a little tricky. As with any print source, the scholar must assess the quality of the work to ensure its reliability. Associations help, such as where the film has aired and how it is distributed, but each work must be assessed on its own merits as well. The journalist Juan Williams worked with Henry Hampton on *Eyes on the Prize* (1987), an outstanding chronicle of the civil rights movement, and foreign correspondent Stanley Karnow was involved in the making of *Vietnam: A Television History* (1983). Both series, along with their companion volumes authored by the journalists named, offer compelling accounts and interpretations of events. Both aired on PBS. As cinematic works of history, both have earned a place in their respective historiographies.

3. If this is a narrative film, where is the history?

A. *History and Biography:* This may be an obvious point, but a narrative film that portrays historical events has to have a script, and unless that script is provided by a historical document that records actual conversation or speeches (a speech on the floor of the House of Representatives, for example), dialogue must be created and scenes staged that only by the most bizarre and unlikely of coincidences could correspond to what actually physically happened. Depending on the intentions of the filmmakers, the script does two things: it presents an interpretation of events, and it does so in the form of a narrative that follows certain rules as to what audiences expect and accept in film storytelling. If historians must use their imaginations to reconstruct and present interpretations of the past—as opposed to simply recording the evidence provided by the documentation—filmmakers have to come up with a movie that people will pay to see. The life stories of famous people are a genre on their own, the "biopic," and the exercise of condensing someone's life story into a two-hour film (perhaps three if the story is compelling enough) requires mashing all the complexity and detail of a person's life into a coherent and entertaining story. In other words, do not expect literal factual truth from beginning to end. The significance lies in how the story is presented and how the person is represented. That aspects of the story are fabricated should not be a great surprise, but the movie must be true in a fundamental sense, presenting the most important realities of that person's life. In general, historical narrative film must not distort these realities or misrepresent people or events. In the interest of narrative, filmmakers may also take liberties with the historical record by adding characters and consolidating the actions of several people into one character. Historians may not accept these liberties, but will be less hostile if the film effectively conveys the essential facts and their significance. Viewers should be ready for anything. While history books are written to advance knowledge of the past, historical films should do the same, but they also must contend with a pressing commercial and artistic agenda.

B. *Historical Fiction:* In this case, the script is a fictional story set in a historical time and place in the past. Adaptations of novels often fall into this category, as do many Westerns. Filmmakers are freed from getting specific facts wrong about central characters, because they are made up. But because the movie invokes a time and place, the historical setting should be as accurate as possible, and characters and actions should fit the time period. Filmmakers have artistic license to use creative anachronisms, but they do not want these to appear unintentional. Mel Brooks' *Blazing Saddles* (1974) is a satirical treatment of the Western that makes deliberate use of anachronism for comic effect, but amidst all the silliness is some socially relevant and historically interesting material.

C. *Cultural Artifact:* Every film is a cultural artifact. The fact that this category includes all the others reminds us that films about the past are also films about the present. Several critics have written that Paul Thomas Anderson's *There Will Be Blood* (2007) is set in the past but full of contemporary significance. It is terrific historical fiction, but its exploration of the ties among entrepreneurialism, obsession, money, religion, and power are certainly relevant to American life today. This category also includes films that deal with contemporary life and would therefore not be considered historical films, but which over time have achieved historical significance because they mark a time period or evoke a special sense of place. Nicholas Ray's *Rebel Without a Cause* (1955) took up the burning contemporary issue of juvenile delinquency, but became a picture of youth culture in Southern California in the 1950s, much as *The Graduate* did a decade later. These films cannot be viewed or studied in isolation, though they are big films: *Rebel* because of its star James Dean, an icon of the 1950s; and *the Graduate* because it is a better film, and it is seen as a major cultural marker of the 1960s.

FOR EXAMPLE . . .

While this book should provide you with the vocabulary and ideas you will need to read movies as historical texts, you will learn these skills best by trying them out yourself on different kinds of movies. While I certainly have my favorites, I also understand that certain movies that I may not like particularly have proven to be very popular. So let us take a few of those to get you watching movies as a historian.

Not truly deserving of this category is a recent popular film that nevertheless has been assessed as *film history*, though the actual historical event it dramatizes has been filtered through the medium of a graphic novel. In the spring of 2007, Zack Snyder's *300* (2006) grossed over $200 million worldwide and appeared to be especially popular with repeat-viewing teenagers "despite" its R rating. The historical basis of this film is the Battle of Thermopylae, which took place in 480 BC, in which, according to the historian Herodotus, a small army of Spartans sacrificed itself in battle against a much larger Persian force, allowing the Greeks ultimately to triumph against the invaders. Whatever actually happened then, the events provided a factual basis for a story that would grow into myth, expressing Greek values of heroism and bravery that would become universal. Herodotus wrote down what he knew of the events themselves, which took place when he was a child, but clearly his views were strongly shaped by the culture of which he was part.

The film likewise should be seen as fitting into the tradition of mythmaking rather than an attempt to reconstruct the events based on historical evidence. That may be a disappointment to those historians who would like to point out that the Spartans did not fight in leather underpants, but it is pretty clear from the outset that this film is using the past to a large extent as a set, to tell a story that blends eroticism and violence in a way that many viewers apparently find compelling. To the extent that the story appears mythical, one does have to take a look at the values it presents to viewers, just as the myths of old presented humanity in all of its complexity in tales of gods and heroes. The BBC described the film as a "valentine to violence," and while the reviewer Daniel Mendelsohn in the *New York Review of Books* (May 31, 2007, 37–39) disputes as historically inaccurate the call to "freedom" that King Leonidas growls as he prepares to fight, for the audience it serves as pretext for the orgy of violence that ensues.

The battle scenes are a little slow in coming, but they appear to be the main attraction of the film. Without the slightest trace of ambiguity or subtlety, our heroes are 300 Spartan men who meet the comic-book definition of masculinity. They are, to a man, heavily muscled fighting machines: the pudgy, let alone the rejected hunchback who betrays them, need not apply. Having somewhat laboriously established a "just cause," Leonidas and his men now do what they do best: rage and destroy. In the end, they die as heroes, and one could interestingly compare the heroic ideal expressed in this film to that expressed by the Greeks themselves centuries ago.

What is sadly amusing about this film and its enthusiastic reception is its obvious homoeroticism, strongly tied to militancy and violence, in a culture and society in which homophobia is being used as a political tool, often by the same people who take a hard line on foreign and military policy. What is disturbing about the film is its presentation of essential masculinity as brawn and violence. What could serve better as a recruitment poster for the armed forces? *300* definitely needs to be analyzed and understood in the context of a controversial, protracted and unpopular war in Iraq. Many viewers may laugh it off—is it not just a visual comic book, after all?—but considering the audience with which it resonated so strongly, the film's moral import is pretty disturbing. Readers are certainly welcome to dispute that point, but while one can look at *300* to some degree as history, its primary interest to historians will be as a cultural artifact. Its impressive visual style makes it distinctive and may make it a classic of sorts, but the context in which this film was released is of obvious significance. To underscore that point, some saw the portrayal of the Persians as offensive to Iran, with whom the United States has engaged in some saber-rattling.

As an example of *historical fiction*, now for something completely different: John Waters' movie *Hairspray* (1988), and the more recent movie based on the musical *Hairspray*, which was based on the Waters movie, Adam Shankman's *Hairspray* (2007). I choose these examples because they stretch the notion of historical fiction quite a bit: a more typical and respectable example would be a film such as Peter Weir's *Master and Commander: The Far Side of the World* (2003), a film based on the celebrated novels of Patrick O'Brien, which are fictional stories set against a careful reconstruction of early nineteenth century British maritime culture. *Hairspray* is a very different phenomenon: less careful reconstruction, but still a story purposely set in the past. One could possibly dismiss *Hairspray* as nostalgia, but while historians try to avoid such wistful portrayals of the past as the "good old days," nostalgia itself is an aspect of human culture that is worth exploring.

John Waters' film, which spawned the musical and its film version, was the most mainstream movie he had made to that time. Films such as *Pink Flamingos* (1972) and *Polyester* (1981) aimed to gross out their audiences as Waters, who as a young person reveled in the tackiest and tawdriest material the film industry could offer, flouted convention, and *Hairspray* actually provides some clues as to why. While the story is almost entirely fictional, it is carefully and deliberately set in Baltimore in 1962, a city still largely segregated between blacks and whites. Rather than take on schools or lunch counters, the iconic battlegrounds of the civil rights movement, Waters focuses on television, specifically the *Corny Collins Show*, a fictional local television show based on the real *Buddy Dean Show*, which featured local teens dancing the latest dances to the popular songs of the day. Waters' portrayal of early 1960s teen culture is over the top, but not by much: there really were dances called the Mashed Potato and the Roach, and hairspray really did immobilize great piles of teased and molded hair into outrageous creations. Waters ascribes political significance to the "hairdo": hair, he asserts in his DVD commentary, was power.

Waters plays up the importance of the show in teenagers' lives, and notes that for white teenagers black music and black dances offered the opportunity to rebel against the more staid, "vanilla" tastes of their parents. Tracy Turnblad (Ricki Lake) is the plump daughter of Edna (Divine) and Wilbur Turnblad (Jerry Stiller), who live in a working-class neighborhood of East Baltimore. Tracy watches *Corny Collins* every day with her Atomic Fireball-popping friend Penny Pingleton (Lesley Ann Powers). Responding to a promotion, they try out for the show: Waters knows that these kinds of shows would not accept heavy teenagers, but with a blend of affection and satire he turns Tracy into the most popular dancer on the show and a local celebrity. Part of her appeal is her outspoken opposition to segregation. Her nemesis is Amber von Tussel (Colleen Fitzpatrick), whose parents (played by Sonny Bono and Deborah Harry) support segregation. While it seems improbable that "dreamy" Link Larkin (Michael St. Gerard) would drop Amber for Tracy, the viewer does not protest.

The film certainly embraces the bizarre: Divine, an obese transvestite whom Waters had helped propel to stardom, plays a straight, conventional mom who supports Tracy's dream. The characters have alliterative, singsong names. But bizarre is part of reality, and unlike many films, this one is set in a very real time and place, with Waters aiming to evoke the Baltimore of his youth. He perfectly captures the sense of importance young people attached to programs such as *Corny Collins*, which had variants all across the country. "Hair hopper" was a local term for someone who clearly spent too much time on her hair. Corny Collins' friend Motormouth Maybelle (Ruth Brown), a black disc jockey, was based on a real person. Baltimore was a test market for new records and dances. Of course, the segregation of city life was all too real, but Waters gives his treatment of the issue the pastiche of an era teen movie such as *Gidget* (1959) with a wickedly ironic twist. None of the conflicts lasts for long, and the villains are ridiculous rather than heinous. Yet at the core of the picture is the very real world of Waters' youth, and that of millions of others at a turning point in American history.

The more recent *Hairspray* is an adaptation of an adaptation and might be more accurately described as historical confection than historical fiction, but it retains some of Waters' comic edge as Tracy sings "Good Morning Baltimore" to a city full of rats and racial tension. As with many major motion pictures, the sense of authenticity with regard to place is lost: though the story is set in Baltimore, the film was actually shot in Toronto and Hamilton, Ontario. The historical reconstruction with respect to sets, costumes, and issues is accurate, but the original songs have been replaced with the musical numbers written for the show, in the style of the 1960s. Both films are best explored as examples of historical memory rather than historical reconstruction, though the latter remains a significant element. The principal historical interest of the films lies in how they correspond to our collective memory (in some cases) or understanding (in the case of those to young to remember) of that era and its significance. Obviously there is a great deal of nostalgia, looking back on the "fun stuff"—songs, dances, candy, hairdos. The material culture of the time is prominently on display. A number of jokes have to do with the "modern conveniences" of 1960s life that have since become dated, if not banned. Hairspray itself was a major source of the chlorofluorocarbons that were subsequently found to be destroying the earth's ozone layer, and today's audiences cringe to see it so freely sprayed and inhaled by its users. One of the film's visual jokes is a group of pregnant women drinking martinis and smoking at a bar, an example of how the liberations of 1960s culture turned out to be incompatible with good prenatal health care.

While the 1988 film remains much more interesting cinematically than the newer version, the latter does manage to cut through the highly stylized conventions of the musical to makes a few significant points. Velma von Tussle (Michelle Pfeiffer) is the chief advocate of segregation, and she is derided throughout the film as belonging to the past. What the film celebrates is the perceived exuberance of the 1960s, a willingness to leave a racist past behind and to celebrate life and liberty and to pursue happiness in venues such as *The Corny Collins Show*. The film's most moving moment is Motormouth Maybelle's (Queen Latifah) number, backed by gospel choir, *I Know Where I've Been*: the music gives a powerful voice to the film's African American characters, and in the end, the newer film manages to portray the integration of the dance show more satisfyingly than the original as the culmination and the heart of the film.

The *Hairspray* films serve well as examples of historical fiction in that they aim for a measure of historical accuracy but also raise, importantly, issues of historical memory. The entertainment imperative is strong in the 2007 musical version, and the film achieved the most lucrative opening weekend ever for a musical. The Waters' original did not have to earn back a big budget, but nevertheless proved highly successful: it earned a total of $6.7 million and became a cult classic; and as we have seen it served as the basis for the highly popular stage musical and second film. The visions of the past that appear in these two films can be compared on the basis of their differences, as independent and studio films. Filmmakers working independently of a studio's control typically have fewer resources to work with, but they are also freer to do their own thing. While some independent filmmakers essentially audition with their work and therefore conform to Hollywood conventions to a greater degree, others maintain a distinct style outside of the mainstream that their followers, at least, find compelling. Waters was definitely less "quirky" in *Hairspray* than in his earlier offerings, but the comparison is still worthwhile and illuminating. The most striking contrast, perhaps, is the casting of Edna Turnblad. Divine certainly was one-of-a-kind, and certainly stood out in the original. If he had not died in 1988, not long after completing his work in *Hairspray*, he probably would have been deemed too old for the newer film. It would be hard to speculate on what his career trajectory might have been, but one would not have been surprised if Hollywood would overlook a real transvestite in favor of a bankable star ready to do a comic turn as one. In the event the studio went with a big star, John Travolta, who certainly tries and has a few moments, but does not ultimately match the Divine "standard."

The final category, *cultural artifact*, contains those films that are not set in the past at the time they are made, but which become historical with age. Some, by the film artists' intention, set out to be important statements; others have "greatness thrust upon them." An example of the former is a film popular with students: Tony Kaye's *American History X* (1998), a powerful and well-acted portrayal of racism in contemporary society that focuses on the relationship between a skinhead, Derek Vinyard (Edward Norton) and his younger brother Danny (Edward Furlong). The title alone prompts students to propose it as a paper topic: though the film itself is not set in the past, the title's use of the word *history* invites the viewer to consider what it has to say in the context of the American experience. A big part of the film's appeal is the fact that it explores the dark side of violent racism through its lead character and attempts to explain how people develop such views and are drawn to fringe groups. It aims for a high degree of realism, and in doing so portrays the ravages of racism in such a way that its R rating is indeed fully justified: this is for mature audiences only, and audiences who will be repelled rather than fascinated by its violence. The film's most shocking moment is the horrific act that sends Derek himself to prison, where he himself is subjected to brutality by his fellow prisoners. Nevertheless, he meets someone in prison who helps him to reexamine his views, and he emerges from prison determined to ensure that his younger brother does not repeat his own mistakes.

The film achieves a candor in parts that is quite remarkable. On issues of race, the movies in general have often preached, but not practiced. Yet on some fundamental issues this film falls short. First of all, it strains credibility to believe that a person as sensitive and intelligent as Derek could be such a vicious racist, though that may also challenge us not to stereotype racism as a form of stupidity. The attempt to root Derek's racism in the past, specifically in his father's racism, makes a significant point, but one that is also a little too obvious. Viewers may disagree on these issues, but *American History X*, even if it is flawed, makes an admirable attempt to explore the roots and ravages of racism, and in doing so, it aims to avoid the simplistic moral pieties that many other films have invoked on the subject. As an example of history in film, *American History X* is best examined as a cultural artifact, one that attempts to capture a significant aspect of American culture at a particular moment in time. The use of the word *history* in the title should also provoke discussion, and while the film is not set in the past (except to flash back to Derek's own experiences), it asserts that racism is a historical burden passed from one generation to the next.

Truth be told, however, to me *American History X* is a powerful film that tries to say something significant about one of the most important subjects affecting our society today, and one which has deep historical roots. But as a focus for historical research, it is still rather limited; I write "still" because it is too recent to work well as a cultural artifact. It is a good example of a movie that students have seen and which they find compelling, but which may not work really well as the subject of historical research.

The purpose of this book is to help you identify and assess the historical content of the movies you see, even the movies you see for entertainment. But just as some documents are of great historical interest, others are not, and most fall somewhere in between Movies likewise run the gamut.

I have discussed *300*, *Hairspray*, and *American History X* as examples of films that can be incorporated into historical studies, but I chose them because, while many students enjoy them, they also may *not* be the best examples of film history, historical fiction, and cultural artifacts. In choosing a movie or movies to study, you must be able to identify a compelling historical element: is there enough in the film(s) to support a sustained and serious discussion of its relationship to the human experience?

MUTINY ON THE BOUNTY: EIGHTEENTH-CENTURY HISTORY AS TWENTIETH-CENTURY CULTURAL PHENOMENON

The history in a movie is often more than what you see depicted on the screen. To illustrate that point, and to describe the different directions a study of history in film can take, I will discuss a set of films that portray events that took place in the late eighteenth century. The popularity of the films and the books on which they are based is a twentieth-century phenomenon, however, holding clues to our own ideals and values. I refer to the famous story of the mutiny on *HMS* (His Majesty's Ship) *Bounty* in 1789, when Fletcher Christian led a revolt against Captain William Bligh near what is now Tonga in the South Pacific. Bligh and his men miraculously survived a journey to Timor in a small vessel, while Christian returned to Tahiti with the *Bounty*. The men who remained on Tahiti were later captured and brought back to England for trial, but Christian left with another group and some of the Tahitian women and was thought to have established a colony on Pitcairn Island. This is now a very famous story, in large part because of the popularity of the 1932 novel *Mutiny on the Bounty* by Charles Nordhoff and James Norton Hall, and the two later novels that make up the *Bounty* trilogy, *Men Against the Sea* (Bligh's story after the mutiny) and *Pitcairn's Island*. There are three major film versions that portray these events: Frank Lloyd's 1935 version of *Mutiny on the Bounty*, starring Charles Laughton, Clark Gable, and Franchot Tone, which won the Best Picture Academy Award for that year, and in 1997 was named by the American Film Institute as one of the 100 greatest American films (#86); an unsuccessful 1962 remake directed by Lewis Milestone and starring Trevor Howard as Bligh and Marlon Brando as Christian; and a 1984 film called *The Bounty*, directed by Roger Donaldson and starring Anthony Hopkins as Bligh and Mel Gibson as Christian. The first two draw largely from the novel, but the title change in the third signifies a return to the historical sources for a more accurate rendering of the facts based on more recent research.

How do you assess the historical content of these films? An obvious and relatively simple approach would be to study the content, production, and reception of the 1984 film. Joseph Roquemore, in his book *History Goes to the Movies*, provides a brief historical sketch of the mutiny that took place on *The Bounty* in 1789, and briefly assesses how accurately each of the film versions portrays the events that took place, and his opinion is that the 1984 film is most historically accurate. He devotes several pages to the subject in his book. Roquemore is not a professional historian, but he has a PhD in English and clearly loves history and film and has produced a useful popular reference book. A book like this comes in handy when you see a film on a historical subject you do not know much about—and do not need to write a paper. It can serve usefully as a point of departure, since it provides reading suggestions and discusses other films that deal with the same subject or theme. Your research, though, is going to have to dig deeper. Books such as this and Frank Sanello's *Reel v. Real: How Hollywood Turns Fact into Fiction* tend to focus on the degree to which the films are historically accurate, according to the known facts, but that is only part of assessing its historical significance. The essay by Greg Dening in Mark Carnes' (ed.) *Past Imperfect: History According to the Movies* (1995) is a good place to begin for a more scholarly approach.

If you wanted to focus on the 1984 film, you would want to research the production history to determine how the filmmakers approached the subject: why they wanted to retell this story in film, and how serious they were about improving on the historical accuracy of the previous films. Roquemore actually provides some titles that you could read to explore the historical backdrop to the story and the story itself. You should check these out in the library, check the catalogue for related titles, and, when you actually go to the stack to retrieve the books, browse the immediate vicinity for other books of possible interest. You also need to check out the journal literature on the subject. JSTOR is a very helpful online search engine that allows you to download full-text articles from historical and other journals. Among the journals it includes is the *American Historical Review*, which since 1990 has included film reviews by historians who are experts in the subjects that the film treats. The *Journal of American History* also has a film review section.

Historians who point out the historical inaccuracies of movies often come under fire for being pedantic: a movie is a movie, not a history lesson. To an extent that is a fair criticism, but the ease with which we accept that point should make us pause and reconsider: why are the two understood to be separate? We can understand that a recapitulation of historical facts does not usually make for a compelling story, one that builds in a conventional manner to an exciting climax and then resolves itself satisfactorily. Historians themselves tell stories, recognizing that we also remember the past in the form of stories, and we approach the past with our own values, ideals and preoccupations, which we trend to impose on our forebears. So we have to ask ourselves how interested we really are in getting to know people and places in the past for who and what they were, versus simply looking for reflections of ourselves.

Another important angle to pursue in your research is the history of the film itself: the story of its production and reception. Who wanted to make this film and why? How did it get made? How did critics and audiences respond to it when it was first released and, if it is an older film, over time? Researching this angle also may give you information about the filmmakers' intentions with respect to the history: do they care about historical accuracy, and, if they do, why and to what degree? What sources did they, or their historical consultants, use? Did critics and the audiences respond to the historical aspects of the film? Focusing more on the content, you might also wish to compare aspects of the three films. In light of recent scholarly work on masculinity, you might wish to focus on how each of the films presents its male characters: the story lends itself to such analysis, given the number of important male characters: who dominates and why? Is there an ideal male type here? How do these men behave away from women and the rest of society? The adventure setting and the conflicts in the story may be thought to bring out these "essential" male qualities.

It may not be necessary to do research in primary documents, but you could actually examine some primary sources very readily. In this case, Penguin Classics has a volume called *The Bounty Mutiny*, which includes Bligh's own account of events, court transcripts, and the correspondence between Bligh and Fletcher Christian's brother. Of course, Bligh's account, while a primary source, should be treated as a potentially self-serving account of events in which he was a participant; it needs to be weighed against other accounts. But if your assignment is to write a paper of fewer than twenty pages, and your purpose is to discuss film representations of the mutiny on the *Bounty*, you do not need to reconstruct the history of the Royal Navy on your own: there are many secondary sources on the topic already, which you should consult and cite as appropriate. The film material itself functions as your principal primary source. Your study of both primary and secondary sources also will give you a better understanding not just of what we already know but also of what we do not know and will perhaps never know, simply because the records do not tell us. In other words, some aspects of this series of events remain a mystery.

Historical accuracy is a major theme to consider in doing research on history in film, but while fidelity to historical fact is of great value, it is not the only value. While you could write a paper praising how the makers of *The Bounty* sought to present a thrilling yet accurate picture of a famous event to the screen, you may want to ask some additional questions or possibly alter the analytical framework of your study to think about the history here in a different way. An important question to ask is about the historical significance of the story. The prologue to the 1935 film talks about how the mutiny prompted the Royal Navy to reform its practices and protocols. If true, that is significant. But another very interesting question is why this is such a famous and celebrated set of events. The Nordhoff and Hall novels made them famous, but what was it about these stories that made these novels successful? This line of inquiry brings in the literary element, which of course relates to the films in very significant ways. In comparing the novels and films to what we know to be true, we can point out factual inaccuracies, but these may not simply be mistakes to be dismissed or disregarded. In watching the 1935 film, I wondered about the fate of Thomas Ellison, the young man impressed into service that left a wife and infant son behind. The ending of the film leaves his fate somewhat ambiguous, but the actual man was among those who were brought back to England and eventually hanged. The filmmakers, or perhaps their studio bosses, apparently could not bear to show his cruel fate, the tragic end to a journey he had never wanted to make, focusing instead on the relatively happy ending for Roger Byam, the main character in the novel, based on the historical character Peter Heywood.

Assessing the historical content of film requires some sophisticated analysis on your part, but, armed with tools to analyze film content and of the different ways in which film can be historically significant, you can begin to experience film as a historian does, able to appreciate film on various levels as a rich historical source. The chapters that follow discuss each of the different categories we have described in the chapter, using examples to deepen your understanding of what film can convey about the past.

Questions for Discussion:

1. Why is the use of reenactment in documentary films controversial? What are the risks of mixing aspects of narrative and documentary film in the same work? What are the benefits?

2. How can a single film serve as an example of more than one kind of historical film?

3. What are the challenges and opportunities of examining highly popular films for their historical significance?

5

■ ■ ■

Documentary Films as Primary and Secondary Sources

The 1970s British comedy program *Monty Python's Flying Circus* frequently made use of the documentary format to purvey its unique style of comedy, playing the dry, authoritative tone of the format against the absurdity of the subject matter. One particular segment, "Storage Jars," lampooned the British Broadcasting Corporation's (BBC) ability to make documentaries on just about any subject, no matter how dull or prosaic, for a captive audience, given the lack of competition for viewers in the days before cable television. But documentary films need not be boring—even "Storage Jars" was pretty good—and they have great potential to reconstruct and interpret the past uncluttered by intentionally fictional elements.

Of all kinds of film, documentaries come closest to replicating in audio-visual form what historians do when they write. They reconstruct aspects of the human experience using various sources of information, including film footage from the time period, still photos, filmed testimonies of eye-witnesses, and the opinions of historians. Generally speaking, documentary is to nonfiction what narrative film is to fiction. However, within the category *documentary*, one finds a great variety of styles and approaches to subjects. To assess any documentary film for its historical content, you need to understand the relationship of the filmmaker to the subject. This chapter examines

* the use of documentary film as both primary and secondary source, and

* specific documentary films of interest to historians, presented in a chronological survey.

Just how a documentary film works as either a primary or secondary source varies greatly from film to film, requiring careful assessment on the part of the historian regarding the nature and value of the evidence. A useful concept to remember in assessing a documentary film in particular is its integrity. While any discussion of a film's morality is likely to get thorny, one can posit that filmmakers should and largely do adhere to a set of filmmaking values that ensure the integrity of the medium and the potential impact it can have on society. The issue of reenactment, raised earlier, helps to illuminate this point. While most people recognize the role that emotions and feelings play in shaping our outlook on a particular issue, we uphold the primacy of reason as the basis for our opinions, especially on matters of public interest. At the risk of stating the obvious, the truth always makes the most compelling case. So the more truthful the filmmaker can be, the more persuasive and compelling the film will be. Truth in film derives from the viewers' belief and confidence that what they see is recorded reality. In the 1990s, several U.S. TV news magazines got in trouble for using filmed reenactments instead of actual footage of events taking place. Since a staple of these programs was exposing wrongdoers "in the act" and "caught on film," trying to use reenactments for the same effect was a violation of the integrity of the program, because these segments were staged and could portray any kind of activity the stagers chose.

The news magazines learned their lesson, but reenactments still appear in documentary films. They can be effective, but as viewers we must remain conscious of what we are watching. As mentioned earlier, the BBC documentary *Auschwitz* (2005) made significant use of reenactments, which, one could argue, insightfully reconstructed aspects of the Holocaust that have not been documented on film, yet for which abundant evidence exists. If the viewer has the critical ability to distinguish between documentary footage and reenactment, the reenactment can be effective. That can be a big "if," but the series offers the opportunity to raise and discuss these issues while also providing excellent narrative and analysis on the subject.

Almost any film can be of interest to historians. Even those Coronet educational films made for post–Second World War health classes are of interest today, and can be seen on the Internet Archive (www.archive.org/details/movies). Films such as *Are You Popular?* (1947) are very amusing to watch today, because they talk about dating and relationships between "boys and girls" that now seem quaint, corny, or lame. But they may also show how times have changed; for social historians, these films can provide clues about everyday life in that period. But one has to be precise about the nature of the evidence: do they represent everyday life, or should they be seen instead as a kind of propaganda, a construction aimed at educating young people how to behave? If that is the case, we may still derive some information about everyday life, but our interest shifts to analyzing and understanding this attempt to engineer human behavior, and how it fits into the broader historical context of American life at that time.

The "reality" a film portrays can be every bit as illusory as any fantasy, and all the more deceptive for its stylistic "objectivity." The documentarian has to determine *how* he or she is going to present the subject (methodology), and the film has to make a case for the argument it presents. The viewer in turn must assess critically the evidence the film provides and the logic it uses. This can be a little easier to do with older films, but it is no less important to do with films in our own day that examine critical issues. The term *propaganda* is easy to throw around, especially once the material becomes ideologically charged, but that term should never be used dismissively. While it has a negative connotation, we can note that during the Second World War, for example, all parties made extensive use of propaganda to build support for their cause, whether it was racial warfare in the case of the Nazis or preserving our democratic systems from the Nazis in the case of the Allies. In other words, one cannot use the term *propaganda* dismissively. Even a film such as Leni Riefenstahl's *Triumph of the Will*, which chillingly glorifies the Nazi regime that had already brutalized Germany and threatened to do the same for all of Europe, must be analyzed critically to determine its historical impact. To the extent that any documentary film presents an argument or promotes a cause or regime, we must identify the connections between the content and the cause.

In this and the chapters that follow, I discuss many different examples of historically significant films that illustrate the type of film under discussion and the kinds of historical issues they raise. Due to their brevity, these discussions do not necessarily serve as good examples of the more thorough research and analysis you will find in books and scholarly articles, some references to which are provided here. Further scholarly references are listed and discussed later in the book.

TRIUMPH OF THE WILL (1935)

Leaders all across the political spectrum embraced film as propaganda. According to historian and Hitler biographer Ian Kershaw in the documentary series *The Nazis: A Warning from History* (1997), Adolf Hitler may have spent more time as dictator watching movies than attending to the affairs of state. One of his admirers, Leni Riefenstahl (1902–2003) was an athletic dancer turned film star. She directed her first film, *The Blue Light*, in 1932. Though she never joined the Nazi party, she was drawn to National Socialist circles and in 1933 filmed the proceedings at the party's annual congress in Nuremberg. The results were disappointing: if the National Socialists hoped to present the German public with a semblance of order, pageantry, and militancy, *The Victory of Faith*, with its primitive camera work portraying the Nazis' primitive showmanship all too honestly, failed to impress, and Nazi leaders suppressed the film. But for the following year's congress, Riefenstahl, clearly still on good terms with the party leaders, made another film, this time with a larger production team and equipment that allowed for more sophisticated camera movement and more impressive angles on the proceedings. The result was a film, *Triumph of the Will*, which portrayed Adolf Hitler as a messianic figure—descending from the clouds (by airplane), no less, in case there was any doubt—bringing order, prosperity, and pride to the German masses.

Having cast her lot with the Nazis, Riefenstahl would spend the rest of her long life after the Second World War defending herself for having supported a regime that brought about history's most destructive war, the worst genocide, and self-destruction for Germany itself. She maintained that she had had no interest in politics, and that *Triumph of the Will* was to her simply a work of art. But no one looking at the film then or now could disassociate the message the organizers of the rally intended to convey from the artistry Riefenstahl used to relay that message to the viewing public. The rally itself was—obviously—a staged event, intended to impress the German public with the order, unity, and patriotism of the movement. The everyday reality of National Socialism was far more chaotic, as Ian Kershaw's scholarship has shown: rival individuals and factions competed for the favor of their *Führer* and, more to the point, the powers he could bestow. Far from being objective, much less truthful, *Triumph of the Will* helped draw audiences into the lies of National Socialism, which contrary to its promises brought chaos, destruction, and shame to Germany. Some Germans were able to see the seeds of destruction in the Nazis' human rights abuses, visited on all Germans, but German Jews in particular: apparently Riefenstahl did not. Instead, she served as the faithful recorder and enhancer of Nazi propaganda: the film titles *Victory of Faith* and *Triumph of the Will* were taken directly from the themes that Hitler himself chose for the party congresses. *New York Times* reporter Frederick Birchall noted the irony in the theme of the 1935 Nuremberg party congress, captured in another Riefenstahl film entitled *Day of Freedom*, which focused on Germany's armed forces.

Whereas the regime suppressed *Victory of Faith*, Propaganda Minister Joseph Goebbels, who saw Riefenstahl as a rival, presented the state's prize for best film of the year to *Triumph of the Will* in May 1935. Not surprisingly, the film was not distributed outside of Germany. Even her less overtly political two-part film about the Berlin Olympics, *Olympia* (1938), was not shown in the United States until much later. When Riefenstahl visited the United States in the fall of 1938, she complained that film studios prevented their stars from meeting with her, and she spent much of her time with the press denying rumors of a love affair with Hitler. Such allegations were perhaps an inevitable, though not excusable, consequence of the fact that Riefenstahl was a woman making her career in a male-dominated profession. Whatever concerns her political affiliations may raise today, the fact that she was a professionally successful woman in a society that, in fact, aimed to turn the clock back on women's rights and roles makes her a remarkable figure. Two biographies on her were published in 2008, one by Steven Bach, the other by Jürgen Trimborn and Edna McCown. Riefenstahl's own autobiography (1995) should be approached with the same caution one would approach any memoir, and the mental tricks she played to live down her past are both visually and verbally evident in the documentary film *The Wonderful, Horrible Life of Leni Riefenstahl* (1993), for which filmmaker Ray Müller interviewed her extensively.

Riefenstahl's work for the Nazis falls into the category of documentary, but it also helps to illustrate what a broad term *documentary* is. Perhaps propaganda really should be placed in a separate category. *Triumph of the Will* is of interest today as a visual record of National Socialism, a skillful cinematic recording of the party's own propaganda exercises and itself a piece of propaganda. What makes it propaganda is the absence of any kind of commentary, positive or negative, that would have presented a detached perspective. Instead, the film served as a mouthpiece for the National Socialist Party. As a historical source today, it can be used as a primary source, a visual record of a propaganda exercise. While angles, camera movements, editing, and other variables in the filmmaking process mean that the film itself is not simply a neutral medium, Riefenstahl's artistry in fact helped to define a Nazi esthetic and this film is the best example of that.

THE PLOW THAT BROKE THE PLAINS (1936) AND *THE RIVER* (1938)

These two films by Pare Lorentz represent a foray of the United States government into documentary filmmaking, with the goal of promoting New Deal programs that addressed the disasters, both natural and human-made, portrayed in the films.[1] These films, which made it onto a considerable number of movie screens in America despite the control of the movie studios over theaters nationwide, examined the origins of the Dust Bowl in the plains states and the impoverishment of the Mississippi valley. Both films aim to instruct, but there is also considerable artistry in the sparse narrative, the visuals and the striking orchestration that accompanies both.

The Plow That Broke the Plains examines the history of America's grasslands, a vast plain stretching from Montana to Texas. The use of the word *broke* in the title carries a double meaning, portending a stern environmental message, accompanied by dissonant music, which cites human error for the Dust Bowl without blaming the individual farmers who suffered most directly from it. From a time when the Nye Commission report essentially blamed the weapons manufacturers, or "merchants of death" for America's involvement in the Great War, the film suggests that war increased the demand for grain and prompted the further exploitation of the plains and exhaustion of its soil. The postwar global economy also takes a share of the blame as expansion kept grain prices high and the intensive farming of the plains profitable. This sequence in the film skillfully intercuts images of moving tractors with advancing tanks, and then victory parades, suggesting an important role for America's agriculture in the Allied military victory. The ensuing Dust Bowl, accompanied by the collapse of grain prices, brought simultaneous natural and human disaster to the plains.

The narrative describes the plight of those forced to flee westward, setting up the case for government programs to assist them. However, the film

---

[1] For a more thorough analysis of the content, production and reception of *The Plow That Broke the Plains*, see John E. O'Connor, *Image as Artifact: The Historical Analysis of Film and Television*. Malabar, FL: Krieger, 1990, 284–301.

viewers see today ends abruptly with images of dead trees on parched earth. An epilogue that described the different programs of the New Deal to address these problems has disappeared, perhaps because of the actual and potential criticism the film faced in Congress, where some saw this as communist propaganda. Of course it was propaganda, but one's view of the film's politics had everything to do with one's views of the New Deal and the role government had to play in addressing the challenges of the Great Depression. John O'Connor writes that the Resettlement Administration dropped the segment of the film that portrayed farmers working cooperatively to address their problems. The year 1936 was, after all, an election year.

In this particular case, the story of the film's abrupt ending turns out to be both interesting and historically significant, shedding light on the political controversies of 1930s America, including the innovations of the Roosevelt administration and the fierce opposition that awaited programs that bore any resemblance to "socialism." O'Connor's formula prompts us to examine the production, content, and reception of a film to determine its historical significance. In this case something that seems not quite right about the content—that is, its abrupt ending—prompts us to investigate further the history of the film itself and to discover and explore the case of the missing epilogue. Pierre Sorlin, who also has written extensively on history in film, likewise encourages the scholar to make sure he or she knows the origins of the print being examined.[2]

Some viewers today may not find the film especially appealing, but there is a real beauty to the black and white cinematography, and the sparse narrative, which includes a lot of deliberate repetition, is rather poetic. The choice and the arrangement of the music also is worthy of further exploration. *The River* similarly is worthy of study for its film artistry, which from a historical perspective should be considered as part of the film's content and significance as a document or artifact of its time. It is structured and presented in ways very similar to the earlier film. The visuals are rich with information about the period: how people lived and worked, how their homes and clothing looked, and what the environment looked like. *The River* not only continues the theme of human responsibility for the problems of flooding and poverty in the Mississippi basin, but also promotes human solutions such as the Tennessee Valley Authority, which controlled the flow of that river and brought electricity to much of the impoverished South.

A question to consider for both of these films is how their esthetic appeal affects the film's message. Does a beautiful film prompt the desired reaction to the problem? To answer the question, consider both the films' production and reception. Lorentz made these films at government expense, and President Roosevelt was delighted with the results. The point of the film was not to promote individual acts of charity and largesse, but rather to build popular

---

[2] Sorlin, "How to Look at an 'Historical' Film," in M. Landy, ed., *The Historical Film: History and Memory in Media*. New Brunswick, NJ: Rutgers University Press, 2001, 38–40.

confidence in the New Deal. If audiences were supposed to emerge from these films feeling good about what the government was doing to address these problems on their behalf, a beautiful film helped to achieve that end.

WHY WE FIGHT (1942–1944)

With movies becoming a prominent feature of contemporary life wherever technology and modest means allowed, the attraction of film to governments as a means of "educating" and influencing public opinion was strong. The Second World War, a truly global conflict in which victory would go to the side that could marshal the most resources, made film propaganda a worldwide phenomenon. British and U.S. propaganda could take a more reasoned and truthful approach to promoting the cause, as they had not initiated the hostilities, and though not blameless in the area of human rights, nevertheless held the high moral ground over the brutal regimes of the Axis powers. Nevertheless U.S. propagandists such as Frank Capra, who during the 1930s had directed many delightful comedy films, recognized the power of Leni Riefenstahl's style and quoted her work in his acclaimed series *Why We Fight*.

The *Why We Fight* series comprised seven films, made between 1942 and 1944: *Prelude to War* presented German, Italian, and Japanese aggression in the 1930s; *The Nazis Strike* honed in on Germany's campaign of expansion into eastern Europe; *Divide and Conquer* covered the German conquest of northern and western Europe; the next three films, *Battle of Britain*, *Battle of Russia*, and *Battle of China*, portrayed the struggles of America's principal wartime allies; the last film, *War Comes to America*, aimed to drive home the threat that the Axis powers posed to the United States.

Presented in a common documentary style, with voice-over narration presenting an interpretation of events that did not insult the intelligence of viewers, the *Why We Fight* series was taken for fact by many viewers for a long time. It went so far as to introduce viewers—mostly armed service recruits—to concepts such as geopolitics: though geopolitics was to become an important word in the cold war lexicon, stressing the importance of land and resources in the global struggle for power and dominance, Capra associated it with a heartless and calculating view of the world characteristic of the Nazi mindset.

Despite the fact that the series consciously aimed to present recruits with a serious and reasoned analysis of events leading up to the war, and the war itself, today the series should be used as a primary rather than a secondary source. While its interpretation of events may still hold true to some extent, it should not be taken as authoritative. It is more interesting to historians as an interpretation from the time period of the war itself, reflective of the stance the United States had taken, the alliances it had formed to win the war, and the government's need to "educate" the public about the nature and significance of the war. One can also find evidence of racial attitudes and the role of women during the war. It is an excellent example of intelligent and effective wartime propaganda, expressive of the patriotic ideals of the time.

Given the dominance of narrative films in the commercial market, the question of who actually saw this documentary series is a good one. The U.S. War Department was the producer, and initially the war department intended to use these films as part of soldier training. However, some of the films found a broader audience. The Hollywood film industry's War Activities Committee coordinated screenings. The first film, *Prelude to War*, was shown in 427 Warner Bros. theaters across the country beginning in May 1943, and the Office of War Information made arrangements with the British Ministry of Information and U.S. companies to distribute the films in Britain, Australia, New Zealand, and South Africa. Domestically, the films also were screened during lunch hours at factories, to educate workers about the war and their role in it. The fifth film, *Battle of Russia*, was the next film to be released publicly, in November, 1943. *New York Times'* reviewer Bosley Crowther described its main theme as "the heroic manner in which the Russian people, as well as their armies, have shattered the horrendous legend of Nazi invincibility." Just as films made during the war could be changed to suit the circumstances, the war department also changed the *Why We Fight* films in preparing them for public audiences. Crowther's review noted that "a significant passage in the original Army film," describing the pre-1941 invasions of Finland, the Baltic States, Poland, and Bessarabia as defensive occupations of territories that had belonged to Russia prior to 1914, had been edited out of the version being shown publicly. The alliance with the Soviet Union was a good illustration of the principle that alliances are shaped by interests, not by affinities. Whereas officials allowed the film to defend Russia's aggression prior to June 1941 for the soldiers, they chose to overlook the matter entirely for the public. *War Comes to America*, the last film in the series, was shown briefly in June 1945 in New York at the City Newsreel Theatre on Fourteenth Street. Director William Wyler believed that the *Why We Fight* series would "live longer than *Gone with the Wind*" and have a greater effect on the development of the medium. Wyler explained that some 10 million men had seen the films. The popular notion that the Axis powers at the time posed a physical threat to the existence of the United States remains strong to this day.[3]

NIGHT AND FOG (1955)

A major aspect of the Second World War that received relatively little public attention until years later was what would become known as the Shoah, or Holocaust: the persecution and genocide of the European Jews and other targeted groups. In 1955 the young French director Alain Resnais made a thirty-minute documentary entitled *Night and Fog*. Using both footage from the

---

[3] *New York Times*: November 15, 1943, 23; and September 16, 1946, x3.

war and contemporary footage of the camps as they appeared ten years later, the narration, accompanied by music, constitutes a kind of essay or meditation on Nazi brutality rather than an explanation of how things happened. Though the film mentions the Jews, it does not emphasize the fact that Nazi war crimes targeted that group in particular.

Nevertheless the film packed quite a wallop, and can still do so today. Resnais used some of the most gruesome film images available from the war. Chosen for screening at the 1956 Cannes Film Festival, the West German government successfully pressured the French to exclude it from the official entries. Nevertheless, with the acclaim the film received in France, including the Jean Vigo award, given to directors for their "spirit of independence and extraordinary style," and with Resnais' subsequent success with the feature films *Hiroshima, Mon Amour* (1959) and *Last Year at Marienbad* (1961), *Night and Fog* gained a wider audience in the early 1960s. The film was not released in the United States until 1960, when it was paired with *Triumph of the Will* and shown at the New Yorker Theater in New York. Not until the later 1970s, however, would the Holocaust become a widely explored event in both narrative and documentary films. While many of these films would answer more specific historical questions about the Holocaust, *Night and Fog* retains a distinct place in the canon as a philosophical meditation on the horror.[4]

The question of whether *Night and Fog* is a primary or secondary source is difficult. Less important than coming up with a clear answer, however, is identifying its value and importance as a historical source. Though it looks at past events and interprets them, it does not so much explain or analyze events as meditate on their significance. As such, it is more philosophical than historical in its approach, and yet because of its connection to actual historical events it retains a substantial historical interest. Certainly in the history of films about the Holocaust, it has a very important place, opening the door, however slowly, to a subject that the film world, and the world in general, had been slow to embrace.

THE SORROW AND THE PITY (1969)

Though France could lay claim to a film that opened the cinematic discussion of the Nazi genocide, its government proved more sensitive when it came to the exploration of French collaboration with the Germans during the Second World War. In the late 1960s, Marcel Ophüls, son of the well-known director Max Ophüls, made a long (four hours and twenty minutes) television documentary about the defeat of France in 1940 and the subsequent dilemmas that the French people faced living under direct Nazi occupation or in the territory controlled by the collaborationist French government seated in the spa town of Vichy. Made in black and white and

---

[4] *New York Times*, June 29, 1960, 27.

consisting of interwoven interviews of about fifteen individuals, this "talking heads" style of documentary is challenging for attention-deficit viewers weaned on television's rapid-fire delivery of advertisements and entertainment. But the film's slow delivery achieves a depth of insight and a sense of humanity that had a transformational effect at the time and remains powerful today. France, then at the tail end of the de Gaulle presidency, had embraced the myth that, like de Gaulle, the people of France had mostly resisted German occupation and influence. Along with a book by the U.S. historian Robert Paxton, *Vichy France: Old Guard and New Order* (1970), *The Sorrow and the Pity* forced the French people to accept a more complex interpretation of their wartime experience. This time the Germans, no doubt grateful for company on the list of European countries with a dark past, embraced the film first. Released in West Germany in September 1969, it was not shown in France until the spring of 1971. It opened a year later in the United States and in 1972, it received a number of international prizes, including an Academy Award nomination for Best Documentary Feature (it lost to a film, *The Hellstrom Chronicle* [1971], which has largely been forgotten).

As a historical source, *The Sorrow and the Pity* is analogous to a secondary source. It does not have the voice of an omniscient narrator, the way a work of written history would: but it presents an interpretation of events in the past, using as its primary sources the recollections of participants in those events. It does not try to produce a neat summary, instead allowing the different voices and perspectives to leave the viewer with a complex and ambiguous picture of the French people's response to the challenges of defeat and occupation.

HEARTS AND MINDS (1974)

For Americans, the Vietnam experience was comparably challenging to tackle in film. The conventions of war films did not suit the subject, as *The Green Berets* had demonstrated in 1968, in large part because the war itself but it was a painful and divisive subject. In 1974, just one year after U.S. troops left Vietnam, Peter Davis' documentary *Hearts and Minds* provided an interpretation of events that critics and audiences embraced. One might expect a film from 1974 to take a strident or impassioned antiwar stance, given that events were still recent. Its stance certainly is antiwar, but even critics would have to concede that it presents a reasoned case and portrays all participants as fully and fundamentally human—not common in portrayals of warfare.

Hearts and Minds begins with a pastoral scene of village life northwest of Saigon and ends with a wrenching Vietnamese funeral ceremony. Some critics charged that Davis was unfair in his portrayal of General William Westmoreland: for example, the film shows Westmoreland saying that the "Oriental" does not value human life the way Americans do, then cuts to a scene of a mother in a state of complete anguish over the death of her child. While Westmoreland later said his words were taken out of context, Davis states in his commentary on the film that Westmoreland made the statement three times and that his meaning was clear.[5]

Hearts and Minds provides a historical interpretation of events in Vietnam, hitting all the principal points of analysis that students would encounter in a typical college course today. In the context of today's politics, it would certainly be attacked by the right, but not easily refuted. It not only takes an antiwar position but also presents the views of those who supported the war. One of the more striking elements in the film is its self-awareness, and Davis' own sensitivity to the potentially exploitative nature of film. Made before the final collapse of South Vietnam, *Hearts and Minds* also serves as a primary document on America in the 1970s. The film met with much critical acclaim and won the Academy Award for Best Documentary Feature. Subsequently, *Vietnam: A Television History* presented the war in much more detail, but both the film and the series retain an interest for historians today. The look of *Hearts and Minds* and *Vietnam: A Television History* is very similar: both use archival footage and contemporary interviews, with an appearance of grittiness and muted color.

HARLAN COUNTY USA (1976)

Vietnam and the Civil Rights Movement coincided with an era of liberal largesse that followed the Second World War. As African Americans successfully overcame the worst excesses of racism, other victims of discrimination pressed for equal rights also, most prominently women. In the film industry, where men usually held the key positions both in the boardroom and behind the camera, women slowly began to make inroads. In 1976, Barbara Kopple produced and directed her first film, *Harlan County, USA*, about the coal miners' strike in southeastern Kentucky in 1974.[6] Here too the camera plays a self-conscious role, but in this case as both instigator and calmer. Initially drawn to the conflict unfolding within the United Mine Workers national organization, Kopple shifted her focus to events in Kentucky, later including the national developments as part of the larger context. In Kentucky, the wives of the mine workers banded together to block the road to the mine, preventing the Eastland Mining Company from bringing in "scab" laborers to work the mines during the strike. A confrontation between men exclusively, and the absence of a film crew, might well have produced a different result. *Harlan County, USA*, is itself a powerful document of the 1970s, reflecting and presenting the empowerment of women. It too won the Academy Award for Best Documentary Feature. Today's viewers without a strong interest in the subject matter or the way the filmmaker handles it may find this film somewhat challenging: at the time Kopple did not set out to make

---

[5] Commentary is included in the Criterion Collection's DVD release of the film.
[6] Also available as a Criterion Collection DVD, with additional features on the making of the film and its significance.

the lives of these people look glamorous or beautiful, and thirty years later it looks even more bleak. But there is a power to this film that is well worth the watching.

KOYAANISQATSI (1982)

All of the films discussed so far have had some connection, either contemporary or looking back, to historical events as we typically understand them: revolutions and wars supply much dramatic material for study, and they do expose a great deal about the nature of humanity and the human condition. But history encompasses all aspects of the human experience, including relations among different groups in society—whether based on race, class or gender, or the relationship between human beings and the natural environment to which they belong. In 1982, Godfrey Reggio's film *Koyaanisqatsi,* using dazzling visuals and a hypnotic score, presented a powerful vision of "life out of balance"—the meaning of the Hopi language title. The film has no narration at all. The visuals present images of nature, much of it shot in the American southwest; slow panning effectively captures the grandeur and beauty of the region. The music, by the popular avant garde composer Phillip Glass, while somewhat slow and repetitive, is quite beautiful to listen to as the images float by. Shifting to civilization, the music becomes more frenetic, and more repetitive as the camera work and editing present modern urban life as bizarre, frantic, and very much out of step with nature. The film's only words appear onscreen at the end the film as *Koyaanisqatsi* is defined as crazy life, life in turmoil, life disintegrating, life out of balance, and a state of life that calls for another way of living.

While the film's message was clear, it may also have had some unintended consequences as well. Some of the scenes of modern urban life were actually quite appealing—lit-up skylines at dusk, the implosion of massive public housing projects and so on, and the intentional skewing of the visuals likewise had appeal. With the advent of MTV in 1981, young audiences in particular, were content to sit for hours watching video images made to accompany their favorite songs, but they would not tolerate the cheesy quality of early videos for long. Reggio's film might be seen as a high-art video, and the visual style proved to be very influential on, of all things, advertising, precisely one of those manifestations of "life out of balance" that Reggio highlighted in *Koyaanisqatsi* and the subsequent films *Powaqqatsi* (1988) and *Naqoyqatsi* (2002). *Powaqqatsi* ("life in transformation") and *Naqoyqatsi* ("life as war") took similar approaches to the developing world and to contemporary warfare, but neither film had the impact of the original. Francis Ford Coppola produced the first, and he and George Lucas coproduced the second. For the third film Reggio had difficulty lining up a producer, but ultimately Steven Soderbergh signed on. One might argue that the innovative element in *Koyaanisqatsi* set it apart in 1982, but its influence was such that the sequels did not stand out. The third film, certainly identifiably part of the series, is a little different from the other two visually. It set out to critique the role of technology in society and in particular to explore the connection between technology and violence. Yet a major element of this film was Reggio's manipulation of the images—speed, color, texture—using, of all things, technology. The result was a film that used technology to criticize technology; some critics suggested that in *Powaqqatsi*, Reggio has "estheti-cized" poverty—made it beautiful. Here he could be said to have made the negative effects of technology into a series of abstract, colorful patterns.

Koyaanisqatsi premiered at the Twentieth New York Film Festival in 1982, on a program that included many documentary films; *New York Times* film critic Janet Maslin attributed the advent of cable television with a surge in opportunities for documentary filmmakers (September 11, 1982, 11). Indeed cable television networks such as the History Channel, owned by the Arts and Entertainment Television Network, and of course the Public Broadcasting System (PBS) made documentary films much more accessible to a growing nation of channel surfers. Also in the 1980s, the VCR became a common household item, making it possible for people to watch films of their own choice whenever they wanted. These changes dramatically transformed the entertainment industry, opening up consumer choices and a vast market.

The Qatsi trilogy illustrates once again how broad the term documentary can be. Without words, they are visual and musical essays on the nature of modern life, humanity's (mostly negative) relationship with the environment, and the general sense that modern life is out of control. Having spent a considerable amount of time living as a monk among a community known as the Christian Brothers, Reggio might be considered a kind of modern-day prophet, calling humanity back from its environmentally destructive ways. Yet while this message resonated with some viewers, Reggio's encounter with mainstream culture also resulted in a triumph of style over substance. While "the look" became common, the message for the most part did not, at least not until the environment re-emerged as a central human concern.

SHOAH (1985)

Claude Lanzmann's extraordinary film runs over nine hours (503 minutes), documenting not so much the events of the Second World War as peoples' memory of those events, and the mass murder of the Jews in particular. It uses no archival footage, instead interviewing at length survivors, bystanders, and perpetrators whom the viewers get to know quite well in a film of this duration. Simon Srebnik, a survivor, describes how he was forced to sing for the Nazis. Later, standing with a group of women outside a church in the Polish town of Grabow, he listens to them talk about how they did not like the Jewish women very much, and it soon becomes evident that many of the beliefs and stereotypes about Jews that we would consider to be medieval live on in these communities. Franz Suchomel, a former Nazi SS (*Schutzstaffel* or "protective squadron") officer, describes in detail how the killings at the death camp Treblinka took place in assembly line fashion. Abraham Bomba, working as a barber in Israel, describes how he survived by working as a barber in Auschwitz. As he describes, in third person, how a man had to cut the hair of his own wife before she was murdered, it becomes clear that Bomba is describing his own experience. Of all the hours I have spent watching films on the Holocaust, this is one indelible moment, not just because of what Bomba's words signify, but because of what his face communicates as he speaks.

Shoah obviously requires a great deal of its viewers, certainly with respect to time, and its length is one way in which it breaks, appropriately, from the conventions of film as entertainment. Relatively few people have seen this film in a theatre as a result; while there have been plenty of documentary series of comparable length, the film is not conveniently formatted for episodic presentation on television, either. Interestingly, the complete text of the film is available in a book of fewer than 200 pages, which suggests that much of the film's significance resides in what the viewer sees (and hears nonverbally). It is not easy, and of course it should not be; but among the thousands of sources on the Holocaust, written or visual, it is essential.

PUBLIC TELEVISION AND DOCUMENTARY SERIES

While Shoah presented obvious difficulties with respect to theatrical screening, the reality is that in most markets people do not normally see documentaries in a theater. *Koyaanisqatsi's* limited theatrical run was rare for a documentary film, facilitated by Hollywood connections, the fact that the film's stunning visuals warranted a big screen, and, most fundamentally, the fact that distributors believed it to be commercially viable. Television was the medium for most documentaries, and PBS (a private nonprofit corporation founded in 1969, to which all public broadcasting stations belong) played an important role in broadcasting major documentaries and especially documentary series, such as *Vietnam: A Television History*, and the two parts of *Eyes on the Prize* (1987). Chronicling relatively recent events in American history, these series, as well as Ken Burns' later series, *The Civil War* (1990), were major events for PBS and drew relatively good ratings for the network.

In 1983, PBS broadcast one of the most ambitious documentary projects any of its affiliates had ever undertaken: *Vietnam: A Television History*. Produced by WGBH in Boston, the series overshadowed an earlier Canadian production written by Peter Arnett known as *Vietnam: The Ten Thousand Day War* (1980). Arguably, with this series PBS hit its stride as a broadcaster of historical documentaries, which quickly became available on videocassette for classroom or private use. Ten years earlier, Jeremy Isaacs' twenty-six-part series *The World at War* had chronicled the events of the Second World War. Masterfully presenting the war from a variety of perspectives, *The World at War* remains an excellent source of information on the Second World War, and its interviews of participants, many of whom have since died, are invaluable. But, though it gained a following over time in the United States,

The World at War was not a major television event. It first aired first on the independent station WOR-TV in New York in 1973 and generated relatively little press compared to *Vietnam: A Television History* one decade later. By promoting and broadcasting nationally, PBS could create a collective experience that was particularly significant when treating subjects that could still generate controversy or strong feelings, such as Vietnam, race relations and the Civil War.

To maintain control of the production of the film series *Eyes on the Prize*, filmmaker Henry Hampton did not arrange with one of the big PBS stations, such as WGBH Boston or WNET New York. Instead, on a modest budget of $1.5 million, his production company Blackside Inc. made the six-part series on its own, and it aired on PBS in January and February 1987. The first series covered the years 1954 to 1965; an eight-part series covering the years 1964 up to the mid-1980s, followed in 1990.

THE THIN BLUE LINE (1988)

Like *Koyaanisqatsi*, the look of Errol Morris' 1988 film *The Thin Blue Line* distracted from the message occasionally, but his reconstruction of the events surrounding the 1976 murder of a Dallas police officer played a major role in reopening the case and getting a new trial for the man wrongly convicted. Morris had earlier made the film *Gates of Heaven* (1978), in which he essentially conducted interviews of colorful individuals associated with a California pet cemetery. In *The Thin Blue Line*, in addition to demonstrating an extraordinary knack for recognizing the cinematic value of allowing peculiar individuals simply to be themselves, Morris adds reenactments of key events. Accompanied by music scored by Phillip Glass, the film was hypnotic on one level, but at the same time, it presented a scathing indictment of a criminal justice system that was preparing to take a man's life for a crime he did not commit.

New York Times critic Janet Maslin wrote that beyond creating a "brilliant work of pulp fiction," Morris created more than a reasonable doubt, not just in this particular case, but toward the justice system as a whole. Drawn to unusual people, Morris was interviewing a Dallas psychiatrist known as "Dr. Death" because of his frequent testimony characterizing murder suspects as dangerous sociopaths. As the film was to include—of course—interviews with a number of these "dangerous sociopaths," Morris came across the case of Randall Dale Adams, serving a life sentence (commuted from a death sentence in 1980), and found his protestations of innocence different from the others he had heard. Shifting his focus to Adams' case, Morris made a film examining the crime and the trial, which revealed that a man with whom Adams had spent part of the day of the crime lied in the trial to save himself.[7]

---

[7] *New York Times*, August 26, 1988, C6.

The film's reception was unusual for a documentary in that it garnered considerable attention and screened in theaters that usually screened
only narrative films. Its distributors, seeing the marketing potential,
labeled it a *nonfiction feature film.* Even more unusual was the fact that the
film led to a reopened trial and a unanimous overturning in appeals court
in March 1989 of Adams' murder conviction. At one point ten years earlier
he had been within days of being executed. Though critics hailed the film
and the New York Film Critics and the National Board of Review named it
the best documentary of the year, the Academy of Motion Pictures Arts and
Sciences (AMPAS) failed even to nominate the film. PBS aired the film in
May 1989, and two months later the John D. and Catherine T. MacArthur
Foundation recognized Morris' talent in July 1989 with their "genius
award." AMPAS at long last recognized Morris' talent in 2004 with an
Academy Award for his film on Robert McNamara and the Vietnam War
entitled *The Fog of War* (2003).

An unfortunate coda to the story of *The Thin Blue Line* illuminates the
challenges of categorizing unconventional films. After being released from
prison, Adams sued Errol Morris over his rights to the story. In a written
agreement, Adams and Morris had agreed that Adams would get $60,000
and 2 percent of profits if Morris made a commercial film; but if the film
were a documentary, Adams would be paid $10. The case was based on
the fact that though labeled a documentary, the film had demonstrated
some commercial potential, though Morris remained $100,000 in debt at the
time of the trial. Morris asserted that he had never claimed Adams rights to
his own story, and the result of the trial affirmed that. Apparently, however,
Morris had not anticipated that a documentary film could have commercial
potential; while this did not end up being a costly error, it did mark a sour
conclusion to an effort by which Morris had saved a man from life in
prison.[8]

The Thin Blue Line helped to open up the commercial potential of documentary film, but it should be added that Morris did so without selling out
the content of his films. Rather, he worked with the medium in an ingenious
way that captured the attention of critics and viewers alike. He continues to
do so, though only *The Fog of War* has been comparable to *The Thin Blue Line*
in its commercial success.

The Thin Blue Line's historical interest is multifaceted. Morris is an
exceptionally gifted observer of culture, and his works are unique cultural
artifacts. *The Thin Blue Line* would be of great interest to students of criminal
justice, and the film also helped to expose the weaknesses of a justice system
in Texas still emerging from the darkest days of segregation (though race was
not a factor in this particular case) and the judicial incompetence associated
with it. The film illustrates the power of film and the media to shape public
awareness, though it also demonstrates that these films have to be made and
distributed within a system that operates according to its own conventions.

---

[8] *New York Times*, August 6, 1989, 23.

ROGER AND ME (1989)

A more controversial director who has enjoyed considerable commercial success is Michael Moore, whose 1989 film *Roger and Me*, like *The Thin Blue Line*, drew unusually large audiences but befuddled those keen on thinking about documentaries in a certain way. Unlike Morris, Moore trains the camera on himself. He aims to gain an audience with General Motors (GM) chairman Roger Smith, in order to ask a few pointed questions about the dismal state of affairs in Flint, Michigan, where GM has been the main industry for many years. Moore grew up in Flint, and his father had worked for GM for thirty-three years. Raised Catholic, Michael Moore attended seminary for a time before pursuing journalism. After running an alternative newspaper, the *Flint Voice*, for ten years he moved to San Francisco to edit *Mother Jones*. One might discern the scathing condemnation of an Old Testament prophet in Moore's work, along with the call to repentance, but he also uses humor to offset situations that are both sad and infuriating. A common theme in Moore's films is the social irresponsibility of corporations, though he does provide them with opportunities to redeem themselves, and the baseness of politicians, especially on the right, who allow this irresponsibility to go unchallenged. In *Roger and Me*, and in his subsequent films *Bowling for Columbine* (2002) *Fahrenheit 9/11* (2004), and Sicko (2007), Moore has taken on corporate greed, the gun industry the Bush administration and the U.S. health care system, embracing a populist style that has proven to be successful both critically and commercially. But their impact is debatable: while *Fahrenheit 9/11* broke box office records for a documentary, it did not achieve Moore's goal of upsetting President Bush's quest for a second term.

Roger and Me documents the impact of economic change and dislocation in a significant year. 1989 marked the upheavals in China and, even more significantly later in the year, the fall of the Berlin Wall and the collapse of communism in Eastern Europe. With the end of the cold war, capitalism apparently stood triumphant, and some might have concluded that corporate America need no longer fear the bogey of communism, long alleged to be lurking in America's unionized labor and an inherent club at labor's disposal. Now capitalism no longer had a rival, and the laws of the global marketplace, heartless as they might be, would allow the rich to become richer and the poor to struggle to hold on to what they had, very much subservient to their corporate masters. Moore's argument is for a little humanity in the face of such harsh realities.

The film has been described as "angry, biased [and] witty." Humor saves the film from being utterly depressing, and much of the humor derives from the pathetic attempts to revive Flint's sagging fortunes. The viewer learns that *Money* magazine has named Flint the worst place to live in America. Miss Michigan waves from a float in a parade that makes its way past boarded up buildings. President Reagan's visit to Flint to treat a dozen unemployed workers to pizza resulted (off camera) in the suggestion that moving to Texas might be the solution to their problem. The film culminates in a Christmas celebration where Moore finally tracks Roger Smith down, and the encounter is crosscut with a scene of an unemployed worker being evicted from his home. The fact that Moore's sarcasm might be considered mean-spirited is not helped by the fact that Moore himself did not attempt to present a balanced picture of GM's role in Flint's economic decline, evading criticism by proclaiming the film a "personal statement." A more reasoned analysis might have been more persuasive, but probably less entertaining. Viewers tend to respond to Moore, therefore, depending on their existing political, social, and economic outlook. While many viewers would readily accept the proposition that corporations were primarily concerned with the bottom line and less concerned with the welfare of workers, Moore's lack of discipline or desire to nail GM on the facts made him vulnerable to criticism, particularly from the right. The fact that, particularly with later films, much of that criticism would come from equally biased individuals on the right does not save Moore from this criticism. But at the same time, the evidence that is there often makes a compelling case.[9]

The reception of the film was unusual by the standards of most documentaries. Once again, critics proclaimed documentaries "hot," despite the fear that the Cable News Network (CNN) would render the documentary obsolete—an absurd concern, in retrospect. The Toronto Film Festival screened the film in the summer of 1989, and it met with a rapturous response, including the prize for most popular film. In September 1989, it appeared at the New York Film Festival, and a bidding war ensued for the right to distribute the film, topping $1 million, which very few documentaries ever had made in box office receipts. It won most of the major documentary awards for 1989, but like *The Thin Blue Line* was not nominated for an Academy Award. Distributed in commercial movie theaters, it did quite well at the box office for a documentary, making $6.7 million when the film had cost only $160,000 to make.[10] GM's own financial woes, culminating in bankruptcy in 2009, have in the meantime intervened to modify how viewers receive this film.

Michael Moore's subsequent films have achieved even greater commercial and critical success, with *Bowling for Columbine* (2002) winning the Academy Award for Best Documentary Feature. In 2004, *Fahrenheit 9/11* took on the Bush administration directly during an election year, with Moore hoping to persuade viewers that ties to Arab oil made the Bush family and the Republican Party less than trustworthy guarantors of the public interest in the so-called war on terror. While it again set a box office record for a documentary, the film could not bridge the sharp political divide for which it held the Bush administration responsible. The political right mounted a campaign against the film, and as a result, it had the effect of galvanizing only those already ill-disposed to the administration. It did not receive an Academy Award nomination, suggesting that, in a climate reminiscent of the early years of the cold war, the Academy declined to embrace the film.

---

[9] *New York Times*: September 21, 1989, D1; September 22, 1989, C1; and September 27, 1989, C15.
[10] *New York Times*: September 28, 1989, C15.

THE FILMS OF KEN BURNS

Though Ken Burns' films do not have the same commercial potential, at least for theatrical release, as the films of Michael Moore, this filmmaker has become the leading historian on public television. Often working in collaboration with his brother Ric, an outstanding documentarian in his own right, Burns tackles major subjects in American history and life. In 1990 his eleven-hour film *The Civil War*, aired over several evenings, earned PBS some of its highest viewer numbers ever. Burns, who had made earlier documentaries for PBS on the Brooklyn Bridge (earning the Organization of American Historians' first-ever Barnouw prize for film and television work dealing with history, in 1983), the Statue of Liberty, and Huey Long, instantly became America's de facto documentary filmmaker laureate. Though this book deals primarily with films on the twentieth century experience, this series cannot be overlooked in a chapter on documentary film, and the series also demonstrated the enduring power and influence of that conflict on American life. With no contemporary footage to work with— motion pictures were invented at the end of the nineteenth century—Burns made skillful use of stills, music, narrations, and perhaps most memorably actors reading contemporary letters to create a compelling narrative. By training not a historian himself, Burns brought in a diverse group of historians to comment.

With the success of *The Civil War*, Burns subsequently undertook other large-scale documentary projects that took up major themes in American life and history: baseball, jazz, and the Second World War. Though at times the attempt to ascribe metaphysical significance to art and sports seems a bit forced, Burns has a knack for identifying and exploring themes that resonate deeply. The jazz series includes some extraordinarily powerful material, especially its portrayal of jazz as an expression of both the pain and the exuberance of the African American experience. That is the focus of the series, and as such it does not explore jazz as a global phenomenon, saying almost nothing, for example, about Latin jazz.

In the fall of 2007, PBS aired Burns' latest series, *The War*, which traced the wartime experiences of a number of Americans connected to four different communities in the United States: Luverne, Minnesota; Mobile, Alabama; Sacramento, California; and Waterbury, Connecticut. While Burns is clearly respectful of what Tom Brokaw called the "greatest generation," these stories bring out the essential or ordinary humanity of those who participated in combat or in efforts on the home front. The film took some criticism in advance for its relative lack of attention to the Latino/Latina experience, and some quick work was done to address that deficiency; the controversy expressed the expectation that in public discourse on the American experience, minorities of appreciable size must be given particular attention. But despite the controversy, Burn's work is both impressive and subtle, with a great variety of experiences ranging from Sascha Weinzheimer's imprisonment as a young girl in a Manila concentration camp to Paul Fussell's recognition, despite the harshness of

daily existence, of the war's broader significance. Burns even felt it important to defy the Federal Communications Commission to include the historically accurate and appropriate statement that daily life for a soldier
during the Second World War normally was pretty "f***** up." The realism of his portrayal makes the ultimate achievement of victory seem all
the greater.

COLD WAR (1998)

To produce a television series on the cold war, Ted Turner of CNN
approached Jeremy Isaacs, by that time a legendary television documentary
producer for his work on *The World at War* (1974) and other series. The result
was a twenty-four-part series that provided a thorough assessment of the
U.S.–Soviet conflict that had dominated the world from 1947 to 1991.
Drawing upon the resources of the Cold War International History Project,
founded in 1991, it aimed for a balanced picture of events. The interviews
with surviving leaders and policy makers allowed for the benefit of hind-
sight, but as the *World at War* series before it illustrated, to have these oral
histories was in itself an invaluable asset. But these public figures also
shed new light on events. *Cold War* also draws heavily upon the experiences
of ordinary individuals whose lives were shaped by these events: an
American woman whose husband was missing in Korea for years; a woman
who escaped from East Berlin; and a Russian woman whose son died
in Afghanistan. As a global history, it does not focus heavily on the American
experience, nor on the diversity of that experience. Aspects of it may seem
dated, as is the case with *The World at War*, but on the essentials, it remains an
witative study of the cold war. Released on VHS at the time, it unfortunately
has not been released on DVD.

REALITY TELEVISION AND THE DOCUMENTARY

The reality television boom of recent years may owe as much to the game
show as to the documentary, but a number of series have placed "contestants" in meticulously reconstructed historical situations. Rather an esoteric
premise for reality television, these programs began with the joint Channel
Four (UK) and WNET New York production of *1900 House* (1999), a show
that placed a contemporary British family of six in a terraced house
(in America, it would be called a row house) in London without central heat-
ing or electricity. While the challenges of running an urban household in 1900
affected the entire family, what became clear very quickly was how much
work it involved for women in a society where the man typically went off to
work outside the home while women looked after the household. The
viewer also understands better the value Victorian men placed on achieving
an income that would permit the hiring of servants. Of course, the Bowler
family could not disappear entirely into 1900, so they had a perspective on

this hard physical labor that their counterparts 100 years earlier would not have had, but history is always a dialogue between past and present. Filmed in the style of more commercially oriented reality shows, complete with talking-head "confessionals" in which the participants reveal their thoughts about the experience as it unfolds, *1900 House* is a narrative created to a large extent in the editing room, where hundreds of hours of footage were cut down to four. It aired on PBS beginning in June 2000, about the same time the first *Survivor* series (2000) became a major television hit.

Subsequently, *Manor House* (2002) recreated the upstairs–downstairs dynamics of Manderston, an Edwardian estate southeast of Edinburgh, *Frontier House* (2002) had three families homesteading in the Montana wilderness, circa 1880, and *Colonial House* (2004) had contestants attempting to establish a viable coastal community in Maine with what would have been available to them in 1628. Each of these series is a remarkable historical exercise, and while they do not present a perfect reconstruction of life in those times, they do ask the contestants and the viewers to imagine life in these different circumstances.

With the vast expansion of opportunities for affluent Americans to view television and film in a variety of formats, the documentary film has not only survived but flourished, perhaps not with huge audiences but with enough commercial success to make this a major conduit for historical information and insights. Whether documentary films capture or attempt to explain an aspect of the human experience, the viewer must consider the circumstances under which the film was made, as well as its content and its reception to appreciate fully its historical significance.

Questions for Discussion:

1. How do documentary films become historically significant?
2. Though documentary films by definition document their subjects, how can and do they address the problems of citation?
3. In your own scholarship, how would you weigh the information and insights presented in documentary films against those presented in written sources?

6

"Based on a True Story"
History and Biography in Narrative Film

When you see a film and the words "based on a true story" or "inspired by actual events" appear on the screen, what do you think? Presumably the filmmaker wants you to know that he or she did not make this up—at least not entirely. He or she has dug into the trove of human experience to tell a story worth telling: the inspiring life story of a revered figure; the lurid tale of a criminal figure; or the stirring heroics of ordinary individuals, taking on a formidable adversary and, we hope, winning. History is full of wonderful stories of people and events that lend themselves successfully to dramatization, and, from a commercial perspective, historical truth is a valuable selling point: people want to be inspired by the examples of others. Yet there is almost always a tension between the artistic and commercial demands of the film medium and the historian's ethical and professional obligation to render the past as it actually happened. But while the historian can easily cry foul when a movie distorts the past, we must acknowledge that writing history also involves constructing narrative. Though not as bound by commercial imperatives, historians must use their imaginations and intellect to interpret events and present them to readers in a coherent and meaningful way. It is a painful cliché, but there is a lot of story in history, too.

History and biography in film present historians and other viewers with elaborate visions of the past, and these visions can both help and hinder the pursuit of historical truth. In this chapter we will aim to

- distinguish between historical writing and historical filmmaking as paths to historical understanding;
- recognize the power of movie visions of the past to stimulate historical thinking and imagination;

• recognize the fact that narrative movies are by definition *dramatizations*, not *documentations*, of the past; and

• account for the artistic and commercial pressures that lead to movie representations that diverge from factual historical record.

Historians know that movies are very different from written studies based on extensive research in archival materials. An article for a journal or a scholarly monograph will be more narrowly focused on a specific topic than any film would be. Likewise, many books on history are monographs that examine specific, narrow topics and are intended for a relatively small reading audience of specialists. Movies cannot afford audiences that small. Nor can movies do what historical writing can. But movies can reconstruct the past with great skill, insight, and beauty.

This chapter is about narrative films that, from the historian's point of view, present an answer to a historical question. A critical analysis of these films should not ask exactly the same questions we would of a written monograph, because we are dealing with a different medium with different modes of expression, intended for a different audience. Reading a history book for a course is not meant to generate the same kind of excitement as reading a thriller; rather it is meant to increase your knowledge and build your critical thinking skills, for your own good and the good of humanity. Watching a narrative film for its portrayal of the past similarly may not generate the excitement of a summer blockbuster. A film's entertainment value is of significant consequence if it is to have an impact as history, but that is not the *primary* consideration if you are looking at a film for its historical significance. I discovered the need to make this point when I used John Sayles' film *Matewan* (1987) in class. This is an outstanding example of a filmmaker's effort to reconstruct history, in this case the coal wars in West Virginia in the early 1920s. Additionally, the students had read Sayles' book *Thinking in Pictures* (1987) in preparation and thus had learned a great deal about the process of making a historical film. So I was greatly disappointed when, in the discussion, students focused on the film's entertainment value rather than how successfully the film had recreated historical people, places, and events. The film's entertainment value for general audiences is not an irrelevant point, but I expect students of history actually to enjoy, or learn to enjoy, how well a movie reconstructs the past and conveys historical insight.

Few films achieve the historical veracity of Daniel Vigne's *The Return of Martin Guerre* (1982), a recreation of a strange-but-true story set in sixteenth-century France, drawn from court records which document the case of a man who appears in a village in southern France in 1560 claiming to be Martin Guerre, returned from many years of army service. Villagers doubt his claims, leading to the court case. Princeton professor Natalie Zemon Davis, a historian of early modern France, played an integral part in the filmmaking. Though obviously some of the story had to be an act of imagination, the outline of the story itself is documented in the court records, as are details of daily life, from other sources. While many films focus on the majestic deeds of leaders and other famous people, this is a good example of social history on film, a reconstruction of ordinary life. Though the film did fairly well for a foreign-language film in the United States, Hollywood later did what it often does with successful foreign language films: Warner Bros. adapted the plot and made a film set in the United States. *Sommersby* (1993), set after the Civil War, would have to be labelled historical fiction, because it no longer could claim to be a true story.[1]

With all of these considerations in mind, the rest of this chapter is a series of discussions that relates these points to specific films, most of which are acclaimed and popular and, depending on the topic of your course, likely to be coming to a classroom near you. Most are worthy of much more extensive discussion. I provide some bibliographical leads both here and in the section on sources at the end of the book, but lay no claim to completeness. These discussions are meant rather

- to illuminate the points raised in the introduction to this chapter;
- to develop more fully your understanding of what we as historians look for in historical filmmaking;
- to familiarize you with some specific and important examples; and
- to promote viewing, discussion, and further research of these and other historical films.

GLORY (1989)

Though Edward Zwick's film *Glory* includes significant fictional plot development and characters, overall the film has done more than perhaps any other film to set Hollywood's historical record straight as to what the Civil War was really about. Movies such as *The Birth of a Nation* (1915) and *Gone with the Wind* (1939) promoted the cause of the South as knights in shining armor battling to preserve their honor. In reality, it was a bitter struggle over a profound human rights crisis in American life, namely the institution of slavery. The film tells the story of the Fifty-Fourth Massachusetts Volunteer Infantry, commanded by Robert Gould Shaw (Matthew Broderick), which in the summer of 1863 answered the skeptics' question of the day, "Will the Negro fight?" Though the assault on Fort Wagner, South Carolina, failed for reasons well beyond the control of these soldiers, their bravery strongly made the case for engaging African Americans in the military quest for their own freedom. As James McPherson, perhaps the foremost living scholar of the Civil War, writes: "Fighting for the Union bestowed upon former slaves a new dignity, self-respect, and militancy, which helped them achieve equal citizenship and political rights—for a time—after the war."[2]

---

[1] Natalie Zemon Davis, *The Return of Martin Guerre*. Cambridge, MA: Harvard University Press, 1984.

[2] See McPherson's essay on *Glory* in Mark Carnes, ed., *Past Imperfect: History According to the Movies*. New York: Henry Holt, 1995, 128–131.

While *Glory* captures the essential truth of the history it portrays, many elements within the film itself are fictional, aimed at dramatizing the story of the regiment's formation and training. While the characters Trip (Denzel Washington, in the role for which he won his first Academy Award), Rawlins (Morgan Freeman), and Searles (Andre Braugher) are made up, they are well-defined characters that illuminate the diversity of backgrounds from which these soldiers came. The fictionalization serves the greater historical good of presenting the accomplishments of the Fifty-Fourth, which were real.

Glory also demonstrates that even anachronisms can be deployed to make a historical point. In one scene, Shaw rides along a path, slashing and destroying watermelons mounted on posts. McPherson points out that one almost certainly would not have found watermelons in Massachusetts during the winter in the 1860s. So what are they doing there? The watermelons certainly grab our attention. Because of their association with a stereotype about African Americans—that is, the assumption that all African Americans are voracious consumers of watermelon—Shaw's maneuver becomes a neat metaphor for destroying old stereotypes, including romanticized, false ideas about the war itself. The end of the film features "the test" itself, as the Fifty-Fourth charges bravely but with no chance of success against Fort Wagner. It was not the end of the story of the Fifty-Fourth's actions in the Civil War, but it answered the question of whether the "Negro would fight" with a resounding yes. The film, meanwhile, ranks among the American Film Institute's "most inspiring films" (#31) and is especially popular among students. Later films, such as *Gettysburg* (1993) and *Gods and Generals* (2003), effectively reenact major battles, but, averaging about four hours apiece, they provide rather plodding military history that appeals primarily to Civil War buffs.

REDS (1981)

While the Civil War has gotten plenty of attention from filmmakers over the years, Warren Beatty's sprawling three-plus hour drama *Reds* takes up a more unusual subject. *Reds* tells the story of Jack Reed (played by Beatty), the American reporter who wrote the famous book *Ten Days that Shook the World* about Russia's Bolshevik revolution in November 1917. To do so it recreates the radical Bohemian culture of New York in the early decades of the twentieth century. Uniquely among democratic, industrialized states, the United States never developed an enduring or permanent socialist movement, but this period was its heyday: the Bolshevik Revolution itself sparked a "Red Scare" in the United States, followed after the Second World War by another strong wave of anticommunism during the cold war that ensured rough passage for any reform that could be denounced as "socialist." The history of the Soviet Union and other communist states would dispel any romantic notions of "from each according to his ability, to each according to his need," but in the very early stages of the revolution, the

Bolsheviks inspired Western radicals, and many remained enamored despite the abuses of Stalinism. In retrospect, the hard-edged capitalism of the United States in particular not only took a pitiless stance toward working men and women, allowing the "invisible hand" to determine wages, but also used force and intimidation to prevent workers from organizing to seek better wages and conditions. Government by and large protected the interests of big business.

Beatty presents the world of such thinkers, activists, and writers as Emma Goldman (Maureen Stapleton), Max Eastman (Edward Herrmann), and Eugene O'Neill (Jack Nicholson) as high-brow but warmly idealistic. Color figures significantly in this evocation, with heavy use of warm shades of yellow, red, and brown. Increasingly, however, the film focuses on the stormy love relationship that develops between Reed and Louise Bryant (Diane Keaton), to the point that its climactic moment has less to do with Reed's political convictions or journalistic accomplishments than with his dramatic reunion with Bryant when she joins him in Russia. Much of that part of the story is made up, and indeed the history might have gotten lost entirely in the melodrama if not for an interesting technique Beatty used to anchor his drama in history: having about thirty different people comment on the times being depicted in the film. This is a common device in documentary films, but it worked well in this narrative film, in part because many of the people were interesting characters in their own right, individuals who had experienced these events themselves.[3]

MATEWAN (1987)

One of America's best-known independent filmmakers, John Sayles has made many films that document contemporary life in specific places and times. In *Matewan*, by contrast, he brings to life the historical coal wars of the early 1920s, imagining how the coal mine strike in Matewan, West Virginia, unfolded. The film certainly stands on its own as a very effective evocation of life in a specific time and place, but what makes it even more useful to historians is the fact that Sayles has written a book, *Thinking in Pictures: the Making of the Movie Matewan* (1987), that describes the filmmaking process and allows the reader to know what in the film is based on documentation and what is imagined, or fictional.[4] With limited documentation, for example, Sayles included some actual historical figures but made up most of the characters. With respect to dialogue, all of the characters use words that may never have been uttered. The film does not pretend to be literally historically accurate. What it does portray effectively is the perils of mine labor at

---

[3] See especially Robert A. Rosenstone's essay "Reds as History" in *Visions of the Past.* Cambridge, MA: Harvard University Press, 1995, 83–108, and his later thoughts on the film in *History on Film/Film on History.* New York: Pearson Longman, 2006, 97–110.
[4] John Sayles, *Thinking In Pictures: The Making of the Movie Matewan.* Cambridge, MA: Da Capo Press, 1987. The book also includes the stills, diagrams, and the shooting script for the film.

that time. First of all, the work itself was physically challenging and dangerous. Yet for local laborers options were few, and mining companies kept
wages as low as the market would bear, rather than at a level that would provide a good standard of living. Faced with this harsh reality, the miners in
the film are drawn to the man who comes to town to organize a labor union,
Joe Kenehan (Chris Cooper), a character that Sayles created to serve as the
film's protagonist. Sayles associates him with the Wobblies, as members of
the Industrial Workers of the World were known, and he makes him a pacifist. The organization of the local miners into a viable union poses significant
challenges, and the conflict between the miners and the company turns
violent before the film is over. Kenehan also confronts the miners with the
fact that their own prejudices and accustomed group identities are working
against them. The company shrewdly exploits these by bringing in African
American and Italian immigrant miners: whether or not this happened
specifically in Matewan, it is a cardinal point of U.S. labor history that ethnic
groups stuck together and posed an obstacle to worker solidarity across
ethnic lines.

Sayles creates a narrative that builds to the violent showdown between
the workers and the company's hired guns. It seeks to defy convention but
nevertheless satisfy the audience's demand for a good story. Sayles creates a
drama that keeps the focus on the historical issues he wishes to illuminate,
rather than a distracting romance. Kenehan, therefore, does not get involved
romantically with Elma Radnor (Mary McDonnell), the widow who runs the
rooming house in which he is staying, focusing instead on his work. By
focusing on the hardships of people's lives and the challenges of standing up
to an exploitative employer, *Matewan* enables its audience to imagine life in
times and circumstances different from their own. Periodically, mining
tragedies in the United States and elsewhere remind Americans that these
circumstances may have changed less than we might imagine.

Matewan bears comparison to earlier and later films about labor issues
in industrial America. An earlier film, Martin Ritt's *The Molly Maguires* (1970),
set in western Pennsylvania's coal mines in the 1870s, has some effective
moments, but actually focuses on the infiltration of the secret society of Irish
saboteurs by a detective from an agency not named in the film, but in real life
the private Pinkerton National Detective Agency. Richard Harris plays James
McParlan, who successfully infiltrates the Mollies, and the film does leave the
viewer guessing as to whether he will betray the workers he has befriended
in the end. The development of a love interest between McParlan and Mary
Raines (Samantha Eggar) also leads the viewer to expect a more conventional
ending.[5]

A film that, like *Matewan*, focuses more specifically on labor issues is
Ritt's later film, *Norma Rae* (1979), for which Sally Field won her first
Academy Award. She portrayed the title character, based on the real life

---

[5] See essay by J. Anthony Lukas in M. Carnes, ed., *Past Imperfect*, 142–145.

actions of Crystal Lee and others who in the 1970s struggled to establish a union for their textile mill in North Carolina. It told a powerful story of empowerment, not just of laborers, but of women. Made on the eve of the conservative Reagan revolution, it marked a high point in the women's movement of the 1970s. A great documentary film from this era should also be mentioned in this context, Barbara Kopple's *Harlan County USA* (1976), discussed in chapter 5. In that film, the women are not the laborers, but their role in a bitter standoff between labor and management in the coal mines of eastern Kentucky is nevertheless crucial.[6]

Labor never organized as fully in this country as it did in other Western industrialized countries, in part because ethnic fissures worked to the advantage of management, but the United States was nevertheless for a time the world's industrial giant, a fact which contributed decisively to the Allied victory in the Second World War. The efforts of millions of laborers, from the mines to the factories, are a vital part of the American experience.

FLAGS OF OUR FATHERS AND LETTERS FROM IWO JIMA (2006)

Though America's role in the First World War was of major consequence economically and militarily, the Second World War proved to be a much longer involvement that had a more momentous impact on America and its global role. During the war itself and subsequently, the Second World War has been a major subject of films made in Hollywood and throughout the rest of the world, particularly Europe. In movies, one can trace shifts in the portrayal of the Second World War that reflect both changes in society and world politics since the war and the evolution of our collective memory of the conflict. Earlier portrayals, for example, reflected some of the prejudices intensified by the conflict itself. During the cold war portrayals of the former enemy, Germany, reflected the fact that Germany had become our ally. Likewise, few films focused on the efforts of then-ally, now-enemy Russia in defeating Nazi Germany in Eastern Europe.

In recent years films about the Second World War have paid homage to the generation that fought the war, as veterans become elderly and pass on. Veneration of veterans reached its height with longtime NBC news anchor Tom Brokaw's book *The Greatest Generation* (1998), which became a huge bestseller. Stephen Ambrose, one of the most commercially successful historians of recent times, wrote many books about the men who fought during D-Day and the Battle of the Bulge in books like *Citizen Soldiers*, *The Good Fight*, and *Band of Brothers* (1998). No one can dispute the significance and importance of what American men and women did to defeat Germany and Japan. A potential hazard of such reverence, however, is that people lose sight of the ordinary humanity of these men, turning them into a patriotic cliché and suggesting

---

[6] On *Norma Rae*, see essay by Robert Brent Toplin in *History by Hollywood*, 204–223.

that subsequent generations do not have "the right stuff." Writer Paul Fussell has described the unbridgeable gap that exists between those who have experience combat and those who have not in his book *Wartime* (1990). That is an important point to keep in mind as film depictions of war become ever more realistic, complete with severed heads, limbs, and guts hanging out. Steven Spielberg's film *Saving Private Ryan* (1998) and the HBO series *Band of Brothers* (2001) not only set new standards for realism in depicting combat, but also reflected meaningfully on the nature of the war and war in general.

In 2006, two films directed by Clint Eastwood, *Flags of Our Fathers* and *Letters from Iwo Jima*, explored the experience of the famous battle on a desolate volcanic Japanese island in the first months of 1945, one from the American and the other from the Japanese perspective. Though they achieved significant critical acclaim, they were not big commercial successes, perhaps because from afar they might appear to come from the same mold as *Saving Private Ryan* and *Band of Brothers*. Visually, they are similar, using the washed-out, grainy look Janusz Kaminski used so effectively in Spielberg's film. But both films break significant new ground as well.

Flags of Our Fathers explores the gap that Paul Fussell describes in his book with its juxtaposition of two definitions of heroism. The story revolves around the famous photograph that every culturally literate American should recognize, Joe Rosenthal's shot of U.S. soldiers raising the flag atop Mount Suribachi on Iwo Jima in February 1945. As was rumored at the time and later turned out to be true, the photograph was not of the first raising of the flag, but of a staged second flag-raising, using a larger flag, so that Navy Secretary James Forrestal could take the first flag as a souvenir. Though the first raising was photographed, it was Rosenthal's image of the second raising that became iconic.

The film does not portray this as a scandal, however. The film focuses instead on three of the men who raised the second flag, who were taken back to the United States to promote the sale of war bonds as heroes of Iwo Jima: Ira Hayes (Adam Beach), Rene Gagnon (Jesse Bradford), and John "Doc" Bradley (Ryan Philippe). Somewhat befuddled by their distinction as heroes, they go along with the publicity tour, understanding the need to raise funds for the war effort. Hayes, an Indian, has the greatest conflict over this role, perhaps because he feels most deeply the hypocrisy of a society that refuses him service in restaurants but nevertheless labels him a hero to sell war bonds. In contrast, Gagnon and his girlfriend-fiancée-wife Pauline (Melanie Lynskey) are happy to pose for the cameras and collect cards from businessmen promising good jobs, emptily as it turns out. Hayes and Gagnon do not get along, and "Doc" is caught between (his son cowrote the book on which the film is based).

In this film about heroes, there are no real villains, just a few schmucks. Eastwood understands the gap between the battle front and the home front, and he portrays the difference between showbiz heroism and heroism as the soldiers themselves understand and feel it without caricature, condescension, or condemnation. The fact that the companion film *Letters from Iwo Jima* focuses on the Japanese soldiers suggests that Eastwood is interested in a truth that is untainted by prejudice or chauvinism. For American audiences especially, the portrayal of Japanese soldiers as individual human beings alone helps to shatter longstanding stereotypes of soldiers mindlessly sacrificing themselves for their emperor. Near the beginning of *Flags of Our Fathers*, the voice of the narrator ("Doc" as an old man) says "Every jackass thinks he knows what war is, especially those that have never been in one. We like things nice and simple, good and evil, heroes and villains." One might easily read some contemporary significance in those words, but Eastwood does not press the point, allowing viewers to draw their own conclusions.

JFK (1991)

Oliver Stone's fanciful blend of fact and opinion packed a powerful cinematic punch in its day, achieving box-office success, critical acclaim, and, remarkably, attention from scholars and politicians alike. Since achieving prominence in the 1980s with the films *Platoon* (1986) and *Salvador* (1986), Stone has become one of the American film artists that scholars take most seriously. Though he has made a number of historical films, he sees himself more as a presenter and explorer of myth. Those perceptions are not as contradictory as they may sound, however, if we consider the term *myth* not as it is commonly used, meaning "untrue," but rather in the sense that we have come to understand mythology: an exploration through stories of the human condition. Greek mythology, for example, resonates with rich insights into what the Greeks believed to be true about themselves and the world around them. Myths are not scientifically, verifiably true, as in people having real-life experiences of gods running around turning each other into beasts, but they are true in the sense that they depict human beings dealing with the essential struggles of life: understanding their own strengths and weaknesses, facing external challenges such as war, and reconciling their individual desires with duty to others and to the community.

So when Stone took on the subject of the assassination of John F. Kennedy, viewers did not get a documentary film that made an argument supported with evidence from documents; nor did they get a docudrama that did the same thing, with allowances made for fictionalization in the name of gaining a larger audience or holding its attention more successfully. They got instead a powerful dramatization that *looked* historical but which did not present as tight a historical argument as one would expect from a book or article, or even in a documentary film. Whether or not that is "all right" depends, to some extent, on one's approach to history in film: *auteur* theory, or a structuralist approach, would emphasize strongly Stone's intentions. But a poststructuralist approach would challenge us to think more about reception, or the impact of the director's work on audiences. Because viewers naturally associate the film's look with documentaries they have seen on television and elsewhere, they are more inclined to infer that what they see is (or is *supposed* to be) the factual, historical truth.

Stone's belief was that the purpose of the Warren Commission, appointed by the new President, Lyndon B. Johnson, to investigate the assassination of President Kennedy, was essentially damage control: to reassure the American public and the rest of the world that the crime was the work of one man, now dead, and that the tragic story was now over. The movie also suggests that, because Kennedy was reconsidering policy toward Vietnam in 1963, he threatened a vast, powerful, and growing military–industrial complex that favored military commitments and lucrative defense contracts. Vietnam had been a divided country since 1954, with a noncommunist South Vietnam struggling to prevent a communist takeover by North Vietnam, led by Ho Chi Minh, who also had a strong militant following in South Vietnam. The United States had backed the anticommunist struggle financially throughout the 1950s, and after France's withdrawal had become the leading foreign presence. Whether or not it was politically possible for Kennedy to stand down from a communist challenge is a matter of historical debate. Under Johnson, however, the United States escalated its involvement to full-scale war, an effort that ultimately failed. Stone himself fought in Vietnam, and his body of work testifies to the profound impact it had on his own life.

JFK is not about Vietnam, really, but Vietnam explains both why Stone made the film and why it is so powerful. The public seemed to accept the assurances provided by their government in the Warren Commission Report. But shocking historical events—such as the attacks of December 7, 1941, and September 11, 2001—produce conspiracy theories, and in *JFK*, Stone consolidates the many theories about the Kennedy assassination into a great political thriller. It does not present a clear or coherent alternative account of what happened; rather Stone's primary purpose was to shatter the complacency of the prevailing myth, that of the Warren Commission, and to reopen the investigation of what exactly happened at Dealey Plaza in Dallas—and in America—on November 22, 1963. Focusing on the activities of New Orleans district attorney Jim Garrison (played by Kevin Costner), Stone focuses on the case Garrison made against New Orleans businessman Clay Shaw, charging that Shaw had conspired with anti-Castro Cubans to assassinate Kennedy. Before the end of the film, however, almost everyone from the Soviets to Lyndon Johnson himself have been implicated, leaving the viewer somewhat confused but amenable to the idea of some kind of conspiracy. Much of the last part of the film is Garrison's closing argument, made with much more drama and conviction than in real life, since the actual case ended quickly in acquittal for Shaw. Costner turns to the camera and says "It's up to you," suggesting to the viewer that if the truth is ever to be know about this case, the public will have to press for it. Indeed the film did reopen discussion of the Kennedy assassination, but despite all the doubt, the questions have not yet been answered satisfactorily. Thus far, a new common consensus has not emerged to replace the Warren Commission myth, even if faith in that paradigm is shaky.[7]

---

[7] Thanks to friends and colleagues Donald Whaley and James Burton for their scholarly insights on Stone's work. For more on *JFK*, especially Robert Brent Toplin, *History by Hollywood* (Urbana, IL: University of Illinois Press, 1996), 45–78; and the Forum on *JFK* in *American Historical Review* 97:2 (April 1992).

THE BIOPIC

One of the major challenges of presenting history accurately on film is the fact that history is messy. Even written history generalizes, summarizes, and simplifies events so that we can remember them and think about their significance. Documentary films can retain some of the complexity of written history, but narrative films face stricter demands with respect to storytelling that often get filmmakers into trouble with historians. A frequent "transgression" is the consolidation of the actions of more than one person into the heroic deeds of one. This corresponds also to Hollywood's star culture, and the impulse to showcase the talents of a few glamorous stars. Biographical films have long been popular, providing movie audiences with portraits of the lives of famous people whose stories can shock, teach, or inspire.

Films focusing on the lives of famous or notorious people have long been popular. *Halliwell's Filmgoer's Companion* lists among the kinds of people memorialized on film: composers, courtesans, entertainers, explorers, inventors, kings and queens, painters, politicians, scientists, soldiers, spies, sportsmen, and writers. We could add criminals, entrepreneurs, saints, and human rights activists. The life stories of famous people, filled with triumph and tragedy, provide the drama that filmmakers seek out. Over time, the biographical film can serve as an index of society's heroes. In the early years of the Academy Awards, many actors won for portrayals of historical figures: George Arliss won for *Disraeli* (1929), the story of the nineteenth-century British prime minister; Charles Laughton won for *The Private Life of Henry VIII* (1933); Paul Muni won for *The Story of Louis Pasteur* (1936) and was nominated again a year later for *The Life of Emile Zola* (1937); Spencer Tracy won for his portrayal of Father Edward J. Flanagan in *Boys Town* (1938). Gary Cooper won his first Oscar for the title role in *Sergeant York* (1941), portraying the reluctant First World War hero as America reluctantly prepared for the Second World War; and James Cagney won the Best Actor Oscar for his portrayal of George M. Cohan in *Yankee Doodle Dandy* (1942), a film that presented a patriotic extravaganza to appreciative wartime audiences.[8]

While playing historical characters advanced the careers of these actors in the early days, only one woman won Best Actress Oscar for a historical role during this period: Luise Rainer, for the role of Anna Held in the *Great Ziegfeld* (1936). More recently, the field has become more even. From 2004 to 2008, four out of five Best Actor Oscars went to men playing biographical roles: Jamie Foxx as singer/pianist Ray Charles in *Ray* (2004), Philip Seymour Hoffman as author Truman Capote in *Capote* (2005), Forest Whitaker as Idi Amin in *The Last King of Scotland* (2006), and Sean Penn as Harvey Milk in *Milk* (2008). Meanwhile, Best Actress went to three women playing biographical roles: Reese Witherspoon as country singer June Carter

---

[8] Interestingly, Muni also had played Tony Camonte in Howard Hawks' 1932 film *Scarface*, which promoters did not mind people associating with Al Capone, though the resemblance to the real-life gangster's life was minimal.

Cash in *Walk the Line* (2005), Helen Mirren as Elizabeth II in *The Queen* (2006), and Marion Cotillard as Edith Piaf in *La Vie en rose* (2007). As stated previously, Academy Awards are not the ultimate arbiters of film quality, but they do crown the work of some film artists as "the best." For the filmmaking community, therefore, one can conclude that biography is very important.

A MOCK BIOPIC: *CITIZEN KANE* (1941)

He lost to Gary Cooper, but Orson Welles was nominated for his portrayal of newspaper magnate and megalomaniac Charles Foster Kane in *Citizen Kane*. Including this film in a discussion of biopics is a bit of mischief that Welles himself might have appreciated: on Halloween in 1938, he was responsible for a radio dramatization of H. G. Wells' *War of the Worlds* that presented itself as a news broadcast and caused actual panic among listeners. The joke here is that Charles Foster Kane was not a real person, and *Citizen Kane*, therefore, is technically not a biopic, but it was made in that style and the characterization was close enough that newspaper magnate William Randolph Hearst took great offense. A famous Hollywood battle ensued.

Orson Welles' *Citizen Kane* (1941) is a perfect example of the biopic, except for the fact that Charles Foster Kane never lived. William Randolph Hearst was not convinced, however. *Source:* Everett Collection

Citizen Kane begins with the death of Charles Foster Kane (played as an adult by Welles himself) at Xanadu, his vast estate. The attempts of a newspaper reporter to discover the meaning of his final word, "rosebud," sparks a series of flashbacks that tell the story of a sad little boy who grows up to become a megalomaniacal newspaper tycoon with political ambitions and an extravagant lifestyle. The associations with William Randolph Hearst were undeniable: he had built up a newspaper empire and spent money lavishly, building a palace at San Simeon, California that became a fabled Hollywood retreat. In the 1930s, Welles and his friends saw Hearst as a right-wing demagogue, and his cowriter on the film, Herman J. Mankiewicz, knew Hearst and his mistress Marion Davies personally.

Hearst took particular offense at the film's portrayal of Kane's second wife, Susan Alexander (Dorothy Comingore) as an aspiring singer without talent. Kane bankrolls her career, but she fails, leading to their embarrassment and social isolation. If Kane was Hearst, then Alexander had to be his longtime mistress, Marion Davies. In real life, Hearst never divorced his first wife, Millicent, and therefore never married Davies, who in fact was a popular and talented comic actress whose career, if anything, suffered because of her association with Hearst, not vice versa. Welles used his portrayal of Alexander in his defense of the film as fictional, but the associations were unavoidable and indelible, and it does not take a thorough feminist critique of the movie to conclude that Davies in fact suffered the gravest insult.[9]

Welles himself was famously egotistical, and making Citizen Kane took a lot of nerve. Though nominated for nine Academy Awards, including Welles himself as actor, director, producer, and writer, Citizen Kane won only for writing, an award Welles shared with Mankiewicz.[10]

Welles would receive only one more Academy Award nomination in his life, the following year for The Magnificent Ambersons. Certainly his own temperament helped to account for his uneven success subsequently, but the history of Citizen Kane also underscores some of the challenges of making biographical films. Most films make a disclaimer at the end asserting that "any resemblance to people living or dead is purely coincidental." Dealing with real history entails walking away from that claim and exposing the filmmaker to potential charges of defamation or libel, or perhaps just negative criticism for inaccuracy or distortion. These realities impede the making of biographical films about some worthy figures and encourage the making of films that turn their protagonists into saints.

---

[9] The film studies literature on Welles and Citizen Kane is extensive, including Laura Mulvey's Citizen Kane (London: British Film Institute, 1993) and Robert Carringer's The Making of Citizen Kane (Los Angeles: University of California Press, 1996). For the history see David Nassaw's multiple prize-winning biography, The Chief: The Life of William Randolph Hearst (Boston: Mariner, 2000), which has a chapter on Citizen Kane, 564–574.
[10] The documentary was shown on PBS and carries the title of the program The American Experience: The Battle Over Citizen Kane (1996); the HBO docudrama is entitled RKO 281 (1999). Pauline Kael's The Citizen Kane Book (Boston: Little, Brown and Company, 1971) includes the shooting script.

Musical Biopics: *The Great Ziegfeld* (1936), *Yankee Doodle Dandy* (1942), and Beyond

Biography has also proved to be a useful tool for stringing together musical numbers to create film extravaganzas, from the beginning of the sound era to the present. The story of an entertainer's life, often fraught with difficulty, provides a necessary narrative thread to what serves primarily as a vehicle for the entertainer's music. Together, *The Great Ziegfeld* (1936) and *Yankee Doodle Dandy* (1942) provide an interesting look at the evolution of the entertainment industry on New York's Broadway in the early twentieth century. William Powell and James Cagney are effective in their roles as Florenz Ziegfeld, Jr. and George M. Cohan. Neither film turns its subject into a saint entirely. But Ziegfeld's divorce from his first wife, Anna Held, is shown almost entirely from her perspective, and the conventional wisdom is that Luise Rainer earned her Oscar for the famous telephone scene in which she bravely and graciously congratulates Flo, whom she still loves, on his marriage to wife number two, Billie Burke (Myrna Loy). No mention is made of her death at the young age of 45.

Similarly, in *Yankee Doodle Dandy*, no mention is made at all of Cohan's first marriage, which ended in divorce, even though the film spanned almost his entire life (he died in 1942, the year of the film's release). The point is that these pictures are less studies of historical characters than life stories that provide linkage for impressive production numbers. In the case of *The Great Ziegfeld*, the Metro-Goldwyn-Mayer (MGM) studio spent $2 million to create spectacular music and dance sequences. Such excess was out of vogue in wartime America, so *Yankee Doodle Dandy* made up in patriotism what it lacked in glitz. Though there are anachronisms, viewers gain impressions of early twentieth century America and its entertainments.

Musical biopics also give filmmakers the opportunity to explore the lives of stars and star culture generally. What drives many of these films is the tension between public stardom, the result of exceptional musical talent and performance, and personal tragedy. Later films did not shy away from the negative sides of their subjects' characters. Of the many more recent examples, Oliver Stone's *The Doors* (1991) explored sex, drugs, and rock and roll in the context of the life of Jim Morrison (Val Kilmer), who died at 28 in 1971. Diana Ross played the legendary jazz vocalist Billie Holiday in Sidney J. Furie's *Lady Sings the Blues* (1972). Depending on the intentions of the film's artists and producers, these films can shed light on the time period in which these artists lived, examining popular culture and the counterculture in the case of *The Doors*, and the hardships and barriers imposed by racism in the life of Billie Holiday, whose song "Strange Fruit" conveys in song the horror of lynching. The pain she expressed in her music also dominated her life; relationships with abusive men and abuse of drugs and alcohol contributed to her personal tragedy and she died in 1959, only 44 years old.

Olivier Dahan's *La Vie en rose* (*La Môme* in France) has very little to say about the major historical events that occurred during Edith Piaf's life (1915–1963), focusing instead on the train wreck that was her personal life (greater indeed than any of today's pop stars). Born in the same year as Holiday, she likewise endured great poverty in her early years, achieved fame with her distinctive singing voice, and died tragically before the age of 50. But aside from a scene set in Paris in early months of 1940, there is no reference to the Second World War at all, even though the Nazi occupation from 1940 to 1944 would have been a significant chapter in her life. The idea warrants further investigation, but the explanation could be that, for French audiences especially, taking on the whole life of Edith Piaf and the Second World War, cannot be done in one film. A sequel, perhaps?

THE AVIATOR (2004)

One of the most acclaimed big-budget biopics in recent years has been Martin Scorsese's The Aviator, starring Leonardo DiCaprio as Howard Hughes, a man whose life story readily lends itself to spectacle: an inventive, daring entrepreneur with ties to Hollywood, who becomes phenomenally wealthy but descends into madness. This film includes the requisite childhood scene that provides clues to the character's psyche, an experience from his formative years that explains his phobia for germs and sets the course psychologically for his experiences in later life. As a young man, Hughes had inherited a fortune, and he turned his attention to filmmaking in the later 1920s, making an enormously expensive movie, Hell's Angels (1930), that can claim to be the ancestor of the summer blockbuster. It did have a story line: two American brothers at Oxford join the Royal Air Force in the First World War, while their German friend ends up on a zeppelin crew; but the movie was really about the special effects. Both color and sound were relatively new, and one of the reasons the film was so expensive to make was that Hughes completely re-shot the film well into its production to incorporate sound. Scorsese's admiration for the film and the story of its production were central to his reasons for making The Aviator.[11]

Hughes went on to make a huge fortune of his own in aviation, becoming one of the richest men in the world, and he romanced such stars as Katharine Hepburn (Cate Blanchett) and Ava Gardner (Kate Beckinsale) before mental illness turned him into an unkempt recluse. The Hollywood connections, the ambition, and tragic end made for a fine cinematic spectacle. For the historian, the political connections are also interesting: Alan Alda plays Senator Ralph Owen Brewster, who allegedly took a bribe to use his influence on behalf of Pan-Am, Hughes' rival; but Hughes played that game himself, and movie provides insight into the early days of what President Eisenhower would later call the military–industrial complex.

---

[11] $3.8 million to make a movie was unheard of in 1930, though in 2006 dollars it would be "only" about $47 million: today's summer blockbusters routinely cost at least three times that. A December release, The Aviator itself cost about $110 million to make, but took in only $103 million domestically; international receipts made the movie profitable, bringing the total to almost $214 million, according to boxofficemojo.com.

DOWNFALL (2004)

Obviously Adolf Hitler was not American, but he was a very important figure in the twentieth century American experience. I must confess an aversion to movies about him, an unambiguously evil character responsible for the deaths of tens of millions of people in the Second World War. Besides his being a chilling character, there is also a more general awkwardness film-maker must address in portraying very famous people of whom we already have a strong impression. Critics have objected to portrayals of Adolf Hitler in particular, fearing that making him human might make him more sympathetic. Oliver Hirschbiegel's *Downfall* (2004) does not tell Hitler's life story, but it is a brilliant study of his character in the last days of his life. Bruno Ganz's performance in the title role is so successful that all of the concerns expressed above are largely put to rest. The film also illuminates the madness of the Nazi vision, still alive as Allied bombs destroy Berlin, Red Army forces close in, and Nazi leaders continue to work and to party while discussing how they will win the war, even as they plan their suicides. The story is told from the perspective of a young woman recruited to serve as a secretary to Hitler, Traudl Junge (Alexandra Maria Lara), a sympathetic and dutiful person who, we must always remind ourselves, works for a genocidal maniac. Ganz does not give Hitler the charm that Forest Whitaker gave Idi Amin in *The Last King of Scotland* (see later text), but he does give him a humanity that does—and *should*—make us uncomfortable. The leading Nazis may have been monsters metaphorically speaking, but they were not literally monsters. The fact that Hitler was quite capable of treating those around him with kindness—though he could just as easily fly into a rage—makes his brutality all the more heinous. The character of Eva Braun (Juliane Köhler) likewise comes to life, a figure who most people have known as the only person crazy enough to marry Hitler. The fact that this film was a German production also reveals something about where the German people are with respect to the Nazi past: certainly in previous decades, a project featuring a portrayal of Hitler would have been greeted with suspicion around the world and in Germany itself. But Germans have done a comparatively good job of confronting their past and recognizing the evils of the Nazi regime. Audiences therefore could expect, and got, an intelligent and insightful film that, while focusing on the last days of the Third Reich, helped illuminate some of the essential realities of the whole experience.

MALCOLM X (1992)

The Civil Rights Movement arguably was the main event in U.S. history after the Second World War, transforming American society from one in which white supremacy was assumed into one in which equality among all citizens became the law of the land. The life of Martin Luther King, Jr. (1929–1968) was the subject of a 1978 television miniseries, *King*, and earlier, in 1970, Sidney Lumet and Joseph L. Mankiewicz made a documentary called *King: A Filmed Record . . . From Montgomery to Memphis*, which was nominated for the Best Documentary Feature Academy Award but is unavailable on VHS or DVD. The only major motion picture, therefore, to portray the life of a civil rights leader has been Spike Lee's *Malcolm X*. Drawing largely on the famous *Autobiography of Malcolm X*, the film tells the life story of Malcolm Little (1925–1965), beginning with his poverty- and tragedy-stricken childhood in different Midwestern cities, then showing the life of crime he led in Boston and New York before he going to jail in 1946. While in jail, he learned of the teachings of the Nation of Islam, and after his release in 1952 he became a disciple of Elijah Muhammad. While he initially preached separation from white society for blacks—he replaced his surname Little with an X to get rid of his slave name—his message became more conciliatory in time, and his charisma and message made him an influential voice in the Civil Rights Movement. He was assassinated in February 1965, many believe by forces from within the Nation of Islam. Having become a martyr, Malcolm X's reputation continued to grow. Compared to Dr. King, Malcolm X had a more radical edge and was famous for the words "by any means necessary" as opposed to King's message of strict nonviolence.

Spike Lee's filmmaking often has a caustic edge (as in *Do the Right Thing*, Chapter 8), but he approached Malcolm X with great reverence, and the film all but tells its audience to sit up straight and listen to what Malcolm X had to say to them. The film generated plenty of discussion upon its release and did modestly well at the box office. The Academy of Motion Pictures Arts and Sciences (AMPAS) could not ignore Denzel Washington's outstanding portrayal of X, but the movie's only other nomination was for costume design. The book still has more power than the movie, in part because Malcolm X was telling his own story to Alex Haley (who later wrote *Roots*), whereas Lee takes a more hagiographical approach that is uncharacteristic of much of his work. At 202 minutes, it was also quite long, even for a biopic. But whatever its flaws, the film is of great historical interest, not just for its content: the production of the film demonstrates the growing importance of African American talent in a still largely white-dominated film industry; and a number of prominent stars contributed funds to its production. And the movie quite obviously was intended to prompt discussion about relations between blacks and whites in contemporary American society, and it did. To underscore the contemporary relevance of the story, Lee used footage of Rodney King, the man whose brutal beating by white police officers in 1991, followed by the acquittal of the officers the following year despite the videotaped evidence, led to riots in Los Angeles.

THE LAST KING OF SCOTLAND (2006)

One could argue that Kevin Macdonald's film about the dictatorship of Uganda's Idi Amin is not a true biopic, since the narrative focuses on a young Scottish doctor named Nicholas Garrigan (James McAvoy), in whom the film consolidates the experiences of at least three different people who worked with or for Amin in the 1970s. But in part due to Forest Whittaker's outstanding portrayal and in part due to the nature of the dictatorship itself, Idi Amin is the dominant character of this film. Kevin Macdonald, formerly a documentary filmmaker, saturated this portrait of early postcolonial Uganda with rich color, contrasting especially the lush green vegetation with the red earth. Garrigan, a recent medical school graduate from Scotland determined to get away from his overbearing father, spins the globe, closes his eyes, and, on his second try, stabs with his finger at what turns out to be Uganda. Initially he signs up to work at a village clinic, but his colleagues find him unsuited for the work, and he is in the process of messing up their personal lives when he meets the new dictator, touring the countryside to build support for his regime. Garrigan is easily swayed by Amin's charming address to the crowd, and the two meet personally after a minor accident, when Garrigan irritably shoots the injured cow with Amin's gun. Amin lures Garrigan to Kampala, where he becomes Amin's personal physician, and, as the occasion suits, his adviser. Amin himself has a charming personal manner, but while he cares enough for the country not to become an outright thief (like Mobutu of neighboring Zaire), it also quickly becomes apparent that Amin is highly suspicious of disloyalty and has no reservations about murdering his closest associates. His affinity for all things Scottish runs to wearing kilts and having bagpipes serenade him in military parades, and of course helps account for his attraction to Garrigan. Garrigan suggests, without any evidence, that the health minister may be conspiring against Amin. When the health minister is killed, Garrigan protests to Amin, but the director has not set this up in such a way as to have the viewer let Garrigan off on grounds of naïveté. Selfish and self-indulgent, he foolishly begins an affair with one of Amin's wives. Caught, he desperately tries to leave, but Amin intercepts him for a horrific showdown at the Entebbe airport, just as the historic 1976 terrorist hijacking is unfolding.

The film dispels the notion that evil characters in history are unambiguous monsters. Whitaker effectively conveys the charm that led people to put their trust and confidence in Amin. Garrigan, a made-up character, demonstrates the lack of discernment, among other weaknesses, including greed, that led real people to become complicit in the actions of an extraordinarily brutal regime. One has to be careful in extrapolating, but while in some ways it is unfortunate that the center of this story is the white guy, the film is a significant piece of postcolonial history, suggestive of the complicity of the West in the bad government that plagued so many African countries in the aftermath of decolonization.

THE QUEEN (2006)

While Forest Whitaker garnered accolades for his portrayal of Idi Amin, Helen Mirren was similarly hailed for her portrayal of the contemporary queen of England, Elizabeth II. *The Queen* takes up a significant historical question, namely the response of Queen Elizabeth II to the death of Diana,

Princess of Wales, in 1997, an event that for much of the world was a prolonged drama in the era of 24/7 news coverage. For the monarchy in Britain
it provided a delicate but significant crisis. Though the film focuses on the
events of a very short period, principally the period from the accident in
Paris to the funeral a week later, the film is very much a study of the queen's
character in which Mirren plays an exceedingly important interpretive role.
Certainly there is enough information about the queen's own response to
the accident and the nation's response to it, but the screenwriter and Mirren
carried out an impressive act of historical imagination to realize this very
intimate portrait of a living, reigning monarch. It is biographical in that it
draws on Elizabeth's own past to explain her disposition during that crisis:
her coming of age decades earlier, assuming the throne from her father, who
was widely perceived to have died young in part due to the challenges of
becoming king instead of his brother, Edward VIII, and helping to guide the
country through the great trial of the Second World War. Elizabeth understood from the beginning that she would have to sacrifice much to fulfill her
duties as queen, a sensibility that few in her own family seemed to share as
the royal family became a soap opera of marriages, affairs, and divorces.
Now the queen was apparently being asked by her people to become
mourner-in-chief. What she perceives as pandering to public sentiment is
also political necessity, as Prime Minister Tony Blair (Michael Sheen) has the
unwelcome duty to tell her. The script imaginatively and intelligently plays
out how this might have unfolded, and Mirren very skillfully brings out
nuances of character, that even if they cannot be verified with documents,
are based on a reasoned assessment of how a person like Queen Elizabeth
might have responded. Her portrayal judiciously balances traits that are
sympathetic with those that are not. Perhaps one day the historical record
will include evidence to prove this particular portrait to be so much tosh,
but in the meantime, viewers have gotten an intelligent, if imagined look
inside a constitutional crisis and the delicate relationship that exists
between the head of state and the head of government in Britain's constitutional monarchy.

The most famous men and women in history remain famous today in
part because of the biopic, which returns to the lives of Julius Caesar, Mark
Antony and Cleopatra, Jesus Christ, Joan of Arc, Elizabeth I, Napoleon and
Adolf Hitler to take renewed measure of their deeds and their historical significance. New interpretations may reflect new scholarship, but they also
reflect broader cultural trends and preoccupations, and the different itera-
tions become the basis for comparison and analysis of changes in perspective over the course of the film era.

Historical films and biopics are obvious places for scholars to study
historical content in film. Presentations of famous events and of important
people can be fact-checked for accuracy fairly easily. These are intentional
explorations of the human record that, despite our insistence on scientific
reconstruction and documentation, correspond to what we do as historians.
The results have ranged from terrific to terrible. But there is a whole lot more

7

■ ■ ■

A Sense of Time and Place
Historical Fiction

Many of the historical movies we see are not about actual historical figures, but they are about actual historical times, places, and events. This chapter explores

* films that we can label as historical fiction, similar to the way we use that label in literature;

* the challenge of thinking through the fictional aspects of such works to discover historical insights; and

* the ways in which fiction actually can enhance the filmmaker's ability to convey historical insights through film.

Historical fiction allows the filmmaker to capitalize on the dramatic, romantic, or exotic circumstances of the past without being bound by known fact in the telling of the central narrative: in other words, the main story can be constructed to suit the norms and conventions of film storytelling that viewers expect, while the characters interact with an environment that may be more or less historical. The fact that the central story is freed from the obligations of historical accuracy allows the filmmakers to construct a narrative that specifically illuminates the historical realities of a particular time and place. Historical drama often has origins in literary fiction, and knowledge of those sources adds to the understanding of the film, though the challenge of any film adaptation is to create a work of film art that can stand on its own (without displeasing those who read the book too much). The connection of the work of fiction to history is worth exploring in its own right, but ultimately the movie has to make its own case for historical insight and significance.

Allowing for artistic freedom, can we suggest rules about the portrayal of historical realities in a work of fiction? We are perhaps better off talking about norms, or what we *expect*, and then allow, and indeed hope, for creative variations. If we are watching an adaptation of a Jane Austen novel, we expect costumes, hairstyles, sets, and the overall look of the film to conform to what we know to have existed at the time. Of course, Austen herself wrote mostly in the 1810s, and filmmakers have in her work alone an important historical resource. In comparison, novels written *about* the past—and their film adaptations—face additional challenges: patterns of speech and behavior should be plausibly of the period; any events discussed should be events of which the characters would have knowledge, and they should represent opinions and attitudes from the time itself, not ones imposed on them from another time.

This chapter argues that critics and audiences normally expect historical drama to represent accurately the period upon which it draws. Errors and anachronisms make the movie look bad and the filmmakers look foolish. But if the filmmakers can pull it off, an intentional creative anachronism can add to a film's historical interest. *Moulin Rouge!* (2001), for example, has loud rock and roll music playing in Paris fifty years before its birth. We can be reasonably sure that director Baz Luhrmann knew that, so what *was* he trying to do? Similar questions greeted Sofia Coppola's biopic *Marie Antoinette* in 2006, which aimed to rescue the ill-fated, Austrian-born queen of France from stale costume drama conventions and establish a fresh connection to the present. While some historians might argue that faithful reconstruction is the best policy, others would assert that the interaction of past and present in these films makes them more interesting, even as history. The anachronisms create a tension that we have to think about; put another way, they give a movie its "pop," or spark that makes the movie unique. Historical dramas, as much as any other kind of film, *should* pop: in reconstructing the past, they should connect us to the past in creative, insightful, and exciting ways.

However much we may wish to be transported completely into the past with a movie, even the most convincing history is not the actual past, but a reconstruction of the past. The fundamental questions to ask of any fictional film set in the past are how the history is presented and for what purpose. How crucial is the historical setting to the meaning and purpose of the story? How much care have the filmmakers taken to represent the past accurately? How important is the historical setting to the film? Are the filmmakers trying to say something about a specific people, place, and time? If the filmmakers do not want to make a historical statement, what impression does the film nevertheless leave? What conventions and stereotypes does it perpetuate?

Without providing an actual historical narrative that reconstructs actual events, films can evoke historical realities by imagining characters living their lives in particular historical circumstances. The filmmakers' motivations and historical interests may vary considerably, and it is up to critics and other viewers to determine and assess fairly the historical merit of any particular film. Intentionally or not, historical dramas help to shape our views of the past. When critics assailed Mel Gibson's 2006 film *Apocalypto* for its brutal portrayal of a self-destructive Mayan civilization, the filmmakers punted, offering that it was just a movie thriller set in an exotic setting. Yet the film opened with a quote from historian Will Durant stating that "a great civilization is not conquered from without until it destroys itself from within," from which a viewer might reasonably expect a historical argument. But what is Gibson saying, and about whom? Did he have a burning drive to pronounce the last word on Mayan civilization, or is he making a point about our own civilization?

The debate over the film should not be between those who, on the one hand, would grant the filmmaker unrestricted artistic license to include anything, real or fabricated, he or she may choose to include, and those who would argue for strict historical accuracy on the other. If a filmmaker invokes history, as Gibson has done by quoting Will Durant, he does have a cinematic obligation to follow through with the history: that includes rendering accurately those aspects of the film that viewers might reasonably assume to be historical, as an aspect of the film's continuity. At the same time, viewers need to be able to distinguish between what we know to be generally true about a time and place and what is made up. Common sense tells us that we cannot know exactly what most historical figures said or did at any particular moment: characters may have existed as real people, but between the script and the actors much of what they say and do must be considered fictional.

Viewers of *Apocalypto* who remember their college World Civilizations courses may be a little surprised to see the Mayan civilization portrayed at the time that the Spanish arrived, since the Aztecs dominated the region at the time, and their destruction at the hands of the Spanish is a central part of the common historical narrative, even the one updated to reassess the old Eurocentric triumphalism. However, despite the dominance of the Aztecs, Mayan civilization did still exist. Much debate still takes place about the role of human sacrifice in pre-Columbian cultures in the western hemisphere, and this appears to be central to Gibson's fascination with the place and time. His dark obsession with suffering, torture, atonement, and sacrifice resonates with some viewers and repels others. Mel Gibson's compulsion to explore the human condition on film draws on specific peoples and places. For the sake of the artistic and intellectual unity of the film, and for the sake of his own argument, these renderings should correspond to what the historical record supports, acknowledging that the record is often incomplete and ambiguous. In portraying a civilization other than his own, Gibson faces criticism from those who feel slighted and/or who know the portrayal to be unfaithful to which we know to be historically true.

However, scholars of all kinds, including historians, study people other than "their own" all the time, and it is important to note, particularly for the discussion that follows, that, though national borders do matter in the film industry, one can never assume any particular film to be exclusively the product of a particular nation. Ever since Hollywood became the world's filmmaking capital, it has drawn talent from all over the world. Indeed, within the United States, that fact has helped to make movies the target of American xenophobia—the fear of that which is perceived to be "foreign." Film is very much an international medium. In recent years, a director born in India, Mira Nair, made *Vanity Fair* (2004), a film about Britain during the Napoleonic era; and the Mexican director Alfonso Cuarón made a film about Britain in 2027, *Children of Men* (2006)—not exactly a historical drama, but a film set intentionally and purposefully in a different time, albeit an imagined future one. The same director directed *Harry Potter and the Prisoner of Azkaban* (2004), another distinctly British cultural artifact.

Though we would not describe the majority of the summer block-busters that dominate the list of all-time box office champions as "historical," historical dramas do make money, and sometimes a lot: the all-time box office champion by far, *Titanic* (1997), obviously draws on history, and one could safely bet that a love story starring Leonardo DiCaprio and Kate Winslet would not have made $1.8 billion worldwide if it were set on a contemporary cruise. But historical films figure even more prominently in the lists of films that have garnered awards, and therefore prestige, for their producers and studios. These and other films leave impressions on their audiences about the past and its significance to the present. It is important, therefore, to acquire a set of critical-thinking tools to assess what historical dramas, and any particular historical drama, can in fact teach us.

VISIONS OF AMERICA'S PAST

Films richly illustrate the history of the United States with countless stories set in the past. In this chapter we focus on films that are fictional, but are set against a backdrop that is more or less historical. The principal critical challenge is to identify what is being conveyed and received about the American experience. Is it principally mythical, a heroic tale that pays homage to the forebears who helped to bring about today's fortunate circumstances? Myth can also explore the darker side of the human experience, and the sense in which we use the term here is a story that, even if fictional, resonates deeply in the culture and is therefore true in ways that historians and fact-checkers cannot verify—though of course they can and should argue about the visions and versions of the past that appear. *Coming Home* (1978), *The Deer Hunter* (1978), *Apocalypse Now* (1979), and *Platoon* (1986) all aimed to present the fundamental truth of the Vietnam experience without a single historical character. But a movie need not tap deep into the American psyche to be of interest to us historically; movies about everyday American life, particularly those with a regional character or set in a particular era, can immerse us in past experiences more like our own.

THE SOUTH

Time has shaped our understanding of the country as being comprised of regions, each with unique characteristics. According to the U.S. Census Bureau, the South is now home to 110 million people, or over one-third of Americans, with the West second (70 million), the Midwest third (66 million), and the Northeast fourth (55 million). Moving pictures have helped to shape our perceptions of the Northeast as quaint New England towns and the big historic cities of Philadelphia, New York, and Boston. Industry built up the Midwest in cities such as Chicago, Detroit, and Cleveland, but "Midwest" also suggests expanses of corn, or green pastures, red barns, and cows. The West means mountains or desert, though clearly it has its major metropolises as well, on the Pacific coast and now also in the southwest.

For the South, stretching south from the Mason–Dixon Line to Florida in the east and Texas in the west, such demographic and economic clout is relatively new, but some of the most compelling chapters in American history have played out in the South or over Southern issues: the bitter debate over slavery, the Civil War, Reconstruction, segregation, and the Civil Rights Movement put the identity that the country had constructed for itself to the test. The tensions and contradictions of Southern life have produced great literature, and the South likewise has a tremendous allure for film, attracting both filmmakers and audiences from the early days of cinema. A romanticized picture of life in the South—colonnaded plantation homes, magnolia trees, Southern belles—has had its allure, but "Southerns" also have enabled filmmakers to explore some of the fundamental issues of American life, including questions of individual freedom and human rights.

The old cliché that the victors write the history does not hold true in the case of some of the most prominent films about the Civil War. In 1915, pioneering filmmaker D. W. Griffith presented the story of the Civil War and Reconstruction in *The Birth of a Nation* largely from his own, Southern, point of view. His film, an adaptation of Thomas Dixon's novel and play, *The Clansman*, will be revisited in a subsequent chapter as an artifact of the time in which it was made, but Griffith took pains to situate his story in history, punctuating the film with historical "facsimiles" that recreated real historical scenes from still photography, including the Confederacy's surrender at Appomattox and the scene at Ford's Theater in Washington, DC, on the evening President Lincoln was assassinated. These are set up as tableaus, very deliberately composed shots that reproduce famous paintings or photographs, live action shots that almost appear as stills. The Civil War battle scenes were unprecedented in scope and realism, and audiences today can still imagine how they would have impressed audiences more than ninety years ago. However, Griffith, confusing the institution of slavery with its victims, blamed African Americans for sowing the "seeds of disunion" and suggested to his audiences that miscegenation, or racial mixing between black and whites, posed a peril to the new nation born of the Civil War. This deeply racist message is obvious to viewers today, and was obvious enough at the time to draw protests and bans, but it also resonated strongly enough in the culture of the time to allow many viewers to either overlook or nod in assent to this noxious view. Certainly its great commercial success suggests that this was true.

The Birth of a Nation held the title as the biggest box office draw in film history until Gone with the Wind, released in December 1939, overtook it. Based on Margaret Mitchell's 1936 novel, which became a worldwide best-seller, the film focused on the transformation of Scarlett O'Hara (Vivien Leigh) from a spoiled Southern belle into a plantation matriarch and the wife of wealthy rogue Rhett Butler (Clark Gable). The first part of the film is a romantic portrait of the Old South, with Technicolor sunsets giving slave life at Tara plantation a rosy hue, while Miss Scarlett's greatest concern is showing off her seventeen-inch waist, the smallest in five counties, to best effect for the Wilkes barbecue. News of war produces excitement and an impetuous decision to marry a man she does not love, while Ashley Wilkes (Leslie Howard), whom she does love, marries the saintly Melanie (Olivia de Havilland). Gone with the Wind portrays the war from Scarlett's perspective: she witnesses no battles, but, as a war widow, she tends the wounded in the hospital, and the film famously and concisely signals the South's defeat with a city square filled with the untended wounded. Rhett helps Scarlett and Melanie escape the burning city and return to Tara, where her mother has died, her father has lost his mind, and the ravaged plantation is near ruin. Her second marriage, to her sister's fiancé, is a heartless, purely strategic move to raise money to pay taxes. She is widowed again as her husband avenges an attempted assault on her. Gone with the Wind did attempt to update the hideous racial views of The Birth of a Nation, but the theme of the Ku Klux Klan protecting the virtue of white women from black men was unfortunately slow to die. Once again widowed, Scarlett agrees to marry Rhett Butler, who seizes the opportunity to propose before it again passes. As Mrs. Butler, Scarlett makes Reconstruction work for her, but she continues to pine for Ashley, whose character is weak and indecisive in contrast to the steely Scarlett. Indeed, one could discuss Scarlett and Rhett as the first power couple of the New South, though of course he famously leaves her at the end of the film.[1]

The history here has to be teased from layers of Hollywood melodrama, and indeed the historian might just as profitably explore Gone with the Wind instead as a cultural artifact of 1930s America. The story of the film's making, the subject of more than one book, is an interesting bit of Hollywood history and has a great deal to say about the interaction of the movie industry with the movie-going public at the time. David O. Selznick aimed to create a phenomenal film from a phenomenal book, and the casting of Scarlett O'Hara, for example, became a drawn out process that the public was invited to follow through the media. With many of the big names in the

---

[1] Catherine Clinton discusses the emergence of Scarlett O'Hara as plantation matriarch in Mark Carnes, ed., *Past Imperfect: History According to the Movies* (New York: Holt, 1995), 132–135.

running, the selection of an unknown British actress was anticlimactic, but Vivien Leigh's performance made it difficult to imagine anyone else playing the role. By the time *Gone with the Wind* was released, Europe was already at war, but while some Europeans would have to wait until after the war to see the film, it would be re-released many times in the United States over the years, allowing ever-younger audiences to see it in theaters. First shown on television over two November evenings in 1976, it drew, according to Nielsen Media Research, ratings that are still among the ten highest ever. Even in the era of home video, *Gone with the Wind* was remastered and had another theatrical release in 1998.

Such an enormous cultural phenomenon had to shape popular perceptions of the South, even as historians documented a different experience and as the Civil Rights Movement raised awareness of the profound injustices suffered by African Americans under the old system of slavery and the newer hardships and indignities of segregation. Yet David O. Selznick was not D. W. Griffith, and Hattie McDaniel's performance as Mammy was the first by an African American to win an Academy Award. Mammy's name came to identify a racial stereotype, that of the faithful servant whose virtue lies in unquestioned loyalty and tireless service to the white master or mistress. McDaniel did not sit at the *Gone with the Wind* table at the ceremony, however, indicating that Hollywood itself had a long way to go. Yet few would deny that her legacy, however ambiguous, was significant in slowly eroding the racial barriers there and everywhere.

Twenty years later, in the midst of the Civil Rights Movement, Harper Lee's 1961 novel *To Kill a Mockingbird* evoked the South of the 1930s, poor and segregated but warm with memories of youth and the acts of courageous individuals. The 1962 film version effectively captured the spirit of the novel, which won the Pulitzer Prize, sold millions of copies and remains a beloved classic: the American Film Institute (AFI) ranked the film as number thirty-four on its list of greatest American films and as the second most inspiring American film ever, after Frank Capra's *It's a Wonderful Life* (1946). AFI also named Atticus Finch (played by Gregory Peck in an Academy Award-winning performance) as the greatest hero in American film. The novel and film tell their story from the perspective of Jean Louise "Scout" Finch (played in the film by Mary Badham), who recalls her life as a young girl growing up in Maycomb, modeled on Lee's own hometown of Monroeville in southern Alabama.

Like the novel, the film draws its audience into Scout's world: the games she plays with her older brother Jem (Phillip Alford) and their friend Dill (John Megna), many of which revolve around legends of their reclusive neighbor Boo Radley (Robert Duvall), and the unique relationship she has with her father, whom she calls Atticus, a lawyer who struggles to raise his children alone after the death of their mother. The film gradually shifts its focus from youthful games to courtroom drama as Atticus defends Tom Robinson (Brock Peters), a black man accused of raping Mayella Ewell (Collin Wilcox), the eldest daughter of Bob Ewell (James Anderson), a poor white drunkard raising his family alone in squalor. As the proceedings demonstrate, the charges are fabricated to hide the fact of Bob Ewell's own physical abuse of his daughter, but that does not stop the all-white jury from convicting Robinson nevertheless and exposing Atticus and his children to Ewell's vengeful wrath.

While the film in part reinforced the images America and the world had of the ugly white racism on display during the struggles over desegregation, it also presented its story in terms almost everyone could relate to: a coming-of-age story set against the very real historical backdrop of segregation and unequal justice. Atticus Finch is a heroic white Southerner, admired by other whites in Maycomb, who sets a powerful example for his own children and challenges them to question the assumptions of the culture in which they are growing up. As a film it was far less grandiose than *Gone with the Wind*. It was made in black and white, which was still fairly common in the early 1960s, but in this case, it was clearly the right choice esthetically to capture the story's intimacy and power. It connects its audience with a vision of the South that is infused with youthful sentiment, but it does not deny its brutal realities, either.

As *To Kill a Mockingbird* portrayed the South in the era when *Gone with the Wind* was made, *Mississippi Burning* (1988) portrays the South in the era when *To Kill a Mockingbird* was made. Made by the British director Alan Parker from a script written by Chris Gerolmo, the film imagines the investigation that followed the murder in the summer of 1964 of three Civil Rights workers in Mississippi. Three men were in fact murdered, but much of what follows in the film is made up. Gene Hackman plays FBI Agent Rupert Anderson and Willem Dafoe plays FBI Agent Alan Ward, dispatched to the small town in Mississippi where the men were working. The men differ greatly in background and temperament, but the friction between them pales in comparison to the extreme tension in the community, where the Ku Klux Klan terrorizes the black population with individual attacks and church burnings. While Ward insists on playing by the rules, Anderson, himself a Southerner, deploys a more personal approach and more brutal tactics to root out the murderers.

Mississippi Burning works very well as entertainment, but critics have challenged the veracity of its historical vision. It faced criticism when it was released for portraying the FBI as champions of civil rights, when in fact its leader, J. Edgar Hoover, was no ally of the cause. It also faced criticism for portraying blacks as fearful and passive, needing white men to come in and save them. In the interest of fairness, one might also note that most of the white people are portrayed as racist, ignorant and, perhaps worst of all, unattractive. Movies face considerable public pressure to portray the past in a positive light, and to use it to teach uplifting lessons about the acts of courageous people. This, however, is a film that portrays racism in a very powerful, visceral, and frightening way. The opposition of Southern whites to desegregation is an ugly chapter in American history, and while this particular fictional story is not particularly nuanced, it makes a powerful point. And, while sit-ins, marches, and other forms of nonviolent protest by African Americans powered the Civil Rights Movement, the government, at that time still quite segregated itself, did have an important role to play in upholding and enforcing the law and protecting the rights of all its citizens.[2]

A slightly later film, Richard's Pearce's *The Long Walk Home* (1990), looks at the beginnings of the Civil Rights Movement in the Montgomery bus boycott, beginning in December 1955. The film focuses not on Rosa Parks, nor on Martin Luther King—we hear him speak, but the viewers are outside the church with the rest of the assembled who cannot get into the packed building—but on two ordinary citizens of Montgomery, Odessa Cotter (Whoopi Goldberg) and Miriam Thompson (Sissy Spacek). Odessa is a domestic, employed for the past nine years by the Thompsons, who live in a shiny white suburban rancher with every modern convenience. Odessa rides the bus to work, following the laws of segregation by entering the front of the bus to pay, then getting off and reentering the bus in the rear, to sit in the back. The point of the law? To protect whites from the risk of having a black person brush past? To prevent the risk of any kind of contact that might lead to sexual contact and the dreaded mixing of the races? Whatever the rationale, this ritual, bizarre to our eyes, visually and viscerally refutes the "separate, but equal" argument used to justify segregation.

In the Thompson home, Odessa has played a key role in raising Mary Catherine (Lexi Randall), who narrates the film as an adult (Mary Steenburgen). When Miriam later looks at a photo album and remembers the domestic who played a key role in her own childhood, the viewer identifies these relationships as very important in helping to break down the walls of segregation. At the same time, it makes clear that many other employers treated their domestics badly. Miriam herself is not blameless in this regard. When a police officer rudely expels Odessa from the park to which she has accompanied Mary Catherine, Miriam demands an apology, but the policeman apologizes to the girl, not Odessa. On Christmas Day, Miriam greets Odessa with a long litany of tasks before remembering, as an afterthought, to wish her a Merry Christmas.

In the meantime, Rosa Parks has taken her stand, or rather her seat. This momentous event is not portrayed in the movie, but Odessa discusses the ensuing boycott with her husband Herbert (Ving Rhames), and, when she decides to support the boycott, she has to walk nine miles from her own modest bungalow to get to work. Miriam's life revolves around managing the home, attending Junior League and playing bridge with Montgomery's other not-too-desperate housewives. For her, the boycott is a nuisance, but when she needs to be downtown, near where Odessa lives, she offers her a ride, a fact that she must keep secret from her husband Norman (Dwight Schultz), who aspires to be a pillar of a white community that becomes increasingly vicious in its efforts to defeat the boycott.

---

[2] See Robert Brent Toplin's discussion in *History by Hollywood* (Urbana: University of Illinois Press, 1996), 25–44.

The Long Walk Home provides a startling picture of life in America when segregation, very much similar to South Africa's system of apartheid, dominated the South. Racism was a national problem, but in the South, the legal enforcement of a system that kept African Americans politically voiceless, economically oppressed, and socially separate was perceived by whites to be necessary for the preservation of society. At Christmas dinner, Miriam's mother-in-law talks openly about "lazy niggers" even as Odessa, who along with another domestic has cooked an entire meal after walking nine miles to work, enters the room and offers her a fresh-baked roll. The viewer yearns for justice (perhaps Odessa clocking the woman with the dish), but dinner proceeds undisturbed with the senior Mrs. Thompson protesting too much about how she is right and does not need to apologize, though certainly everyone feels the awkwardness of the moment. The viewer knows that, but for those "lazy niggers," she would have had to cook her own damned Christmas dinner. Miriam's "challenge" to this affront is to accept a roll when offered and to extend the courtesy of a thank you, hardly a revolutionary act. The viewer is forced to share the indignity and to understand why Odessa essentially turns the other cheek, but the tension builds.

Moments such as this illuminate the historical realities of life in the segregated South, and the extraordinary difficulty African Americans faced in challenging it. The law enforced a society in which African Americans assumed complete deference in the presence of white people. In this context, the decision of Odessa's daughter Selma (Erika Alexander) to defy the boycott and ride the bus is taken by three young white men as justification to harass her for being "uppity." To his credit, the bus driver kicks the boys off, but they then assault Selma, who has fled, and when her brother Theodore (Richard Habersham) arrives in a taxi to help, they beat him up, too. The taxi driver (Afemo Omilami) arrives with a tire iron to drive the boys away, but warns that the situation could escalate into a lynching. It does not, but the point is clear that in this society, blacks faced harassment while simply going about daily life, with no recourse or protection from a legal system that catered exclusively to whites.

Miriam's moment of truth comes relatively late in the film, when her husband discovers that she has been giving Odessa rides, thereby supporting the bus boycott. He orders her to stop, and she obeys. When she tells Odessa that she cannot give her rides anymore, she explains that it is her husband's fault, that he cannot see another way of life than segregation. But Miriam is slowly recognizing that she cannot treat Odessa this way and decides to defy her husband openly, asserting her authority in the management of the household. But soon she is not only giving Odessa a ride, she joins the carpool that provides rides for other boycotters, and the viewer sees that for Miriam it is no longer a matter of convenience or self-interest but of principle. The film ends with a tense confrontation between a gang of white men, including Miriam's husband and brother-in-law Tucker (Dylan Baker), and the group of mostly black women gathered at the carpool headquarters. Tucker berates and hits Miriam, who has been "exposed"; Norman attacks

Tucker, but as the black women sing, gradually silencing the shouts of the white men, Miriam joins hands with the women, and Norman stares impotently from the crowd of snarling men.

The film ends with a postscript on the bus boycott, which ended with a new law allowing all passengers to sit where they chose, but also acts of violent acts by whites aimed at intimidating blacks. As the film discusses, the boycott addressed a single aspect of segregated life, but in fact challenged the whole system of segregation. The "look" of the South in this film is not colonnaded porches and blooming magnolias, but a city and suburbs quite recognizable to many Americans. Actually filmed in Montgomery, locations in 1990 looked much as they had in the 1950s, including a downtown that looked as if nothing had been done to it since that time.

Of course, no one film can capture all of the history and diversity of the South, and there is no film that really attempts a grand narrative, but one lovely television movie from 1974, *The Autobiography of Miss Jane Pittman* (1974), based on the novel by Ernest J. Gaines, and directed by John Korty, captures much of the African American struggle for freedom from the Civil War to the Civil Rights Movement, using the fictional character named in the title. Cicely Tyson plays a 110-year-old former slave who recounts her life to a *New York Times* reporter (Michael Murphy) in Louisiana in 1962. Filmed on location, the settings were authentic. The flashbacks initially take the viewer back to 1865, when Ticey (Valerie Odell) is told of her freedom by Union troops, and she discards her slave name for Jane. Thwarted in her efforts to migrate northward, she struggles to survive, witnessing lynchings and murders along the course of her long life. Her marriage to Joe Pittman (Rod Perry) ends with his tragic death, and the efforts of her adopted son Ned (Thalmus Rasulala) to educate members of the community are snuffed out when Elbert Cluveau (Will Hare), dispatched by the white community, kills him. But Jane perseveres and, in the end, after Civil Rights worker Jimmy (Arnold Wilkerson) is murdered in nearby Bayonne, she defiantly rides into town and makes her way to a whites-only water fountain for a drink. The film ends as the truck in which she is sitting on a chair in back slowly pulls off, and a crowd begins to follow. The history here is largely symbolic, but the details illuminate the profound challenges African Americans struggled with in the South after the Civil War and show how the bitterness and resentment felt by whites translated into the policies and practices of segregation and racial violence. The movie won seven Emmies, including two for Cicely Tyson in different categories and Outstanding Special: Drama or Comedy. In the often maligned genre of made-for-TV movies, this production stood out for its quality and power. Originally aired on CBS, it ran 110 minutes, with just one commercial break.

Forrest Gump (1994), the enormously popular and critically acclaimed Robert Zemeckis film has its fictional title character edited into history (Woody Allen had done it in 1983 with *Zelig*), an amusing technique that helped propel this film to tremendous commercial success—two-thirds of a billion dollars worldwide. Then, somewhat surprisingly for a summer blockbuster, the film went on to win the year's major awards, including Oscars for Best Picture, Director, Actor (Tom Hanks), and Adapted Screenplay, plus two others. Forrest Gump is a simple-minded but good-hearted person who grew up in Alabama, and who tells his life story to people while waiting for a bus in Savannah, Georgia, sometime in the 1980s. He has unwittingly interacted with some of the most significant historical figures in American history during the past decades, including three U.S. presidents, but appears oblivious to the role he has played. The film takes Forrest Gump from the 1950s to the 1980s: he serves with distinction in Vietnam; he plays ping-pong (very well) in China; he witnesses the break-in at the Watergate; and he makes a fortune investing in Apple Computer stock before the onset of the PC revolution. Fatherless Forrest loves his motherless childhood friend Jenny (Robin Wright), but the currents of life and history separate them. Her life, in contrast to his, is a series of failures: unlike Forrest, whose mother (Sally Field) loves him deeply, Jenny's father is abusive. During the Vietnam War, she hangs with the counterculture and her drugged-out 1960s idealism devolves in the 1970s into just being drugged out and abused by one man after another. She does have a child as a result of one encounter with Forrest, but contacts him only after she finds out she is ill with what the audience knows to be AIDS. Forrest, who has lost his best friend in Vietnam and his mother, now loses Jenny, but not before he tenderly nurses her through her illness. The ending is very much a tearjerker, but there is enough going on in this movie to ensure that the sentiment is not cheap. The history is part of that: part of the film's joy is the recognition by viewers of the events they remember from earlier in their own lives, the major events, the cultural touchstones, the trivial but common, easily recognizable features of American life. It does not teach history, but it definitely invokes it, and it does so in a very entertaining way. Younger viewers will not recognize the history specifically presented here, but with a little explanation from their parents or teachers they can at least pick up on the notion of a shared experience, presented here with wit and warmth. People can look at this film in a lot of different ways. It does not have a strong ideological edge to it, nor is there any clear pronouncement on American life during the latter half of the twentieth century. It has a literary feel to it, and it is probably a film to be felt more than thought about, uncomfortable ground for a historian. But there is a feel to history, particularly our own, and that is worth exploring. Nostalgia may be a bad word to historians, but it is part of the human experience.

THE WESTERN

The Western is a recognized genre of film, very popular from the early days of the movies until the 1960s, when it became less common as big-screen fare, though TV series like *Gunsmoke* (1955–1975) and *Bonanza* (1959–1973) remained popular and probably helped to tire out the genre. Occasionally a big-screen Western still does appear, and Clint Eastwood's *Unforgiven* (1992) became the first Western since *Cimarron* in 1930 to win the Best Picture Academy Award, though Kevin Costner's *Dances With Wolves* (1990), a Best Picture winner in 1990 has been called a "liberal Western" for turning the genre on its head and making the Indians the heroes—in addition to himself, of course.

The Western is most significant historically as myth rather than as an accurate reconstruction of the history of the western part of what is now the United States, often telling a story that aims at defining America's national identity more than a regional identity. Told from a white perspective the Western portrays the expansion of Anglo European civilization into the western territories, focusing often on an isolated individual whose heroic deeds as a lonely warrior pave the way for gentler folk to establish a foothold for civilization under a system of law and order. Indians were often the "bad guys," though white cattle rustlers and other villains (the Mexican presence often figures here) populate these films heavily as well. Western adventures often allowed their heroes and heroines, perhaps with troubled pasts, to experience a new beginning or a form of redemption.

There is a great deal of literature on the Western in film studies, but an indispensable source to the historian is Richard Slotkin's *Gunfighter Nation: The Myth of the Frontier in Twentieth Century America* (1993), an exhaustive study of all forms of entertainment, including popular literature, to shape a collective view of the past that is best described as myth. While popular usage of the term *myth* suggests untruth, myth in this sense is very much like the myths of ancient times: they draw on actual experience, but through retelling assume certain common characteristics that correspond to popular tastes and shared values. Stories of the "Old West" were retold in stories and later represented in film in ways that were not attempts to reconstruct the historical realities of the time, but which are nevertheless historically significant for what they reveal about a society's sense of identity and values.

Slotkin describes how, for example, the Hollywood studios deliberately attempted to revive the Western as a genre in the late 1930s, as an attempt to answer the popularity of recent historical "prestige" pictures, often dealing with European historical figures, with history that was distinctly American. Dictatorships and the threat of war also called for the expression of American identity and patriotism in movies. To that end the story of westward expansion served as the story of America, a narrative that demonstrated the bravery, hard work, and virtue of ordinary people. In other words, the studios were not so much interested in history as we understand it, but rather in presenting the myth of the frontier as a way of boosting public morale in times that were still hard and potentially menacing. Films like Cecil B. DeMille's *Union Pacific* (1939) for Paramount and Michael Curtiz' *Santa Fe Trail* (1940) for Warner Bros. put history to patriotic duty.[3]

---

[3] Richard Slotkin, *Gunfighter Nation: The Myth of the Frontier in Twentieth Century America*. New York: Harper Perennial, 1993, 278–279.

Ironically, John Ford's *Stagecoach* (1939), which had more modest ambitions, would become the greatest classic Western from this period. In general, Westerns were cheap to make, since the necessary backdrops were close at hand in Hollywood and the sets were simple, so before television there were lots of B Westerns. However, some directors, John Ford in particular, made films that have become culturally very significant, again less for portraying an authentic historical set of events than for reflecting what Americans believed to be true about themselves and their experience as a people. *Stagecoach* (1939) is one of his many great films, about a group of travelers who run a dangerous gauntlet from Tonto to Lordsburg. This was the first of many films he shot in Monument Valley, in northeastern Arizona, and the actual journey the stagecoach follows makes no geographical sense, but the dangers the travelers face allow them to redeem themselves from troubled pasts through acts of heroism.

John Ford made many great films, but *The Searchers* (1956) is a classic, though significantly unconventional, Western that still appeals to students today as an introduction to Ford's vision, style, and views of the past. In the AFI's 2007 list of the one hundred greatest American films, it moved up eighty-four positions from the previous poll (1997) to twelfth. Ford had shot many of his Westerns in Arizona's Monument Valley prior to this, but the landscape now stunned audiences in dazzling Technicolor. Ethan Edwards (John Wayne) is an angry, vengeful veteran of the Civil War, searching with his nephew Martin Pawley (Jeffrey Hunter) for his niece Debbie Edwards (Natalie Wood), who has been kidnapped by Indians. Younger audiences more accustomed to Kevin Costner-like Western heroes may feel a little uncomfortable with a central character so hateful toward Indians, but of course the story of the West would have been very different if the "heroes" of the West in fact had been more like Kevin Costner and less like John Wayne. But the hatred is in many respects the point of this film. In Ford's and Wayne's earlier work, the violence was largely unexamined, assumed to be justified and necessary. In contrast, Ethan Edwards is an antihero whose hatred clearly menaces and destroys.

The long-lived popularity and the common elements of the genre make the Western greatly interesting to historians, not just for the history it depicts, but also for the times they reflect. Though producers resisted analyses of *High Noon* (1952) as a cold war allegory, the analogy persists, and it is important to remember that a film is more than the sum of its intentions. In 1969, Sam Peckinpah's *The Wild Bunch* portrayed a gang of outlaws working in southern Texas and northern Mexico during the time of the Mexican Revolution and the First World War. William Holden and Ernest Borgnine are not men in white; in fact they are "bad guys" wearing U.S. Army uniforms at the beginning, and the gun battle in the southern Texas town does not clearly establish heroes and villains. Yet the audiences root for them as they steal munitions and weapons from Pershing's army; the men are ambivalent about selling them to the Mexican government, and an interesting historical detail is the presence of German advisors working to incite Mexico against the United States. In the end the Wild Bunch supports one of its own, Angel (Jaime Sanchez), and the final blood-bath is a suicidal assault on Mexican government forces on behalf of the local rebels. The film defied conventions of movie violence, showing the gory consequences of gun violence and not sparing the "womenfolk" from the carnage. Though it stops short of drawing the children into the battles, it is extremely clear from the earliest sequence that the children, who glee-fully watch red ants attack a scorpion and then set fire to them all, need no instruction in cruelty. Peckinpah suggests that the violence is not inciden-tal, but a central aspect of what is happening, the means by which people get what they want. At a time when the most prominent film actually *about* Vietnam, *The Green Berets* (1968), took a "hawkish" position, *The Wild Bunch* made a more profound statement about the war without even mentioning it, playing on the conventions of the Western to confront audiences with their penchant for violence.

The Western faded in popularity during the 1970s, but occasionally returned to the screen. Lawrence Kasdan's *Silverado* (1985) was an entertain-ing compendium of Western conventions updated for the 1980s—no Indians, and an African American among the good guys. Despite its high spirits and a talented cast, including Kevin Kline, Scott Glenn, Danny Glover, and Kevin Costner, the film did not do well enough commercially to warrant a sequel, and the subsequent high-profile Westerns of the early 1990s, *Unforgiven* and *Dances with Wolves*, have been called anti-Westerns for inverting the old myths entirely. Except for those completely in denial, sto-ries of the Old West featuring white people bringing order and civility (even-tually) to an untamed wilderness, and defeating the savages to do so, no longer fit with the public memory, let alone the historical record, of how Westward expansion actually unfolded.

A recent film that has some of the look of the Western, and which its director has described as taking place at the tail end of the "wild, wild West," is Paul Thomas Anderson's *There Will Be Blood* (2007). Daniel Plainview (played with ferocious intensity by Daniel Day-Lewis) is an "oil man" obsessed, driven by a manic competitiveness to find and control oil under the desert in southern California. The son of a rancher, Eli Sunday (Paul Dano), is similarly entrepreneurial, but plays a histrionic fundamentalist preacher who struggles with Plainview for a share of the action and for power in the community. The director has identified John Huston's *Treasure of the Sierra Madre* (1948) as an influence, and this film likewise depicts the destructive power of greed. But the film is far more than a morality play, and as history it presents a more ambiguous picture of economic development and the relationship of money, religion, and power: though it taps into uni-versal themes, it is also powerfully realized vision of America's past, leaving viewers with a lot to think about and discuss. While the words historical drama may to some viewers suggest a static tableau, this film is extraordi-narily vital and powerfully suggestive of how major forces in life and in history intertwine and clash.

OTHER AMERICAN HISTORICAL NARRATIVES

The Western is an easily recognizable genre, to which cultural historians have added the notion of a Southern. Together, the Northeast and the Midwest made up the most heavily populated parts of the country in the past, with the result that movies set in mainstream America often have the look of a Midwestern or northeastern town. *The Best Years of Our Lives* (1946) was set in a fictional town modeled on Cincinnati, but was actually shot in the Los Angeles area, as is evident from some scenes, including the occasional palm tree. Production costs still account for the impulse to film on sets close to the studio or in places such as Vancouver, British Columbia, that cater specially to the movie industry. Currency exchange rates also can help reduce production costs. But historians and other film viewers value the sense of place that a film can provide by not just filming on location, but also by capturing the qualities that give a place a unique identity.

California's mild climate was a major factor in attracting the filmmaking industry to begin with, and ever since the state has appeared in the movies in various guises, from a land flowing with milk and honey, as in the *Grapes of Wrath* (1940), to seedy and sinister, as in Roman Polanski's *Chinatown* (1974) and Curtis Hanson's *L.A. Confidential* (1997), both of which draw on the film noir tradition and presented southern California as less than heavenly. Set in the 1930s, *Chinatown* portrays the efforts of a private detective, Jake Gittes (Jack Nicholson), as he sets out to investigate a domestic matter but discovers far more about rampant corruption and the politics of water. *L.A. Confidential* is set in the 1950s and similarly uncovers police corruption and sleaze in the entertainment industry. For both look and sensibility, both films are indebted to such film noir classics as Billy Wilder's *Double Indemnity* (1944) and Howard Hawks' *The Big Sleep* (1946).

The Plains figure prominently and beautifully in Terrence Malick's *Days of Heaven* (1978). Set in the 1910s, the story beings in the slums and steel mills of Chicago, where the laborer Bill (Richard Gere) kills a foreman, to the west, where Bill, his sister Linda (Linda Manz), and his lover Abby (Brooke Adams) seek refuge working on a farm. With allusions to contemporary events, such as the outbreak of the First World War, and visual motifs that emphasize the mechanization of rural life, Malick, in an oblique and subtle way, relates the lives of these individuals to the broader currents of history. The tragic outcome of the story suggests that the quest for individual happiness and security is highly vulnerable to these larger forces.

New York has been the location for thousands of movies that have both explored and developed its character. The 1933 version of *King Kong* gave a starring role to the new Empire State Building, itself a "Wonder of the World." John Guillermin's 1976 version of the film moved the climactic scene to the relatively new World Trade Center, giving viewers today a different experience of the film from that of viewers before September 11, 2001. Unlike the two predecessors, Peter Jackson's version (2005) sets the story in the past, in fact in the era of the first *King Kong*. Despite the hardships of the Great

Adding to the thrill and spectacle of *King Kong* in 1933 was the fact that the final showdown between man and beast took place atop the world's tallest building, the new Empire State Building in New York.   *Source:* Getty/Bettmann.

Depression, New York appears in its former glory, with heavy use of yellows, reds, and browns to evoke a warmly nostalgic picture of the past.

Of course, as a center of both American finance and American culture, New York was the setting for movies that portrayed some of America's wealthiest and most glamorous people. Milos Forman's *Ragtime* (1981, see Chapter 2) reconstructed the different strata of New York society in the early twentieth century. Though America may have offered greater economic and social mobility than European societies, *Ragtime* clearly portrays the social and economic divisions that did exist, often determined by ethnicity and reinforced by prejudice. The movie presents characters from diverse parts of American society: the real-life character of Evelyn Nesbit (Elizabeth McGovern), who consorted with several prominent men and figured in a famous scandal involving the murder of the architect Stanford White (Norman Mailer); an affluent family living in the suburbs of New York. But a two-hour film—and in this case a little over two-and-a-half—cannot provide audiences with a satisfying exploration of as many characters as the novel had done, with the result that the film focused quite heavily on the character of Coalhouse Walker, Jr. (Howard E. Rollins, Jr.), an African American man living in New York. Through him, Forman places a heavy emphasis on the issue of race. A pecking order exists, and the film shows how the Irish, themselves spurned by Anglo-Americans, themselves mistreat African Americans. Ethnic prejudice is certainly a major topic of discussion in our own time, as it was when *Ragtime* was filmed. So while we know, and can verify from other sources, that the forms of discrimination depicted in the film did indeed take place, the singling out of this issue for examination is an act of historical interpretation, a focus that reflects the concerns of later generations.

Francis Ford Coppola's *Godfather* trilogy tells the story of a Sicilian-American crime family in America, beginning just after the Second World War, but flashing back to earlier days both in the "old country" and in America. During his career, Coppola has made smaller pictures, but he is best known for his filmmaking on a grand scale: the first two *Godfathers* were his first big films and remain, along with *Apocalypse Now* (1979), his greatest. The first, *The Godfather* (1972), focuses on the aging godfather, Don Vito Corleone (Marlon Brando), who "does business" in the Old-World style, though it becomes clear that times are changing and that, while Don Corleone continues to receive the deference and respect due the head of an extremely patriarchal family, younger mobsters are eager to develop new markets in drugs. Bound to the family estate in New York, with a powerful attachment to the old country, Vito Corleone sees the burgeoning crime world of Las Vegas as a world away.

Elder son Sonny (James Caan) would appear to be the heir to the title of don, but Michael (Al Pacino), who enlisted to fight in the Second World War to escape the family and its ways, returns and finds himself drawn into its dealings, and toward the end of the first film moves his family to Nevada. Michael is the central character in *The Godfather: Part Two* (1974), though the film also traces the career of the young Vito (Robert De Niro), ruthlessly working his way to the top in the sepia-toned New York of the 1920s. Both films share great visual richness, and—of particular interest to the historian—the second film has a great sequence set in Havana, a glamorous den of iniquity, literally on the eve of the Cuban Revolution in the late 1950s. While these two films were enormously influential in spawning a new generation of movies about organized crime (recalling such 1930s films as *The Public Enemy* (1931) and *Scarface* (1932) exploring the similarly fascinating underworld of Chicago), they can also be seen as explorations of the notion of the American Dream. While Michael certainly comes off as a ruthless and brutal figure, he also pursues respectability and recognition for his financial success and acts of charity.

Whether or not the Corleones could be considered the quintessential American family, their saga is certainly an American story, tapping into themes of immigration, ethnic identity, and assimilation, and achieving great financial success. Leaving Michael all-powerful but alone at the end of the second film, it is not entirely clear that a *Godfather: Part III* was necessary, and in retrospect, the production history, the content of the film and its reception made it unworthy of its predecessors. Made eighteen years after the original film, *The Godfather: Part III* (1990), with adjustment for inflation, cost about as much to make as the two previous films combined, and even then Paramount's efforts to contain spending diminished the end product. Robert Duvall, who had played Tom Hagen, the lawyer who had been brought up as a member of the family, was replaced by George Hamilton, who had only a fraction of Duvall's screen presence, playing an inconsequential character. Most notoriously and unfortunately, Coppola's own daughter Sofia was brought in to replace Winona Ryder in the pivotal role of Michael's daughter Mary. Still a teenager, she had little acting experience and could not redeem a weak character near the heart of the film's narrative. The story is set ten years in the past, (the late 1970s), but does not have the deeper ties to the past that the earlier films had, again perhaps because of the cost of adding period sets and costuming. While the film garnered major award nominations (including Best Picture and Best Director Academy Awards), it disappointed audiences. At the box office, adjusted for inflation, it made only half of what *The Godfather: Part II* had made and one-sixth of the original. *The Godfather*, which in its day became the top-grossing film of all time, remains among the most highly regarded of American films, passing *Casablanca* to claim the number 2 spot in the 2007 AFI survey, lagging now only behind *Citizen Kane* (1941).

It would be fitting to discuss *Citizen Kane* here, as it traces the story of a fictional character through decades of American history, but in a deliberate attempt to blur lines and distinctions, I discussed it as a biopic in Chapter 6, even though the subject of the film is fictional. In any case, Welles' next film, *The Magnificent Ambersons* (1942), is a better example of a historical drama, set entirely in the past and aiming through fictional characters to illuminate realities of American life at the end of the nineteenth century. Adapted from the Booth Tarkington novel, which won the Pulitzer Prize for fiction in 1919, the film tells the story of families whose fortunes rise and fall in the boom-and-bust days of America's Gilded Age. The Ambersons are a wealthy family living in the fictional Midwestern city of Midland: Eugene Morgan (Joseph Cotten) courts Isabel Amberson (Dolores Costello), but she marries a safer, more socially acceptable choice, Wilbur Minafer (Don Dillaway). Years later Eugene returns, a widower, but having achieved success in the young automobile industry. When Isabel's husband dies, Eugene tries again, but is now opposed by Isabel's bratty son "Georgie" (Tim Holt), whose behavior leads everyone to wonder when he will get his "comeuppance."

A film about upward and downward mobility, *The Magnificent Ambersons* is one of the great classic historical dramas of American film. Given that it was made by Orson Welles, it has a stormy production history that in itself is historically significant. An *auteur* who did not work well with Hollywood's studio system, Welles left the country for Brazil to aid in the war effort by making films promoting hemispheric solidarity for Nelson Rockefeller, President Roosevelt's Coordinator for Inter-American Affairs. While he was gone, the RKO studio had editor Robert Wise (who would become a celebrated director later on) cut fifty minutes from the film, and the ending was redone to make it less gloomy for wartime audiences. The result was a film significantly different from what Welles had intended, but one which nonetheless bears his unique style and sensibility. The film got some acclaim, but awards that year went to movies dealing with the war or more upbeat,

8

■ ■ ■

Capturing the Moment
Narrative Movies as Historical and Cultural Artifacts

From the previous chapters, it has become evident that, whatever a film may say about the past, it also exists as a product or an artifact of its own time and place. This chapter examines

* movies as cultural artifacts, revealing significant aspects of contemporary life;

* movies whose content may be set in the past, but that nevertheless reveal concerns and preoccupations of the time in which they were made; and

* movies that are not merely artifacts, but icons of a particular time.

Even movies that on the surface have nothing to do with real life—movies set in the future such as William Cameron Menzies' *Things to Come* (1936), about life in the future after a devastating war, or an epic fantasy such as Peter Jackson's trilogy *The Lord of the Rings* (2001–2003)—are cultural expressions that can be very relevant to contemporary life. One of the challenges of historical scholarship, however, is to find enough material to support the topic. So, before you ask if you can write a paper on Judd Apatow's *The 40 Year Old Virgin* (2005), read on.

While academic historians may take issue with the historical interpretations of popular films, they embrace much more readily the notion that a film may capture aspects of a time period or phenomenon that a lecture, reading, or discussion never could. But even if the viewer does not have to worry about the accuracy of a film's reconstruction of the past or the validity of its interpretation, assessing the historical significance of a film as a document of its time nevertheless requires careful analysis and discussion. A fan of old movies can have a great deal of fun with *Casablanca* (1942) as a reflection of America and the world in the Second World War, or with *The Graduate* (1967) as a reflection of 1960s American culture, but one still has to sort through the inherent and intended artifice of the medium to identify a film's real historical significance.

The clearest example of this kind of film is one that treats a contemporary issue and thus becomes a means for audiences today to gain insight into the preoccupations and concerns of the past. Films from an earlier era also capture the look of their time: cityscapes, cars, styles, home interiors, and so on. This chapter moves through the twentieth century, selecting a variety of films for discussion that illuminate key points and serve as a model for the kind of analysis and discussion that you could pursue in your own research and writing, bearing in mind the three aspects of production, content, and reception. Also crucial to bear in mind are the cultural, social, economic, political, and cultural circumstances in which the film was both made and viewed.

With very little effort we can identify those films that, as a society, we have embraced as particularly representative of a particular time and place. Using the term *iconic* to describe a moving picture is a little ironic, if one thinks of icons as the static religious paintings one might see in an Eastern Orthodox Church. But in the sense that icons are meant to represent or symbolize, we recognize that some movies are more than just movies: they can represent a time or place, or a larger body of similar works. The Library of Congress' National Film Registry (http://www.loc.gov/film/filmnfr.html) has distinguished a number of the films discussed below, including *The Birth of a Nation* (1915), *The Freshman* (1925), *My Man Godfrey* (1936), *The Grapes of Wrath* (1940), *Casablanca*, *The Best Years of Our Lives* (1946), *Rebel Without a Cause* (1955), and *The Graduate* (1967) for their cultural, historical or esthetic significance.

THE BIRTH OF A NATION (1915)

In our definition of icons, we did not say that they had to be beautiful. Anyone familiar with this film may wonder what it is doing in *this* chapter. D. W. Griffith's portrayal of two families, one Northern and one Southern, during the Civil War and Reconstruction periods would appear at first to be misplaced in this chapter. But it serves to make the general point that the memory and understanding of the past is part of the present. More specifically, as a fictionalized depiction of past events, *The Birth of a Nation* does not set out to depict or capture visually the look of 1915 America, but it does document a contemporary view of race relations that drew upon the pseudoscience of eugenics and contemporary notions of social Darwinism to reinforce the legal segregation of American society and help stimulate a revival of the Ku Klux Klan. It also helped to create an enduring popular myth of Reconstruction as a brutal and unnatural occupation of the South by vengeful Northern forces. Essentially, it suggested that reconciliation in the divided country was to be achieved through shared vilification of African Americans and the pursuit of racial purity through segregation. In Griffith's view, racial equality in the wake of the ban on slavery would lead to miscegenation (marriage across racial lines), offspring of mixed race, and therefore degradation of the white race. At the time, many states had laws banning miscegenation, and the U.S. Supreme Court had upheld these laws on more than one occasion; only in 1967 did it strike these laws down permanently. The study of eugenics, a branch of genetics aimed at "improving" the race by selective breeding, aimed to lend scientific credibility to these views. Hollywood "did its part" as well: in the 1930s the Production Code banned the portrayal of miscegenation in the movies, reinforcing the taboo.

The climactic moment in *The Birth of a Nation* comes when Gus (played by white actor Walter Long in blackface) pursues the young Flora Cameron (Mae Marsh) through the woods with the intent, presumably, to rape her. "The Little Colonel" Ben Cameron (Henry B. Walthall) arrives too late to save his sister from jumping off a cliff to protect her virtue, but the tragedy stirs up a rage in him that leads to the formation of the Ku Klux Klan. The film ends with the Klan riding into the Camerons' South Carolina home town to restore "order." The film's prejudice is explicit and obvious, but viewers may not immediately pick up on the central message of the film, that equality between blacks and whites, whether political, social, economic, or sexual, poses a danger to America's progress as a nation. In 1915 not everyone in "Progressive Era" America defined progress the same way. Griffith's racism drew criticism both at the time, and the film has been controversial ever since. But, while it was actually banned in some cities, this blockbuster, arguably the first, nevertheless became the top-grossing film in U.S. film history for almost twenty-five years, until it was surpassed by another Civil War epic, *Gone with the Wind*, released in December 1939. Nasty as his film's message was, Griffith was a pioneer of cinematic storytelling, creating a long film that kept audiences in their seats far longer than they were accustomed; for that reason, *The Birth of a Nation* remains a classic, and the American Film Institute (AFI) listed it among the one hundred greatest American films, at number forty-four in its 1997 survey. Ten years later, it was gone from the 2007 survey, though *Intolerance* (1916), the film D. W. Griffith made in response to what he felt was unwarranted hostility toward *The Birth of a Nation* (yes, you read that correctly), came in at number forty-nine. This film used examples from ancient Babylon and Judea, early modern France, and contemporary America to show the destructive impact of intolerance through history.[1]

---

[1] (http://www.afi.com/tvevents/100years/movies.aspx).

THE FRESHMAN (1925)

The economic impact of the First World War on Europe had enabled the United States to consolidate its global dominance as an economic superpower. The film industry itself was an example of this dominance, and films in turn portrayed America to the world as the land of wealth, opportunity, and high spirits. Film comedians became world-renowned. Along with Buster Keaton and Charlie Chaplin, Harold Lloyd was one of the great film comedians of the silent era, and this film, thanks in part to beautiful restoration, captures college life, football culture, and the look of 1920s California in an entertaining spectacle featuring Lloyd's extraordinary physical comedy, directed by Fred C. Newmeyer and Sam Taylor. Harold "Speedy" Lamb (Lloyd) enters Tate University, lacking the physical attributes or athletic ability of a "big man on campus," but he is determined nonetheless to succeed socially and sets his sights on the lovely Peggy (Jobyna Ralston). Though his efforts lead to many comic mishaps and much ridicule from his classmates, the film ends happily, of course. Obviously, many aspects of the film are over the top and not intended to portray college life realistically, but the main features of college life, then and even now, are present, and in the film's quieter moments one can observe aspects of 1920s American life that the filmmaker may not even have set out to capture, and which may therefore be truer than a more deliberate attempt. There may not be enough in this film alone to warrant a study of its historical significance, but one could certainly examine a larger sample of Lloyd's work to analyze the picture of American life that emerges. For example, *Safety Last!* (1923), also directed by Newmeyer and Taylor, is another comedy that takes Lloyd out into Los Angeles to pull off amazing stunts, including the famous one that has Lloyd, as "The Boy," dangling from a clock face high above the street. "The Girl" (Mildred Davis), fresh from the country, stares in amazement at the array of goods in an urban department store, an image that captures the transition from rural to urban (and consumer) life for many Americans. While *Safety Last!* and *The Freshman* were not necessarily made with the most serious of intentions, the location photography documents contemporary life, making these frames worth studying for historical purposes.

CAVALCADE (1933)

Consistent with America's dominance of the world film industry, the apparently all-British melodrama *Cavalcade*, which won the 1933 Academy Award for Best Picture, was in fact a Hollywood production. This film takes audiences through several decades of recent British history, from the 1899 to 1930, but effectively portrays the confused and weary patriotism that followed the First World War. Notably, it was made the same year that the hyper-nationalist National Socialists gained power in Germany. Based on a Noel Coward play and starring big-name British actors, *Cavalcade* follows an affluent middle class family, the Marryots, and their help, the working-class Bridges family.

Focusing on the long-suffering matriarch, Jane Marryot (Diana Wynyard), the film takes the audience through the Boer War, the death of Queen Victoria, the sinking of the Titanic, and the First World War, up to the New Year's celebration for 1930. Today, *Cavalcade* looks rather stagy, and even primitive in comparison to earlier U.S. films that had taken on the subject of the First World War, *All Quiet on the Western Front* (1930) and *Wings* (1927). The film condemns war, but embraces the same patriotism that had been invoked to urge men to enlist in 1914. The song that Fanny Bridges (Ursula Jeans) sings at the end, "Twentieth Century Blues," written by Coward, is probably the film's most enduring element, asking the question: "Why is it that civilized humanity must make the world so wrong? In this hurly burly of insanity your dreams cannot last long."[2] Noel Coward took a casual approach to history and contemporary life, but *Cavalcade* was emblematic of an approach to international politics that reached far beyond the stage and into the corridors of power. The film premiered in New York on January 5, 1933; at the end of that month, Hitler became chancellor of Germany. But six years would pass before British foreign and defense policy reflected the reality that, to defend its European and global interests, Britain would have to be ready to fight another major war. *Cavalcade* documents the antiwar sentiment behind the appeasement that would characterize Britain's approach to Germany during the first years of the Nazi regime.

IMITATION OF LIFE (TWO VERSIONS, 1934 AND 1959)

The high cost of filmmaking makes the industry risk-averse and wary of innovation. Though audiences may roll their eyes at the notion of the sequel, and older viewers may wonder why classic films like *The Manchurian Candidate* (1962) or *The Thomas Crown Affair* (1968) needed to be remade (in 2003 and 1999, respectively), the box office numbers do suggest that, in a risky business, proven hits warrant remakes and sequels. For historians, remakes offer an interesting opportunity to take the pulse of society at different points across the decades. *Imitation of Life* is a good example of how the remake situates essentially the same story in two different times or places. The 1934 film starred Claudette Colbert, one of the biggest stars of the 1930s, as Bea Pullman, a widow raising her daughter Jessie (Rochelle Hudson) and trying to survive economically. She takes in Delilah Johnson (Louise Beavers) as a domestic, and the two achieve financial success marketing Delilah's delicious pancakes. Delilah also has a daughter Peola (played as a young woman by Fredi Washington), and the film thus draws parallels between the experiences of black and white women in 1930s America. Peola is light-skinned enough to pass for white, and her struggle with her identity produces a heartbreaking split with her long-suffering mother. Bea and Jessie, meanwhile, experience romantic conflict over the same man.

---

[2] Noel Coward, *Cavalcade*, Part III, Scene 2. *Plays: Three* (London, 1979), 198.

Based on the successful "women's" novel by Fannie Hurst, *Imitation of Life* marked significant progress from the days of *The Birth of a Nation* by casting an African American woman in a leading role and bringing that story to white audiences: not bad for 1934. But one has to note also that whereas Bea is youthful and beautiful enough to compete with her own daughter for the love of a handsome man, Delilah's feminine virtues lie in loyalty and hard work. While *Imitation of Life* portrays working women positively, one must also note the inequalities in the partnership between Bea and Delilah, which appear to have been taken for granted.

The 1959 version was directed by Douglas Sirk, who under the name Detlef Sierck, had directed films in Nazi Germany before fleeing with his Jewish wife in 1937. Working in Hollywood from 1943 onward, he directed a number of gloriously soapy films in the 1950s, including *Magnificent Obsession* (1954), *Written on the Wind* (1956), and *Imitation of Life*, his last film. The first two films starred Rock Hudson, one of the biggest stars of the 1950s, in films that took melodrama to delightful excess. Sirk's irony was not contemptuous, however; all three of these beautifully finished films presented to the world Technicolor spectacles of postwar American affluence. A more recent film, Todd Haynes *Far from Heaven* (2002), was an acclaimed *homage* to the work of Douglas Sirk.

Sirk's black heroine, Annie Johnson (Juanita Moore), is still a domestic, but the white mother, Lora Meredith (Lana Turner), is an actress this time around. One would need to draw in other films from the period to substantiate the argument further, but in comparing the 1934 and 1959 versions of the film, one could note that Claudette Colbert played an intelligent woman succeeding in the male-dominated world of business, whereas Turner plays a self-centered woman in a profession where looks trump intelligence and even acting talent: hardly a step forward for women. The prevailing conservatism of the 1950s pushed women, who had been empowered in particular by the economic opportunities of the Second World War, back toward traditional domestic roles, and one could argue that a glamorous actress was less a role model for women than a fantasy subject for magazines read during an afternoon break on the sofa. While Sirk's portrayal of the African American experience is sympathetic, it also suggests that little has changed in twenty-five years. While it shows little sign of an impending women's movement, one can explore the film for signs of the growing Civil Rights Movement.

MY MAN GODFREY (1936)

Turning back to the 1930s, the label *screwball comedy* belies the fact that *My Man Godfrey* makes significant social commentary on American society in the Great Depression. This 1936 film begins with Irene Bullock (Carole Lombard) dragging the hobo Godfrey (William Powell) from a New York City shanty to a fancy party as part of a scavenger hunt. This thoughtless game satirizes the attitudes of the idle rich, who view the great city as their playground. Godfrey becomes the Bullock family's butler, and while romantic tension builds between Godfrey and Irene, Godfrey spars with Irene's cold and calculating sister Cornelia (Gail Patrick), while the parents, Alexander (Eugene Pallette) and Angelica (Alice Brady), carry on in comic oblivion. The joke is that, while the Bullocks grumble about the 60 percent income tax and congratulate themselves on their charity, Godfrey is their "better": he has been hiding out from own family in Boston, superior in wealth and pedigree to the Bullocks.

My Man Godfrey, still entertaining today, is a stinging social satire from a time when the disparities between rich and poor were at their most profound since the Gilded Age, due to the ravages of the Great Depression. The New Deal addressed those inequities to a degree, though the wealthy aimed to protect their fortunes from "that man" Roosevelt. During the cold war, producing this kind of satire might have provoked an investigation by the House Un-American Activities Committee, or, if made more recently, the far right might attack it as politically incorrect for its portrayal of a minority—in other words, the very rich—as foolish and undeserving of their great fortunes. But even at the time its rapid-fire comic approach, and the great (and enduring) charm of the actors, especially Lombard and Powell, helped to disarm critics, even while a clear populist message supported (somewhat) greater economic equality. Those qualities make *My Man Godfrey* an iconic film of the 1930s.

THE LADY VANISHES (1938)

Though Hollywood produced many outstanding films in the 1930s, some of which had great social and political relevance, very few films took up the subject of the prolonged international crises in Europe and Asia that eventually would draw the United States into the Second World War. With very few exceptions, the studios, which produced hundreds of films every year, accommodated a public mood of isolationism. One exception, *Confessions of a Nazi Spy*, premiered in late April 1939 to considerable acclaim, though the production history of the film suggests that a considerable fear of reprisal surrounded the making of the film. Though nativist sentiment resented the "foreign"—sometimes less politely expressed as "Jewish"—influence in Hollywood, the film industry was in fact virtually silent on the subject of the Nazi persecution of the Jews, before, during, and for a long time after the war, and had very little to say about Nazi Germany more generally.

The most important filmmaker to sound the alarm in America was Alfred Hitchcock, whose work in film and later television would make him the legendary "master of suspense." The most important foreign influence in American cinema was British, particularly since the absence of a language barrier made British films more marketable in the United States and British talent more at home in Hollywood. Especially after September 1939, when Britain was at war with Germany but the United States clung to stringently defined neutrality, the British government aimed to win the hearts and minds of Americans to the Allied cause. But no foreign subsidies were necessary to bring *Foreign Correspondent* (1940) to the screen. Producer Walter Wanger (president of the Academy of Motion Pictures Arts and Sciences from 1939 to 1945) had been working on a film about the Spanish Civil War, but it ended before the film could be made. Instead, *Foreign Correspondent* presented a picture of Nazi treachery in a thinly disguised version of the neutral Netherlands, and ends with a direct appeal to the camera for Americans to wake up. Starring Joel McCrea as a naïve American reporter who gets drawn into the intrigue, the film contains several classic Hitchcock action sequences.

A much more charming film, however, is the romantic comedy thriller *The Lady Vanishes*, made in 1938, which has Margaret Lockwood and Michael Redgrave searching for poor Miss Froy (Dame May Witty), a kindly governess, who has disappeared on a train making its way across Europe. Though the film does not have the attractive production values that would enhance Hitchcock's Hollywood films, this film is driven forward by the energy of the lead performers and the director, and neatly presents a British perspective on the looming crisis in Europe. The opening shot, enjoyably fake, presents a charming mountain resort in central Europe, but events quickly show that sinister influences are everywhere. The film challenges the indifference and complacency of British public opinion with a story line in which plucky Iris (Lockwood) pleads with her fellow travelers to help her address the crisis of the vanished governess. She wins Gilbert (Redgrave) as her ally, but must continue to work on the other passengers. The film works beautifully as call for vigilance and preparedness in the face of the Nazi threat, in part because it also entertains so successfully.

THE REAL GLORY (1939)

Few films deal with the U.S. colonial experience in the Philippines or elsewhere, and this particular film is interesting historically on several levels. *The Real Glory*, directed by Henry Hathaway, looks back to the early days of U.S. colonial rule in the Philippines. Made as a historical drama, the film should not be taken at face value as history; its principal interest lies, rather, in its depiction of colonial rule in general, and specifically in its portrayal of American *intentions*. After the United States defeated Spain in what Theodore Roosevelt called a "splendid little war," it took over Spain's colony in the Philippines. Though controversial at the time—should a country that had shaken off colonial rule to become independent now colonize other lands?—the United States did acquire territories without the assent of the indigenous peoples. In the Philippines, in fact, they encountered armed resistance from Emilio Aguinaldo's independence movement. The deployment of U.S. forces to the Philippines became a protracted struggle and America's first Asian war. *The Real Glory* does not address that struggle, but instead presents a justification of colonial rule as a means of empowering the Filipinos to help themselves.

Made in the style of adventure films such as *Beau Geste* (1939) and *Gunga Din* (1939), and mimicked later with greatly advanced special effects in the *Indiana Jones* movies, *The Real Glory*, starring Gary Cooper, David Niven, and Broderick Crawford, set out to thrill audiences but also to present a positive vision of colonialism. Viewers must compare this representation with the historical realities as described in print sources to determine the relationship of the ideals to the realities. Some may be inclined to dismiss the film as propaganda, or a whitewash, but its defense of American colonialism is precisely what makes it historically interesting. Students exploring this film will want to research how and why this film got made and how audiences responded to it. What happened in the Philippines during the Second World War would preoccupy Americans greatly during the war, but who was paying attention in 1939? Examining further the historical context for the film, one does not get the impression that the Philippines ever loomed very large in the American public imagination, the way India did in Britain, for example, though of course there we are talking about a much longer time period as well. But even in the case of Hawaii, a colony that became a state, the fascination was much greater. The other irresistible point that the film raises is the issue of terrorism, and the fact that the Americans ostensibly are in the Philippines to get the indigenous people to defend themselves against terrorists will invite comparison to contemporary world politics.

THE GRAPES OF WRATH (1940)

If *My Man Godfrey* offers wry social satire from the Great Depression, *The Grapes of Wrath* earnestly expresses what would become its central historical narrative: that the economic victims of the Great Depression were not to blame for their hardship, and that the government needed to intervene to mitigate its most brutal effects. Darryl F. Zanuck, the founder of Twentieth Century Fox and one of the legendary producers of the old studio system, had a strong hand in the adaptation of John Steinbeck's controversial but acclaimed 1939 novel, modifying its dark radicalism in favor of a more optimistic message. He assembled great talent for the project, including screenwriter Nunnally Johnson, cinematographer Gregg Toland, composer Alfred Newman, and director John Ford, and, by the end of the year in which the novel was published, the film had been shot in locations from Oklahoma to California.

The film follows the Joad family from their shut-down farm in Oklahoma to the fruit-producing region of California, focusing on eldest son Tom (Henry Fonda), on parole after serving four years for killing a man in self-defense during a barroom brawl. The journey claims both Grandpa and Grandma Joad, and Pa Joad, shattered by his experience, no longer leads the family. That economic circumstances have defeated good men are tragic, but the film is more hopeful than the novel. Ma Joad (Jane Darwell, in an Oscar-winning, classic performance), a powerful embodiment of feminine strength and heart, leads the family alone and expresses the film's philosophy: "We'll go on, because we're the people."

The Grapes of Wrath is regarded as one of the best American films ever made (number twenty-one on the American Film Institute (AFI) list of the one hundred greatest in 1997, twenty-three in 2007), an iconic film that captured the time in which it was made and did so with great artistry. Its optimistic message also spoke for the film industry: though film could not provide hope for the most desperately poor in the Great Depression, it was an inexpensive source of entertainment for millions, and thus provided comfort and hope in very hard times. The Grapes of Wrath demonstrates the power and significance of the moving picture on every level: culturally, historically, and esthetically.

CASABLANCA (1942)

Still popular with audiences today and second only to Citizen Kane among the AFI's 1997 list of one hundred greatest American films (it dropped one spot in 2007), Casablanca owes some of its great charm to the fact that it did not set out to become a great film. A product of the Hollywood studio system, it combined the talents of outstanding writers, actors, and an energetic director in a film that both entertained audiences at the time and presented a very serious message. The pairing of Humphrey Bogart and Ingrid Bergman as the romantic leads succeeded brilliantly, though the film could just as easily have paired Ronald Reagan and Ann Sheridan, which even the most devoted of Republicans would have to agree would have made for a very different film experience. The film used the conventions of screen romance to pose audiences with a serious question about the tension between personal happiness and the fulfillment of duty in wartime. But there is enough comedy in the film as well to drive the film forward to its rightful conclusion.

This is a quintessentially American film, but it also represents an awakening from the isolationism that had characterized the country in the years leading up to the Second World War. It reflects the fact that, since the First World War, Hollywood had drawn talent from all over the world to become the world's filmmaking capital. Director Michael Curtiz was Hungarian, Ingrid Bergman was Swedish, Paul Henreid was Austrian, and much of the supporting cast hailed from across Europe, from Britain to Russia. The story focuses on Rick Blaine (Bogart), determined, after an ill-fated romance with Ilsa Lund (Bergman) in Paris early in the war, "to stick his neck out for nobody." His casino club in Casablanca provides a respite for desperate travelers, many of them refugees from Europe awaiting papers to move on to their true destination: America. Casablanca is a hard place, governed by a Vichy regime wavering between pledged collaboration with Germany and a possibly beautiful new friendship with the Allies. Service providers like Rick can exploit the refugees for material gain, or they can actually help, but kindly sentiment does not generally help the bottom line.

Made as America entered the Second World War, *Casablanca* (1942) tells a compelling story of characters sorting through the complex and conflicting demands of love, loyalty, heroism, and other ideals. A brilliant example of the old studio system at its finest, the film became a classic thanks to a witty and intelligent script, crisp direction (Michael Curtiz), and the chemistry and fine performances of its actors, including (left to right): Paul Henreid as Victor Laszlo, Ingrid Bergman as Ilsa Lund Laszlo, Claude Rains as Captain Louis Renault, and Humphrey Bogart as Rick Blaine. © CORBIS All Rights Reserved.

Rick believes that Ilsa ditched him as they fled Paris in June 1940, and when she arrives in Casablanca, with her husband Victor Laszlo (Paul Henreid) no less—she was married at the time of her romance, but believed he had been killed—he is more determined than ever to look out only for himself. But Victor Laszlo is a hero of the resistance, whom the Germans are determined to kill. The films plot places two exit visas in Rick's hands, and he must choose between his mantra and the call of duty. The particular circumstances of the love triangle make the dilemma particularly acute for Rick. The film's conclusion twists the conventions with skill and wit, but in ways that audiences readily accepted. In addition to being great entertainment, the film fulfills a patriotic duty as well. The patriotism expressed is not cloyingly sentimental or chauvinistic, but genuine and cosmopolitan. Some have described *Casablanca* as an early example of film noir, a style that would characterize many films of the later 1940s and 1950s: dark in look, tone, and theme, a look that reflected Hollywood's encounter with the brutal realities of war and its harsh demands. America's entry into the Second World War knocked isolationism onto the ropes and forced the country to deal with its inclinations toward xenophobia and nativism, racism, and anti-Semitism. With its own cultural diversity, Hollywood could help in the effort, but it was not immune to these influences itself.[3]

THE BEST YEARS OF OUR LIVES (1946)

At the end of the Second World War, producer Sam Goldwyn wanted to make a movie that captured the real-life challenges of veterans returning to civilian life. The result was *The Best Years of Our Lives*, an immediate critical and commercial success that retains much of its power and poignancy today. Goldwyn called upon the industry's top talent, including director William Wyler, writer Robert Sherwood, and cinematographer Gregg Toland, to tell the story of three veterans, of the army, navy, and air force, who return to the fictional city of Boone City (loosely based on Cincinnati, Ohio, but actually filmed in the Los Angeles area) to resume their lives, only to find themselves haunted by their wartime experiences and hard-pressed to deal with those who have not experienced what they have. Army veteran Al Stephenson (Fredric March) returns to a happy family and a well-paying job at the bank, but struggles with the bank's conservative lending policies and his own tendency to drink too much. Sailor Homer Parrish (Harold Russell) has lost both his arms at the elbow and faces an uncertain future both personally and professionally. Bomber pilot Fred Derry (Dana Andrews) returns to the wrong side of the tracks and his floozy war bride, and finds that his military distinction does not easily translate into professional success at home.

Though there are certainly melodramatic moments, the film is realistic and frank in its handling of the issues, including such uncomfortable topics as restoring intimacy, overcoming the traumatic experiences of the war, and facing the sometimes humiliating challenges of readjusting to civilian life. Viewers should also note that the film is instructive also for what it does not portray, namely the ethnic diversity of American society. The Second World War had marked many significant developments in relations among different ethnic groups, but while these developments would become major themes in the history of the American experience in the Second World War, America itself remained largely segregated in the immediate aftermath of the war, and Hollywood itself reflected that segregation.

GENTLEMAN'S AGREEMENT (1947)

Like *The Best Years of Our Lives*, many of the studios' "prestige" pictures of the later 1940s took up pressing social issues of the time. Billy Wilder's *The Lost Weekend*, winner of the Best Picture Academy Award for 1945, took up alcoholism, and Anatole Litvak's *The Snake Pit* (1947) exposed outdated and cruel practices in care for the mentally ill. While many of these films appear

---

[3] Susan A. Brewer has written extensively about wartime propaganda and specifically about the emerging internationalism evident in this film. See her book *Why America Fights: Patriotism and War Propaganda from the Philippines to Iraq* (New York: Oxford University Press, 2009), 111–114.

dated to today's audiences, they remain interesting for the moments they capture in the history of attitudes toward these problems. As discussed earlier, the 1949 film *Pinky*, directed by Elia Kazan, aimed to expose racial prejudice in the South, but the film's producers themselves declined to cast an African American actress in the title role (Lena Horne demonstrated an interest in the role), fearing that audiences would feel uncomfortable with a "colored" actress playing opposite a white romantic leading actor. As a cultural artifact, the film represents a particular moment in the history of race relations, revealing both complacency and courage.

The *Snake Pit* and *Pinky* were Twentieth Century Fox films, and its founder Darryl F. Zanuck led the drive for social relevance in American movies. He also produced *Gentleman's Agreement*, which took on the subject of anti-Semitism in American life and won the 1947 Academy Award for Best Picture. It may surprise audiences today that the film made no mention of the persecution and genocide that Nazi Germany had perpetrated against the Jews of Europe over the previous fifteen years, but on that subject Hollywood had been silent and would remain silent for a long time to come. The film was really about the more "polite" form of anti-Semitism that continued to permeate affluent American society even after that catastrophe and would continue to exist, even legally in the form of housing discrimination, for decades to come. Moved by the revelations of what had happened in the death camps, Zanuck made the film over the pleas of Jewish film producers who did not want to draw attention to the problem. He was determined to bring to the screen the novel Laura Hobson had written in response to an incident in which Congress applauded the comments of the overtly anti-Semitic Senator John Rankin (D-Mississippi).

In the film, Gregory Peck plays Philip Green, a reporter who goes undercover to assess and expose the attitudes toward Jews held by the affluent people of New York and Connecticut. The film goes well beyond the clichés of anti-Semitism—"some of my best friends are Jews"—to address the unfortunate truth that anti-Semitism was part of the unexamined culture of people who otherwise obeyed laws and conducted themselves with civility and decorum. Green even finds that his girlfriend Kathy (Dorothy McGuire) harbors prejudices, despite an otherwise kindly disposition. While it would take Hollywood more than a decade to take up the subject of the Holocaust, *Gentleman's Agreement* demonstrated the insidiousness of anti-Semitism without invoking what had happened so recently in Europe. While one can validly identify dated elements, far more remarkable is the degree to which the film gets inside the far more familiar kinds of prejudice Americans are likely to express or experience even today. A commercial and critical success in its own time, *Gentleman's Agreement* documents a discussion on prejudice that still has something to say to contemporary audiences.

THE DAY THE EARTH STOOD STILL (1951)

In the 1950s, Elia Kazan became embroiled in the anti-Communist hysteria that devastated the careers of individuals in the film industry who were blacklisted for alleged communist sympathies. Anti-Semitism also played a role in Congress' pursuit of the film industry and its "foreign" influences. The response of the film industry itself at the time was to retreat to safe ground. The best place to look for film artifacts that document the fear and hysteria of the time is in the genre of science fiction. Many of these were low-budget "B" films made without well-known talent. One exception was the Robert Wise film *The Day the Earth Stood Still*, which enjoyed modest commercial and critical success at the time and has become a classic. It cost about $900,000 to make and earned about $1.8 million at the box office, in a year when only the top five films earned over $4.5 million. Movie attendance was still dropping precipitously as more and more homes got television.

The Day the Earth Stood Still is one of the earliest films to use the science fiction genre to explore cold war themes. A flying saucer space ship arrives from a planet 250 million miles away and lands on the Mall in Washington, DC. After soldiers injure him in the initial encounter, the "alien," Klaatu (played by Michel Rennie), to all appearances human, escapes hospital custody. His mission is to warn Earth that it will be destroyed if it does not abandon its destructive ways. The president of the United States attempts but fails to arrange a summit of world leaders. Klaatu, using the pseudonym Mr. Carpenter, meets Professor Barnhardt (played by blacklisted actor Sam Jaffe) and persuades him to convene a summit of the world's greatest minds. In the boarding house where he resides, he befriends a young widow, Helen Benson (Patricia Neal), and her son Bobby (Billy Gray). While the film does not explore the possibilities of interplanetary romance, the portrayal of these relationships provides a core of human decency and goodness around which the more dramatic events revolve.

As a historical artifact, *The Day the Earth Stood Still* is a remarkable statement on the cold war, considering the time in which it was made. The Soviets' use of the term *peace* in their own propaganda had made it a bad word in some circles in the United States, particularly the extreme right. Spy scandals and a general "Red Scare" enabled some politicians, most notoriously Senator Joseph McCarthy(R-Wisconsin), to achieve prominence and power by exploiting those fears. This film does not single out any earthling as particularly villainous, except perhaps Helen's selfish boyfriend (Hugh Marlowe). Instead, it states that the present course of humanity will lead to its destruction. Somewhat ironically, Klaatu tells the earthlings that his own planet has a technology that will automatically destroy any planet that poses a threat to its neighbors.

A modest commercial and critical success, the film got no Academy Award nominations, but did garner a Golden Globe Award for Best Film Promoting International Understanding. To the extent that the film addresses the subject of international politics—hardly box office magic, sadly—it attempts to present the cold war as a global problem requiring an international effort to resolve rather than a struggle between two adversaries that only one side can win. The film production itself got embroiled in the politics of the day when producer Julian Blaustein refused, under pressure, to fire the blacklisted actor Sam Jaffe from the cast. Twentieth Century Fox boss Darryl F. Zanuck supported Blaustein, and Jaffe stayed.

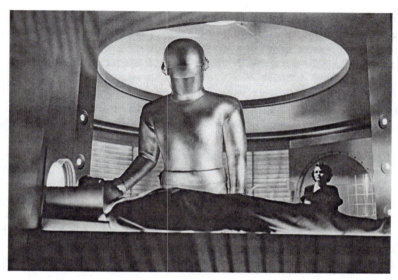

The Day the Earth Stood Still (1951) is a good example of a movie that explores cold war themes through science fiction. The special effects give it a hokey charm for today's viewer, but its message is a relevant piece of cold war history. *Source:* © John Springer Collection/CORBIS.

REBEL WITHOUT A CAUSE (1955)

James Dean was twenty-four when he played the juvenile delinquent Jim Stark in Nicholas Ray's overwrought examination of teen anxiety and violence. Challenging the perception that crime emerged from poverty, the film portrays affluent white teenagers from Los Angeles engaging in dangerous and illegal activities as an escape from loveless or overly materialistic families. Writer Stewart Stern added the psychoanalytic element of a cold, domineering mother and a weak father to explain Jim's own rebelliousness. *Rebel Without a Cause* takes up the issues of white middle class life in the 1950s and gives it the Hollywood treatment, but its greater significance derives from the presence of James Dean, who defined youth and masculinity during his brief career and for a long time after his death in a car crash in September 1955.

Jim Stark's family has had to move because of the trouble he has caused, but he soon finds himself in trouble again with "the kids" at his new high school. He establishes a friendship with Judy (Natalie Wood) and Plato (Sal Mineo), and the three form a "lateral family" that allows Jim to express to Sal the kind of paternal affection that he does not get from his own father. Replete with the popular psychology of the day, *Rebel Without a Cause* also aimed to define the youth of the 1950s, and while switchblade fights and "chickie runs" were not common among America's teenagers, this film, and James Dean in particular, identified a spirit of coolness that both reflected and promoted an affluent teen culture. While these teenagers do not suffer from any kind of physical want, the film suggests that they are very needy emotionally, and the planetarium presentation early in the film also suggests a cosmic sense of alienation and the fragility of life, which one might also associate with the threat of nuclear destruction that characterized the cold war.

Rebel Without a Cause is important for the presence of James Dean, who in life was becoming a major star but in death became an iconic figure in popular culture worldwide. In the first Palomar Observatory scene, Jim suggests to Buzz that he's been reading too many comic books, and Jim proceeds to redefine the masculine ideal not just as physical toughness—though he possesses that—but also the achievement of emotional security and maturity. In other words, it is not unmanly for Jim to try to understand his feelings and to form caring relationships with other people. This certainly appeals to Judy, with whom a romance develops, but it is also clear that Plato is in the mix as well. Jim becomes the father to Plato that his own father has not been to him, but one can reasonably infer that Plato is in love with Jim, and some have suggested that the character represents Hollywood's first gay teenager.

James Dean died before the film was released, adding to its tragic appeal, and naming Sal Mineo's character Plato alluded to the classics. Though not among the most critically acclaimed films of the year, it received Academy Award Supporting Actor and Actress nominations for Mineo and Wood, and director Ray was nominated for Best Writing, Motion Picture Story. It did modestly well at the box office, but was not among the year's top draws. Like James Dean, both Mineo, who was murdered in 1976, and Wood, who drowned in 1981, died young under tragic circumstances, adding further to the aura of the film.

THE UGLY AMERICAN (1963)

The Ugly American, released in 1963, presented audiences with a screen adaptation of William J. Lederer and Eugene Burdick's well-known 1958 novel of the same name. Starring Marlon Brando, the film did not do well commercially, nor did it garner any Academy Award nominations, usually a sign of positive critical reception. The book, still in print, is more readily available than the film, though the latter is available both on DVD and VHS. Set in the fictional Southeast Asian country of Sarkan (Vietnam thinly disguised) and filmed largely in Thailand, the film is entertaining almost solely from a historical point of view. Brando plays a journalist-turned-diplomat named Harrison MacWhite (the name could not have been a coincidence), who, after a heated Senate confirmation hearing becomes the U.S. ambassador to Sarkan, where he had fought with freedom-fighting guerillas against Japanese occupation during the Second World War. He meets up again with his old friend Deong, who has become a charismatic nationalist leader, but whom some American suspect of having communist leanings.

Of course, the story presented is fictional, so how is it helpful to the viewer as history? Indeed the viewer wonders from the outset what the film is really trying to say, and that in fact is the film's mystery, which Marlon Brando's character resolves with an extended soliloquy at the end of the film. The film begins with a construction scene, featuring a U.S.-sponsored infrastructure project called "Freedom Road." For native Sarkanians, the dilemma is whether this is a project that will improve life for Sarkanians, or whether it is a tool of U.S. imperialism that will benefit perhaps a few Sarkanians but primarily will facilitate the expansion of U.S. corporate interests and secure Sarkan as a U.S. ally in the cold war. The murder of a U.S. worker, and the injury of several Sarkanians by communist saboteurs, threatens to stall the project and brings the opening sequence to a dramatic close.

In the meantime, Harrison Carter MacWhite (Brando) undergoes a Senate hearing in which his credentials come under fire, because he is a journalist and because his friendship with the nationalist leader Deong, dating back to resistance activities in the Second World War against Japan, trouble conservative Senators. But he is confirmed nonetheless, and as he prepares to take up his post with his lovely wife Marion (Sandra Church), Deong organizes a welcome that is intended to protest the Freedom Road construction, yet welcome the new ambassador. The new ambassador's arrival, however, turns into a riot, underscoring the difficulty of both Deong and MacWhite's positions. But MacWhite quickly defies any sense that he may be soft on such native unrest by whipping the embassy into shape, transforming it from a country club of complacency and incompetence into a professional operation in the course of a meeting that takes place within hours of his arrival.

That same evening he reunites with Deong, and the two reminisce about old times and the challenges that confront them now. However, Deong is opposed to the construction of the road, while MacWhite believes it should go forward. His own tour of the project later confirms that the road brings modern services, particularly health care, to the native population. An affable American project manager, Homer Atkins (Pat Hingle), his Sarkanian assistant (uncredited), and Homer's wife Emma (Jocelyn Brando, Marlon's older sister), a heroic nurse who runs a clinic, confirm the film's own position on the road as a good thing. Yet Deong insists that it must stop, and he falls in with conspirators who promise to make him the country's leader in a coup. MacWhite, meanwhile, boldly proposes that the road be rerouted toward the north as a direct challenge to communist rebels there. He also meets with the president and prime minister of Sarkan and helps to negotiate a transition toward greater democracy. He uncovers the plot into which his friend Deong has been lured, but Deong is betrayed by his own closest aide and dies in MacWhite's arms after he is shot.

The Ugly American essentially presents a cold war fantasy in which America's global role serves the interests of freedom, democracy, and development in the best interest of all concerned. The communists are the unambiguous villains, but that would not surprise audiences then or now; the film's message is directed at Americans, suggesting that support for dictatorships and economic selfish exploitation are not American values. In a televised speech, MacWhite invokes the values on which the country was founded, and insists that those values must be upheld as America assumes a global role. Yet the film ends on a surprisingly rueful note, one which suggests that the filmmakers do not believe this message will be heeded. The film was not a great commercial or critical success, and, of course, the real events of 1963—chaos in Vietnam and the assassination of President Kennedy—confer a sadly ironic tone on the film for viewers today. As in the movie itself, where a viewer turns off the television, Americans ignored this movie.

While the film obviously does not provide documentary evidence of the origins of the Vietnam War, it presents a debate active in American society at the time and which can be traced back to the days when the country began to project its growing economic power outward. Worth discussing as well is the fact that the embassy staff is all-male and all-white. Among the American women we meet only Mrs. MacWhite, who displays courage, intelligence, and compassion but whose role is to help her husband, and Emma Atkins, the saintly wife of the road construction project manager. The Atkins are a professional team in the tradition of Christian missionaries, though in this case the salvation they bring is improved health care and economic prosperity.

THE GRADUATE (1967)

Mike Nichols' satirical look at affluent middle-class life in southern California became an iconic film of the 1960s. A critical success and a commercial smash, it starred Anne Bancroft as Mrs. Robinson, Katharine Ross as her daughter Elaine, and Dustin Hoffman as Benjamin Braddock, the film's central character who, having graduated recently from an unnamed elite Eastern college, returns home without any sense of purpose or direction in his life. One of his parents' friends famously advises Benjamin to go into "plastics," but these friends come off as shallow, materialistic and, in the case of the Robinsons, unhappy. The comically neurotic Mrs. Robinson seduces Benjamin, and they begin an affair that is driven essentially by a shared sense of loneliness and boredom. Benjamin's parents pressure him to settle down, suggesting that he date Elaine Robinson. Unable to duck this awkward situation, he treats her badly on their date, but feels remorse and they develop a mutual attraction. What would have been a perfectly conventional relationship becomes forbidden because of the affair, and the rest of the film plays out the consequences of Benjamin's unhappy predicament.

The Graduate explores the boundaries of conventional morality, not at the corner of Haight and Ashbury in San Francisco—the most famous address for the counterculture movement—nor in any other bastion of 1960s liberalism, but rather in the all-white, affluent and presumably Republican suburbs of Los Angeles. Beautifully filmed, it captures California's "good life": attractive modern homes, manicured lawns, swimming pools. But it is by no means a complete picture. The 1960s were a time of liberal reform in favor of civil rights and the emergence of a counterculture that rejected the materialism of affluent postwar America, but little of that is evident in this film. Of course, it would not be fair to assert this as a criticism of the film; it is important to the historian rather to identify what this film does or does not portray or address. One might even suggest that the absence of any kind of ethnic diversity in the film is intended to intensify its satirical portrayal of affluent white society.

DELIVERANCE (1972)

This John Boorman film, based on the bestselling novel by James Dickey (who also wrote the screenplay), is about four men from the suburbs of Atlanta who take a weekend canoeing trip on the Cahulawassee River (played by the Chattooga River) in the northeast corner of Georgia. Alpha male Lewis (Burt Reynolds) leads Ed (Jon Voigt), Drew (Ronny Cox), and Bobby (Ned Beatty) on a journey that turns into a disastrous struggle against the primitive forces of nature that they encounter. Contemptuous of the "hillbillies" they meet early in the film, the men later come under assault from a couple of mountain men, and in the ensuing violence the men, whose normal pursuits involve selling insurance, real estate, and soft drinks, discover their more primal survival instincts. The river itself plays an interesting role in the film: one of the main reasons the men choose to go on the trip is that it is about to be dammed for hydroelectric power, and Lewis' voice is strongest in opposing this assault on the environment. The river itself is presented as a manifestation of pristine beauty, though shots at the beginning and the end show the river "drowning" as a result of the damming project. In the meantime, however, it carries the men both into and out of danger, it hides the evidence of their actions and it washes them clean of the blood on their hands. Though *Deliverance* takes up universal themes in a myth-like tale, the film also presents a strong sense of place. Boorman is a British filmmaker, but the novelist and screenwriter James Dickey was a Southerner writing at a time when intellectuals were lamenting the end of the South as a distinct region of the United States. The conflict between the suburbanites and the mountain men does not exactly make the case for the older way of life, but the looming transformation of the river certainly does.

Deliverance is a study of humanity, mainly of the masculine kind, in its environmental context. Especially when viewed today, the characters raise some interesting questions. Lewis is all testosterone, charging headlong into the wilderness in his Confederate flag-adorned sport utility vehicle, but he is also most critical of what is planned for the river. Audiences today might be surprised to see this pairing, because in the culture war that has ensued over the environment, care for the environment has been assaulted as, among other things, unmanly. The other vehicle the men use is Drew's station wagon: suffice to say that the station wagon was the 1970s version of today's minivan, and a symbol of a man's capitulation to the supposedly emasculating demands of domesticity and suburban life. Drew is a great guy, though, and initially he connects with the alien world of the mountain men through his improvised duet with the haunting figure of the banjo player. Bobby becomes the victim of the initial, most humiliating assault, but Drew and Lewis fall victim as well, leaving Ed, who emerges as the film's protagonist, to assume the role of alpha male, thus undergoing the most profound transformation of all the men. Since 1972, seeing the film *Deliverance* has itself become a rite of passage, particularly for young men, but for women also it provides an enlightening exploration of masculine fears and obsessions. It certainly should be understood within the cultural context of the early 1970s, but it also aspires to the status of myth, a more timeless portrayal of humanity.

The film's theme "Dueling Banjos" became a number two hit and a selling point for the movie, which was the fourth biggest box office draw of 1972, earning more than $20 million over its relatively small $2 million budget. Advertising drew attention to the fact that the film was shot on location (through river and place names were changed). Other facts about the film's production also underscore the themes of adventure and masculinity: the film was shot in sequence, more or less as it would have unfolded in real life, and the men performed without stunt doubles, meaning that they really charged those rapids and went over that waterfall, and Jon Voigt really scaled a cliff without any of the fancy equipment rock climbers would use today. It met with great critical acclaim as well, though for the year it was overshadowed by *The Godfather*.

ANNIE HALL (1977)

Few cities have been so thoroughly documented in film as New York City, which for much of the twentieth century was a symbol of American greatness. While that may sound triumphalist, millions immigrated to the United States through New York's Ellis Island, filled with hopes of achieving success and a better life for their children than seemed possible in the lands left behind. The city itself offered tremendous excitement, drawing not just immigrants but ambitious Americans from across the country. By mid century, it had claimed the titles of world financial capital from London and world arts capital from Paris, and its forest of skyscrapers and bright lights gave physical form to the dynamism and energy of the world's largest city. It became a character in countless great films, including *My Man Godfrey, Miracle on 34th Street* (1947), *All About Eve* (1950), *On the Waterfront* (1954), *The Apartment* (1960), and *West Side Story* (1961).

The 1970s, however, were a tough decade for New York—it narrowly avoided bankruptcy in 1975—and several excellent films from that decade explore its grittier side: Gordon Parks' *Shaft* (1971), William Friedkin's *The*

French Connection (1971), Sidney Lumet's *Dog Day Afternoon* (1975), and Martin Scorsese's *Taxi Driver* (1976). Yet the city would spring back from the problems of the 1970s, and the films of Woody Allen, beginning with *Annie Hall*, presented the city as a great place to live. Allen's characters are urbane and sophisticated, if also deeply neurotic. Alvy Singer (Allen) and Annie Hall (Diane Keaton) have a romance that seems improbable (until we remember that Allen and Keaton had a relationship themselves) and which goes through a series of trials until it finally falls apart. As the film's narrator, Alvy tells the story of the relationship, which includes a number of social gatherings that humorously skewer the pretentious and those who have left New York for the sun-dappled unreality of Los Angeles. Though very funny, the film overall has a bittersweet feeling, and in the end Alvy, or Allen, is resignedly philosophical about the fleeting nature of human relationships, able to appreciate the happy times despite the ultimately unhappy outcome. *Annie Hall* captures a moment in the history of love, or sentiment, which can be fruitfully compared to other films that explore relationships meaningfully. It might be considered a romantic comedy, but it defies the conventions of that genre. Of course, Allen's personal life subsequently overshadowed his work, at least for a time, but this was his most critically and commercially successful work, winning Academy Awards for Best Picture, Best Director, Best Actress and Best Writing (directly for screen).

E.T.: THE EXTRA-TERRESTRIAL (1982)

Watching this film today, one might be a little surprised that this film rose to become a phenomenal commercial success, topping the list of all-time U.S. box office hits for the next fifteen years. It certainly has retained much of its charm and entertainment value, but it is surprisingly intimate for a blockbuster, a term we associate with adventure, fantasy, and disaster, and indeed with its director, Steven Spielberg. His films, such as *Jaws* (1975) and *Raiders of the Lost Ark* (1981), drew huge crowds, especially in the summer, and helped to define the culture of the period. Its title character notwithstanding, *E.T.* was a very human drama and serves as a document of contemporary life in southern California, portrayed from the perspective of the child Elliott (Henry Thomas), growing up in suburban sprawl in a family that reflected the high divorce rate that had become characteristic of American life. The film was not in denial about the challenges of contemporary life, particularly for children. The fact that Elliott's mother Mary (Dee Wallace) is completely overwhelmed as a single parent helps to facilitate the necessarily unsupervised development of the relationship between the child and the alien.

Of course *E.T.* was not intended to be a chronicle of contemporary life, and the quest for the film's historical significance must also include exploration of the film's enormous popularity. The notion that extraterrestrial life would be friendly seems to belong to that era: *Close Encounters of the Third Kind* (1977) and *Starman* (1984) took a similarly liberal view of the otherworldly. Though the cold war had turned frosty again, space aliens no longer stood in for godless communists (with films like *Independence Day* (1996), aliens would again turn nasty in the 1990s). Advancements in special effects also made it possible for *E.T.* to become a real and realistic character, and the film certainly enabled viewers to experience the sense of awe that one could imagine would accompany meeting a real alien.

DO THE RIGHT THING (1989)

Director Spike Lee achieved prominence with *She's Gotta Have It* (1986), an entertaining black-and-white film with a distinctive look and feel. Three years later the brilliantly colorful *Do the Right Thing* had viewers debating issues of racial tension in the summer of 1989. Set in Brooklyn's predominantly African American and Puerto Rican Bedford Stuyvesant neighborhood, the movie powerfully evokes the enervating heat and humidity of a New York summer. The street life is vibrant, and characters such as Da Mayor (Ossie Davis), Mother Sister (Ruby Dee), Buggin' Out (Giancarlo Esposito), Radio Raheem (Bill Nunn), and Mister Señor Love Daddy (Samuel L. Jackson) give the street, and the movie, an unusual energy and exuberance. Lee himself plays Mookie, who delivers pizzas for Sal (Danny Aiello), and at the restaurant he works with the boss' sons Pino (John Turturro), who is openly racist, and Vito (Richard Edson), who has a friendlier relationship with Mookie. There are plenty of strong feelings on race and ethnicity all around, and the movie culminates in a chain reaction in which tension gives way to violence. Why it happens and how it unfolds can be debated at great length, and there is a lot to be learned about our own assumptions and attitudes in the process. While it documents a time and place in American history, the issues it raised remain highly relevant today, and its ambiguities make it a great teaching and learning film.

Do the Right Thing was a commercial success: it cost $6.5 million to make and earned over $27.5 million at the box office. The critical reception of the film is also worth examination. The Academy Awards rewarded a more heartwarming movie about race, *Driving Miss Daisy*, that year, while *Do the Right Thing* was nominated only for Best Supporting Actor (Aiello) and Best Original Screenplay, winning neither award. It did not make the AFI's 1997 survey of the top one hundred American films, but it appeared on the 2007 survey at number ninety-six.

At the time, some critics suggested that the film irresponsibly promoted rioting. Lee could and did point out that it did not. Moving pictures did play a role in the next major rioting that took place in the United States, in 1992, after a Ventura County jury acquitted four Los Angeles police officers who had been caught on tape the previous year beating Rodney King. The video documented the reality of police brutality. What immediately sparked those riots, however, was the strong signal from the criminal justice system that equal justice for African Americans under the law was still a dream and not the reality. That, unfortunately, was the truth, Ruth.

Do the Right Thing sparked a lot of discussion about race in the summer of 1989. Its production, content, and reception mark it as one of the most historically significant movies of the 1980s. *Source:* MCA/Everett Collection.

THE BONFIRE OF THE VANITIES (1990)

In the mid-1980s, critics hailed Tom Wolfe's satiric novel *Bonfire of the Vanities* as a perceptive and incisive look at wealthy New York society in pursuit of wealth, masculine security, thinness, and eternal youth, while the broader society teemed with poverty and other more serious problems. Film adaptations of gazillion-selling novels face a serious challenge in high public expectations: big budgets are a requirement, and because of the investment at risk, the industry draws upon its most reliable talent and most bankable stars. That can become a heavy burden. Instead of inspired, adaptations often end up being plodding or overwrought. Tom Hanks, a very popular actor who would win two Academy Awards in the 1990s for two very different roles, was miscast in the lead role as Sherman McCoy (fifteen years later, Tom Hanks would be similarly "elected" to play Robert Langdon in *The Da Vinci Code*, 2006), but other casting choices and alterations to the plot and characterization from the novel would face even more criticism.

Satire enables an author to address serious problems and human folly with irony and humor. The title *Bonfire of the Vanities* refers to the action of Florentine leader Girolamo Savonarola, who in 1497 led an attack on the lifestyles of Florence's wealthy middle class by gathering up their luxury goods and burning them publicly. But Florence revolted against him, and less than a year later he was tried, tortured, and eventually burned to death on the same spot where the bonfire of the vanities had taken place. The book and the film suggest that America's wealthiest people are engaged in vain pursuits, but whereas Wolfe maintains sense of humor, the film fails to carry over the book's satiric edge. Brian de Palma, a skillful director of thrillers, did not have the comic touch required for this material. Still, the movie serves as a document of the way Hollywood works, and *Wall Street Journal*'s Julie Salamon wrote a book describing this process in detail. The title of the book, *Devil's Candy: Anatomy of a Hollywood Fiasco* (1991) refers to DePalma's sole concern with casting an actress with great sex appeal in the role of Maria Ruskin, the woman with whom McCoy is having an affair. The fact that, in the book, the woman was very much a Southerner was apparently lost, and Melanie Griffith ended up playing the role with a distracting and unconvincing Southern accent. With these flaws, the film became a legendary critical and box office failure: it was nominated only for Razzie awards for worst film achievements; and with a big budget of $47 million, it earned less than $16 million in the United States. Of course, this fact now draws the curious, and it is worth examining both the book and the film to understand how the Hollywood "system" both succeeds and fails in documenting American life, intentionally and unintentionally.

GRAND CANYON (1991)

More earnest than *Bonfire of the Vanities*, Lawrence Kasdan's *Grand Canyon* takes viewers across the country to the West Coast for a look at contemporary life in southern California. It is a better written film, with a strong ensemble cast that today's viewers inevitably will compare to the 2004 film *Crash*. Set in Los Angeles, the film takes on issues of race and violence in a complex weave of stories. Written by Lawrence and Meg Kasdan and directed by Lawrence Kasdan (who had written, among many other noteworthy films, *The Empire Strikes Back*, 1980, and *Raiders of the Lost Ark*), *Grand Canyon* examines contemporary urban life through the stories of a number of individuals: Davis (Steve Martin), a director of hyperviolent schlock films; his friend Mack (Kevin Kline), an immigration lawyer; Mack's wife Claire (Mary McDonnell), sadly facing an empty nest; Mack's secretary Dee (Mary-Louise Parker); her co-worker Jane (Alfre Woodard); the tow-truck driver Simon (Danny Glover) who rescues Mack from a tense confrontation with gang members in South Central Los Angeles; and Simon's sister Deborah (Tina Lifford), who needs a safer place to live with her children.

Returning from an L.A. Lakers game, Mack takes a short cut to beat a traffic jam; when his car breaks down, a gang of thugs hassles him until the tow truck arrives and Simon defuses the situation. The men establish a friendship that the highly segregated nature of the community would not otherwise favor. Though Simon does not need well-meaning Mack's help, he can help Simon's sister Deborah find a safer place to live for her family. Less nobly, Mack has a brief affair with his lonely secretary Dee. Claire, meanwhile, who is at a loose end after their only son Roberto (Jeremy Sisto) goes to camp, finds an abandoned baby while she is out jogging. Davis gets shot in the leg as a mugger steals his Rolex, and mends his ways, briefly, as he recovers from this trauma. Each of the characters is stressed out in one way or another, living in a vast city that also seems to be living on the edge of chaos, whether it is due to human-made violence or natural disaster. The connection to Hollywood filmmaking makes the film self-referential, questioning the role of entertainment in shaping and reflecting the broader society, quoting reverently from Preston Sturges' classic film that did the same in 1941, *Sullivan's Travels*.

This discussion illuminates how many films can be studied as documents of the time period in which they were made, even if they in some cases do not portray contemporary events. Many factors, from its production history, to its content, to its critical and popular reception, shape a film's historical significance. The study of any particular film cannot include just the film itself, but the primary and secondary sources that document and describe the film and the times in which it was made. This survey concludes with the early 1990s, in deference to the notion it takes some time to determine the historical significance of films that document contemporary times. Even the National Film Registry stipulates that films must be ten years old before they can be added to the list. While films like *Crash* are valuable for the kind of discussions they prompt, we do not yet have the kind of distance in time we need to explore them critically as historical documents, even if we can sense that they may be historically significant in the future. Availability of resources is another consideration that argues against studying very recent titles, though the Internet has weakened that argument to some degree. That can be disappointing news for a student looking to do research on a recent favorite film, but it is definitely advisable, for best results, to focus on older materials.

Questions for Discussion

1. What makes some movies more historically valuable than others as cultural artifacts?
2. How do movies become iconic representations of their time?
3. Could you imagine writing a history paper on *The 40 Year Old Virgin* in twenty years?

■ ■ ■

9

Around the World in Eighty (or So) Movies

Thus far the focus of this book has been primarily on films that illuminate the American experience—though we have recognized that much of the world's ethnic diversity is present in the history, culture, and society of a country made up of largely of immigrants from every continent on Earth. The fact that, over the past century, the United States has become a super-power with global interests is another reason for Americans to learn about the world beyond their borders. Furthermore, while the United States produces hundreds of movies every year that have an enormous impact on the global movie marketplace, thousands more are produced outside the United States. Both India and the European Union typically produce more films in a given year than the United States.

As an increasingly accessible medium that can both educate and entertain, movies from all over the world offer viewers the opportunity to gain insights into almost all cultures and traditions. This chapter will examine

* cinematic traditions, with well-known examples, from around the world; and

* ways in which different cinematic traditions have produced cultural markers and works of cinematic history.

The films discussed here serve as an introduction. If you were to study any particular tradition further, you might well find that other films, less well-known internationally, capture better the special characteristics of that country's history and culture. The films discussed here are, generally speaking, available for purchase or rental in the United States, which means that they were deemed by a distribution company to have a potential market in the United States.

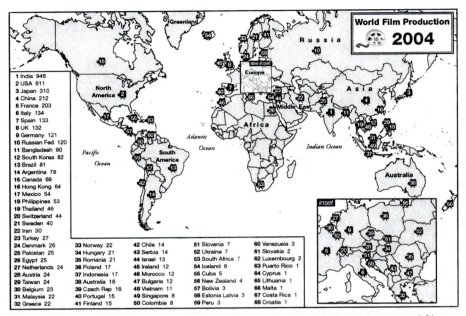

The numbers on this map represent commercially produced and/or state-supported film productions released in 2004. Do you find any surprises here? What questions do these numbers suggest about film industries in different parts of the world?

A film may achieve that status for various reasons, but the reason it is available to us is that the film's distributor believed it would please an international audience. In other words, unless one travels outside the United States or studies the film of a particular country and makes considerable effort to acquire or access copies of the films from outside the United States, the international films we are likely to see have found their way to us through international marketing. At worst, these films may be done in a fluffy vein, made to please crowds without probing any issues too deeply, and perhaps not telling us much about anything. But it may also be a superb example of filmmaking that international audiences will recognize and appreciate. If it is a historical film, the history likely will have to be somewhat familiar outside the country. In the twentieth century, some of the major historical events have been global in scope, such as the world wars and the cold war. The discovery of other historical film material will require further study and greater resourcefulness. For example, for a long time I have wanted to see Fons Rademakers' film *Max Havelaar* (1976), a Dutch film version of the classic nineteenth century novel by Multatuli (*Eduard Douwes Dekker*) about the colonial experience in what is now Indonesia. The book was very influential in its time, and is available in English in the United States, but the film adaptation, released on DVD in the Netherlands in 2003, is not available through the most common channels: to see the film, I would have to order it from Amazon.co.uk, and, as, a European import, it would not play on a standard North American DVD player, since it is in the PAL region 2 format.

I had better luck with Andrzej Wajda's 2007 film *Katyn*, about the massacre of thousands of Polish officers by the Soviets after they occupied eastern Poland in the fall of 1939. Though, as Anne Applebaum points out in the *New York Review of Books* (February 14, 2008), the film focuses on an event of particular significance for Poland (and Wajda himself), this film is available on DVD in the United States. Wajda is a world-renowned director who received the Lifetime Achievement Award from the Academy of Motion Pictures Arts and Sciences (AMPAS) in 2000. The Second World War carries broad interest, and this specific episode achieved international notoriety as well. With an Academy Award nomination for Best Foreign Language Film (2007), *Katyn* by definition has had a U.S. release.

This international survey is organized broadly according to nations of origin, but it is important in discussing both film and history to recognize the limits of national boundaries. Nationalism is a force in modern times, and it has shaped many communities of people into countries according to a common ethnic identity and culture. While we hope that every country's customs and laws respect and uphold universal standards of human rights, we recognize also that customs vary significantly from country to country: how people dress, what they eat, what they enjoy doing for recreation, and so on. But while we may easily identify a dirndl as German and a kimono as Japanese, we also would expect to see little difference among the ways teenagers dress on any given day in Berlin or Tokyo—or Cleveland. Very few people these days can claim, or would want to claim, their culture to be ethnically "pure." Battles may rage over multiculturalism, but in fact every modern culture has been shaped by many others despite the efforts of some to retain a sense of purity. Depending on a wide variety of factors, a film might speak specifically to the national community in which it was produced, but it can just as well address a larger, more global audience. In the period between the two world wars, Germany struggled over whether its movies should promote German culture specifically or appeal to an international audience. In that case, the marketplace argued for broader appeal, but the social and political currents, of course, favored hypernationalism, and as a result, much of Germany's filmmaking talent left the country.

It is probably most helpful to think of filmmaking internationally as clustered in different areas or countries of the world, so that it is relevant and useful to speak of a *national cinema* in Argentina, France, or India. Government support for the film industry, intended to foster the domestic film industry in the face of overwhelming competition from the United States and to promote a national culture, certainly also makes the term *national cinema* relevant and useful. But one always has to bear in mind the very significant ways in which the production, content, and reception of films involves significant movement of goods and services across national borders. In discussing the content of films, it may be helpful to distinguish between qualities within a film that make a film uniquely, say, Italian,

Japanese, Senegalese, or Brazilian, versus qualities that give those same movies universal appeal.

Movies are an expensive medium, and the history of world cinema has been shaped by disparities in wealth across the world. The film industry emerged at a time when the United States was in a period of phenomenal economic expansion, and Hollywood, drawing talent from abroad, became the world capital of filmmaking. Many other countries nevertheless developed significant film industries of their own, and often with state support helped sustain these industries as a form of national cultural expression in the face of overwhelming competition in the marketplace from American films. Some even suggest that the predominance of American film in the world market is a manifestation of cultural imperialism. There is, however, a significant difference between dominating and exploiting people militarily and economically and putting out forms of entertainment that people willingly consume. One might still argue that there is a relationship among military, economic, and cultural factors, but it remains important to define these terms carefully, especially when they are politically charged. The U.S. film industry is large and complex, and it responds to a variety of forces, including political and cultural currents in society; but it aims above all to produce movies that will return a profit, not just in the United States but worldwide.

While movies cannot replace books as a source of information and insight on different cultures in different times, they can certainly provide splendid visual and auditory evocations that books cannot. Narrative films cannot quote the historical sources the way a scholarly book or article can, but they reach much larger audiences and, in a time of increasing global interconnection, promote intercultural understanding and more cosmopolitan world views. While Hollywood and its well-heeled rivals can produce lavish spectacles such as Bernardo Bertolucci's *The Last Emperor* (1987), complete with historical inaccuracies, many countries have their own film industries that have produced films with global appeal. Though by the numbers American audiences tend to prefer American films, foreign language films occasionally catch on popularly, and some have made a significant impact on American culture. Abroad, most countries contend with heavy, if not overwhelming, competition from American films. To compete, domestically produced films often must match the high production values and popular appeal of Hollywood films.

In this international context, it is helpful to raise again the question of a Hollywood style. Of course, that is a very broad and somewhat vague notion, but the question to consider here is whether that style is intrinsically American. As we have discussed, the norms and conventions of Hollywood filmmaking have developed in a commercial setting, but there are powerful incentives as well for Hollywood to produce films that respond to artistic considerations as well, including innovation. Yet the popularity of different genres, such as horror films, suspense thrillers, and romantic comedies, push risk-averse studios toward the tried and true. Internationally, movie industries contend with the same irresolvable tensions. Obviously with film, we are dealing with questions of culture, but politics and economics are powerful forces as well. Unless a country can shut out competition from the United States entirely, American film is a powerful force in its market. Domestic filmmakers are under considerable pressure to produce the same crowd-pleasing results that Hollywood does. In some cases, the state supports filmmaking, on the rationale that filmmaking is an important mode of expression, and that issues of national importance and cultural significance can and should be dealt with in film. The United States does not need such protection for its film industry. But even states that have subsidized the film industry face substantial pressure to make films that satisfy esthetic criteria and also return the investment.

Considered internationally, Hollywood style becomes more appropriately the popular style, vague as that may sound. Hollywood itself is a world filmmaking capital as much as it is an American one. And the kind of movies Hollywood has produced tend to be seamless in appearance, avoiding as a rule any technique that draws attention to the medium itself or reminds the viewers that they are watching a movie. The popular style focuses more on storytelling and less on exploration of the medium. At one time, critics distinguished between Hollywood films and art films, but that tends to suggest that Hollywood films are not art, or at least not "high" art: that is not a fair distinction to make. Hollywood has commerce to consider, but every form of art, high or low, responds in some way to the marketplace. High art, after all, contends with and responds to market forces as much as any other commodity.

What follows is a survey of different cinematic traditions around the world, along with a description of how they have dealt with the past. It is not meant to be a history of world cinema, such as Robert Sklar has written, but rather an introduction to how you may use film to enhance your understanding of world history, or U.S. history in its broader global context.[1]

ASIAN CINEMA

Japan

Asian countries have developed their own filmmaking traditions, fueled in part by the emergence of the Pacific Rim as a global economic force. Among the Asian countries, Japan has had the longest sustained cinematic relationship with the United States, which developed in conjunction with its transformation from enemy during the Second World War to ally in the later 1940s and 1950s. The film that introduced Japanese cinema to the world market was Akira Kurosawa's *Rashomon* (1950). Set in medieval Japan, it tells, and then retells three more times, a fairly simple story of a robbery that takes place in a forest. The complexity and interest of the film derives from the variations that emerge as the different versions of the story unfold. Without turning the film into a pedantic exercise, Kurosawa, who also wrote the screenplay, raises fundamental questions about how film narrative works: rather than present a scientific, objective reality, film always presents a point of view.

---

[1] See Robert Sklar, *Film: An International History of the Medium.* Englewood Cliffs, NJ: Prentice-Hall and Harry N.Abrams, Inc., 2001.

Kurosawa would remain the best-known of Japanese directors internationally, and he certainly figures among the greatest directors ever. His work was subject to American censors during the occupation, but he found their scrutiny less debilitating than Japan's own wartime censors had been. He lived and worked through the Second World War, Japanese defeat in 1945, and a six-year occupation of Japan by the United States. Ultimately he achieved in film what appears to be a hallmark of Japanese culture and history: the ability to adapt foreign influences with unique success, retaining a distinctly Japanese esthetic and sensibility, while matching or surpassing the world's best filmmaking for quality. His dark views of the past, dealing mostly with the feudal era and Japan's Samurai tradition, were often presented as adaptations of Western literary works, including adaptations of Shakespeare tragedies: *Throne of Blood* (1957), a version of *Macbeth*, and, late in his career, *Ran* (1985), a retelling of *King Lear*. One of his most popular films remains *The Seven Samurai* (1954), in which the narrative, again set in sixteenth century Japan, has very much the feel of an American Western. Made less than ten years after the end of the Second World War, it also documents a time of Japanese economic renewal and political alignment with the United States during the cold war.[2]

Kurosawa's *The Seven Samurai* (1954) is an entertaining historical fiction in its own right, but also bears additional interest as a cultural artifact of 1950s Japan. *Source:* AF Archive/Alamy.

---

[2] See John Dower, *Embracing Defeat: Japan in the Wake of World War Two.* New York: Norton, 1999, 426–427.

China

The two largest and most enduring civilizations of Asia, China and India, have emerged more recently as film producers of global stature. During the first decades of communist rule, dominated by Mao Zedong from 1949 to 1976, Chinese filmmakers, working under severe censorship, mostly produced films that served the propaganda aims of the communist regime. Cold war politics also ensured that any material suitable for a worldwide audience received limited distribution. Only with the opening of free markets after Mao's death did conditions begin to favor the development of a film industry with global potential. In the early 1990s, films by Chen Kaige and Zhang Yimou surprised audiences with their often veiled and sometimes explicit criticism of the early days of Chinese communism, particularly since the regime had cracked down hard on demonstrators in 1989. Indeed filmmakers continued to contend with censorship, and Zhang Yimou's 1994 film *To Live* was banned because of the way it portrayed the Cultural Revolution. *Ju Dou* (1990) and *Raise the Red Lantern* (1991) were set further in the past, but sometimes made allegorical references to more recent times. High-class martial arts films such as Ang Lee's *Crouching Tiger, Hidden Dragon* (2000), and Zhang Yimou's *House of Flying Daggers* (2004) evoke the splendor of China's imperial past and showcase the country's natural beauty in uncontroversial ways. With its phenomenal economic growth and a worldwide market for historical Chinese films with a martial arts flair, China has the resources to support a huge film industry. In southern China, Hengdian has emerged as a major filmmaking city with a dozen movie sets that include a replica of Beijing's Forbidden City that is larger than the original. Films such as *Hero* (2002) and the miniseries *Marco Polo* (2007) used the sets in Hengdian. Filmmaking is one manifestation of China's reemergence as a major economic world power, and the view of its own history as presented in films for worldwide distribution is well worth exploring.

Hengdian, with its magnificent period sets, illustrates the importance of history in Chinese film. Zhang Yimou's *Curse of the Golden Flower* (2006), the most expensive film project in China to date, was filmed there. Set during the troubled period between the Tang (618–906) and Sung (960–1279) dynasties, the film portrays conflict within the family of the fictional emperor Ping (Chow Yun-Fat) and his wife the empress Phoenix (Gong Li). The plot is melodramatic, with the screenplay derived from an opera of the 1930s. An intricate web of intrigue has the emperor and empress trying to outwit one another, after the empress discovers that the emperor is slowly poisoning her. The sets and costumes are extraordinarily lavish, though almost certainly inaccurate for the period. The palace bears a striking resemblance to Beijing's Forbidden City, but is never identified as such: a good thing, as that particular complex would not be built until the 1400s, during the Ming Dynasty. Needless to say, the prominent cleavage of Gong Li and other women in the court also serve purposes of entertainment rather than historical accuracy. In other words, this film is a good example of deploying history to present a dramatic story in a visual feast, and shows that

Hollywood does not hold a monopoly on taking liberties with the historical truth. And yet there are some interesting historical observations to make. The dynamics of court life certainly could be full of drama, particularly in a time of transition and upheaval such as this was. In this case, a fictional emperor, having worked his way up from army captain, manages to cling to power, but loses his three sons and potential heirs in the process. From the film itself, one does not get a sense of the cyclical view of history inherent in the notion of the Mandate of Heaven; the focus is on the intricacies of the family strife itself rather than its larger meaning or purpose. The establishment of an imperial dynasty is exceedingly difficult, and while the emperor manages to outwit and outlast the rest of his family, he is left without a family to succeed him, leaving a major question in the end about the succession. The story therefore fits metaphorically into this period of Five Dynasties and Ten Kingdoms (907–960).

Obviously one does not describe today's China in dynastic terms, but it remains an authoritarian state that exercises power in ways somewhat similar to the emperors of yore. Though the film broke box office records in China itself, a film made on this scale also has to set its sights on the international market. While the Chinese government did not have a direct hand in the making of the film, one can conclude that it enjoyed the government's favor, as it became China's official entry for the Best Foreign Language Film Academy Award. It did not receive a nomination for that prize (but was nominated for costume design). Nor was the film as successful, commercially or critically, as *Crouching Tiger, Hidden Dragon, Hero,* or *House of Flying Daggers* were. All of these films are fictional stories set in the past, evoking timeless themes of power, love, loyalty, and betrayal. While they do not teach us the specifics of Chinese political history, they present us with an attractive picture of Chinese civilization. They may also subtly remind audiences that, compared to the West, China has often been the more advanced civilization in the past. With its extraordinary economic expansion in recent times, China is once again a leading world civilization. Whereas, in the West, different powers have cloaked themselves in the glory that once was Rome, China can dig into its own history to make cinematic statements about its present ascendancy.

India

The other giant among Asian civilizations, India, has a huge film industry that rivals, and in numerical terms often surpasses, Hollywood in production of films, most of which are made for the domestic and expatriate market. India, however, is often seen in the West through the filter of colonialism. It is familiar to most Western film audiences as the British Empire's "Jewel in the Crown," romantically captured in such major productions as Richard Attenborough's *Gandhi* (1982) and David Lean's *A Passage to India* (1984). Though the directors were British, these were coproductions of U.S., British, and Indian studios. Both films focus on the late colonial period, the injustices of colonial rule, and the growing tension within India. A BBC TV miniseries called *Jewel in the Crown* (1984, based on novelist Paul Scott's *Raj Quartet*), was popular with American public television audiences in the 1980s. Renowned French director Jean Renoir made one of his later films, *The River* (1951), in India. Remarkable especially for the color cinematography of his son Claude, which lives up to the family name of the great Impressionist painter, the film again is an adaptation of a literary work, in this case a memoir of an Englishwoman, Rumer Godden, who grew up in India.

For a more exclusive focus on the experience of Indians apart from British rule, several Indian films stand out. Among classic films, Satyajit Ray's Apu trilogy—*Pather Panchali* ("Song of the Little Road," 1955), *Aparajito* ("The Unvanquished," 1956), and *The World of Apu* (1959)—follows the character Apu from childhood in a Bengal village in the first film to adulthood, marriage, and parenthood in the subsequent films. Though these films were set in the past, they have little to say about the broader sociopolitical context of Apu's life—British colonial rule, for example—and focus instead on the details of his personal life. Life in a Bengal village is hard to imagine for many in Western audiences, yet Ray's close observations create intimacy and strong identification with the central characters and a realistic picture of their lives. Sometimes compared to the work of Italian neorealists such as Vittorio de Sica and Roberto Rosselini, the films' look is simple and straightforward, with black and white cinematography that nevertheless has an attractive and distinctive style. The nature of everyday life is a primary focus of social historians, and this film provides plenty of evidence of that. Of particular interest is the transition from rural to urban life.

A poster for *Pather Panchali* (1955), the first film in Satyajit Ray's celebrated Apu trilogy, which captures the timeless patterns and rhythms of village life in India. *Source:* © Dorling Kindersley, Courtesy of BFI Stills, Posters and Designs.

AUSTRALIA

Many of Australia's top actors are well known in the United States, including Cate Blanchett, Russell Crowe, Hugh Jackman, Nicole Kidman, and Naomi Watts. Three directors, Gillian Armstrong, Bruce Beresford, and Peter Weir, helped bring Australian film to world prominence in the late 1970s and early 1980s. Armstrong's *My Brilliant Career* (1979), Beresford's *Breaker Morant* (1980), and Weir's *Picnic at Hanging Rock* (1975) and *Gallipoli* (1981) are all set in the early twentieth century, either in Australia, or away at wars in which Australia fought for the British Empire. The forging of an Australian national identity is a theme that can be traced through these films as well as others set in more contemporary times, such as Weir's *The Last Wave* (1977). Weir and Beresford have done a lot of work in the United States as well. Beresford directed *Driving Miss Daisy* (1989), a Best Picture Academy Award winner, and Weir's most interesting historical work in recent years has been his *Master and Commander: The Far Side of the World* (2003), an adaptation of the popular Patrick O'Brien books, in which Captain Jack Aubrey (Russell Crowe) and Dr. Stephen Maturin (Paul Bettany) represent two distinct kinds of men in the world of the nineteenth century: the naval hero, so pivotal to Britain's dominance of the seas and the world, and the scientist, whose research and discoveries advance society further into modern times. Made with great attention to historical detail, *Master and Commander: The Far Side of the World* is a standout work of recent film history.

AFRICA

Cote d'Ivoire, Algeria, and Senegal

Like India, Africa in film history has tended to serve as an exotic locale for drama or adventure movies focusing on the white colonial experience. Some of these capture well the atmosphere of colonial Africa. John Huston's classic *The African Queen* (1951) was set in East Africa, and actually filmed in Uganda and the Congo, then British and Belgian colonies. Primarily an adventure story set during the First World War, the film's comic and romantic spark derives from the tension between the uncouth river trader Charlie Allnut (Humphrey Bogart) and the prim Rose Sayer (Katharine Hepburn). The adventures build toward a confrontation with the Germans late in the film. Though it does not focus on the indigenous African experience of colonialism or the First World War—that would have been a surprise in 1951—it nevertheless presents viewers with the strange spectacle of Europeans fighting each other thousands of miles from Europe.

A later film that presents more of an African perspective on the same war is Jean-Jacques Annaud's *Black and White in Color* (1976), an Ivory Coast (now usually called by its French name, Côte d'Ivoire) production that won the Academy Award for Best Foreign Language Film, the first such award for an African film. This film is set in and around a dusty outpost of the French Empire in western Africa in 1915, where news of the outbreak of war in

Europe arrives about five months after the event. The local French population attempts to assemble local Africans to fight for France against the Germans, whose territory lies just across a little brook nearby, and whose German inhabitants actually did their shopping at the French post—until now. The film is not exactly funny, but it does draw out effectively the tragic absurdities of the situation, at the heart of which is the noxious assumption that Africans exist to do the bidding of their European colonial masters, even if it means dying for those who exploit them.

One of the best films about the struggle against colonialism is Gillo Pontecorvo's *The Battle of Algiers* (1966), an Italian–Algerian coproduction sometimes mistaken for a documentary because of its gritty, realistic style and the sense of immediacy it creates. The film was made in 1965, just three years after Algeria gained its independence from France. Filmed in the streets of the Algerian capital, *The Battle of Algiers* portrays a portion of the long struggle (1954–1962) against French colonial rule. The Front for National Liberation (FLN, the French initials by which it was known internationally) used terrorist tactics against the European French population of the city, but the suppression of that violence by French military forces only intensified the struggle for independence. France, which defined Algeria as an integral part of the country, had to rewrite its constitution in 1958 to empower its government to deal effectively with the crisis. It took no less a figure than war hero Charles de Gaulle to return to public political life to guide France through the trauma of losing its colony. This film, however, tells its story from the streets of Algiers, where France's "civilizing mission" was a far cry from the brutal tactics of its military personnel and police. Though the struggle was over in 1965, the French government banned the film, and some of the torture scenes were censored in Britain and the United States, but the film nevertheless made a vivid and powerful statement that remains relevant in the postcolonial world. The *New York Times* reported in 2003 that the Pentagon showed the film as an example of how one could fight terrorism effectively but still lose popular support. The situation was not precisely analogous to that in Iraq, but was relevant nevertheless.

Among the best-known of African directors was Ousmane Sembene from Senegal. His first feature film, *Black Girl* (1966), told the story of a Senegalese woman, Diouana (Mbissine Thérèse Diop), who goes to work as a maid for a French family in Dakar, then rejoins them after they move back to France. But in France, she feels trapped in the family's apartment in Antibes, and she becomes ever more desperate in her unhappiness. Made in a realist style similar to that of contemporary French New Wave directors such as François Truffaut, the film refers to and serves as a metaphor for Senegal's recent independence from France in 1960. Diouana's boyfriend (Momar Nar Sene) admonishes her not to walk playfully on the memorial to those Senegalese who have fallen in service to the French Empire, curbing her spirit in deference to the French. In the end, she refuses payment from her French employers and takes back the mask she has given them as a gift: in her final tragic act, she declares her own independence. The film suggests that the French remain the masters, but in the final scene a young boy (Ibrahima Boy) pursues Diouana's former boss (Robert Fontaine) out of Diouana's old neighborhood wearing the mask he has returned to her family along with the rest of her possessions. Sembene could have chosen to portray an even uglier face of colonialism, but instead he chooses a fairly ordinary French family, albeit one with a rather unpleasant wife/mother, to portray a more common, but no less dehumanizing, face of colonialism.

Later films, such as the more recent *Moolaadé* (2004), retain a primary focus on the experiences of women, taking on powerful issues with a thoughtful, subtle approach. *Moolaadé* is about a movement within a village in Burkina Faso to oppose the practice of female genital mutilation, a practice common in Muslim societies in Africa. Always concerned with the interaction of modern, Western influences and African traditions, Sembene shows that there are traditional grounds for opposing this practice. The advocates of the practice are not portrayed as totally evil or savage, and in the end the community finds a way to resolve the conflict. Though a couple of scenes are difficult, the film is not graphic, and Sembene manages to handle the issue in a way that is delicate yet unambiguous, within the context of a film that celebrates traditional African life but also accepts change.

EUROPE

Europe has been a principal source of foreign and foreign-language films for North American audiences, with substantial movie industries in Britain, France, Germany, and Italy, and legendary directors of international stature hailing from across the continent: surrealist Luis Buñuel from Spain, Ingmar Bergman from Sweden, and Sergei Eisenstein from Russia to name just three examples. The list of films exploring the sweep of European history is very long. The worlds of ancient Greece and Rome, the knights of medieval times, explorers in the early modern period, adaptations of literary classics, especially English ones, and wars and revolutions in modern times have inspired cinematic historical visions that appeal to large audiences across the world.

When film was invented in the late nineteenth century, Europe still dominated much of the world. Though Latin America was mostly independent, Spain and Portugal held on to portions of their once extensive empires. Among the European rivals for colonial power, Britain and France had the sharpest elbows in Asia and Africa, but the newer powers Germany and Italy had joined the fray, and tiny Belgium and the Netherlands controlled territories many times their own size. To the east, Austria, Russia, and the Ottoman Turks controlled vast domains that included many different subject ethnic groups. After a relatively peaceful nineteenth century, rivalries among all these powers portended trouble in the early twentieth century, and European dominance of the global economy now faced a serious challenge from across the Atlantic as the United States emerged as an economic superpower.

As a new technology with capacity to awe and entertain the masses for great profits, film was an industry bound up with national pride in an era of intense nationalist rivalries. So, for the Europeans, the competitive dominance of the United States was difficult to accept. The French, after all, had invented photography, and the Lumière brothers were among the first moviemakers. But American business savvy and a huge domestic market made the United States a powerhouse in the film industry as in many other industries, though few others had as public a face.

It certainly makes sense to talk about national traditions in filmmaking, though the focus on Europe prompts us to explore a little further the significance of the term *national*. Many of the films described in this chapter have reached a global audience, and many of the bigger films are coproductions involving several countries. Hollywood itself draws talent from all over, and Americans likewise work in a global marketplace for film. One of the best films of 2007 was a U.S.–French coproduction with the American artist Julian Schnabel as director, *The Diving Bell and the Butterfly*.

Our survey cannot include every European country, though many have had several great directors who have contributed to the exploration of history in film. Discussed earlier in this chapter, Poland's Andrzej Wajda is an especially notable film historian, from his 1950s works on the Second World War experience—*Kanal* (1957) on the Warsaw uprising in 1944 and *Ashes and Diamonds* (1958) on the last days of the war—to his *Man of Marble* (1977) and *Man of Iron* (1981), bold films that challenged the Communist party line and, in the latter case, marked the emergence of the Solidarity Movement. Czech filmmaker Milos Forman made films in his native country that could be related to the events of 1968 in Czechoslovakia, though he left after the crackdown and has worked in America ever since, on movies such as *One Flew Over the Cuckoo's Nest* (1975), *Amadeus* (1984), and a film we have already discussed, *Ragtime* (1981). In recent years, Romania has distinguished itself with several films that take up its recent history: Cristian Mungiu's *4 Months, 3 Weeks and 2 Days* (2007), set in the last days of the Ceausescu regime; and Corneliu Porumboiu's *12:08 East of Bucharest* (2007), set in the present but suggesting that Romanians already have forgotten both the story and the significance of the 1989 revolution that ended the Ceausescu dictatorship.

France

Answering the question "who invented film?" is a complicated one, given that the development of a system whereby people would gather in a specially outfitted room to watch moving pictures for entertainment involved a number of inventions and innovations. Strictly speaking, it is more a question for film history than an issue of history in film, but the origins of the medium and its history enhance our understanding of the historical information we can derive from film. U.S. inventors, including Thomas Edison played key role, but the French can make a solid case for having invented cinema. The brothers Auguste and Louis Lumière developed the *Cinématographe*, which could both record and project images, and in 1895 they began regular screenings of their work, starting with the riveting

Workers Leaving the Lumière Factory. The use of the term *riveting* is a little face-tious, in that more than a century later, the scene itself seems very ordinary, but it makes us think about what a thrill it was for audiences to see pictures move, even if the pictures themselves were not so sensational. Before long, the Lumière brothers were capturing events such as a flood in Lyons and the Russian czar's visit to France, introducing the newsreel and what would eventually become the television news report. Importantly, unlike many inventors, the Lumière brothers also were entrepreneurs: within several years, the *Cinématographe* was amazing audiences in Russia, Egypt, India, China, Japan, and Australia, and a global industry was born. A French magician, Georges Méliès, began to explore the more illusory properties of the new medium, essentially inventing special effects with films such as *A Trip to the Moon* (1902), and beginning to mark the distinction between narrative and documentary film.[3] Before long, however, the Americans would prove themselves to be fierce competitors, both as filmmakers and entrepreneurs in the U.S. and world markets, but cinema would endure and grow as a hallmark of France's national culture. The early French films are very significant historically, and French filmmakers and critics would exert an important influence on the world film scene. Today the Cannes Film Festival, an annual event held in May on the French Riviera, can still claim to be the world film industry's Olympics.

But what can we learn of French history from its movies? Much of the twentieth century was brutal for France. During the First World War, the Western Front cut through northeastern France, and the brutal trench war-fare fought for more than four years from 1914 to 1918 claimed more than one million French lives. French film production was minimal during the war, but the experience of the Great War in France has been the subject of several great films. Jean Renoir's *The Grand Illusion* (1937) has been listed among the greatest films ever made, a powerful antiwar statement that may be more significant as a pacifist document of the 1930s than as a depiction of the historical realities of the war itself. While some may fault the filmmaker for denouncing war as the threat of another one loomed from across the Rhine, the film effectively conveys a warm and powerful sense of humanity such as one would not find publicly expressed in Nazi Germany.

Bertrand Tavernier's *Life and Nothing But* (1989) is a beautiful film that compellingly portrays the stunning effect of the First World War on France. Philippe Noiret plays Major Dellaplane, who is in charge of finding and identifying missing French soldiers in the immediate aftermath of the war. Two women, Irène de Courtil (Sabine Azéma) and Alice Vallier (Pascale Vignal), unknowingly are looking for the same man, but the artifice of that plot device helps to illuminate different responses to the experience of the war, addressing issues of class, race, and gender, that is, the same issues with which historians deal in their scholarly work. Tavernier's film is an intelli-gent mediation on the nature of wear and of this war specifically, and it

---

[3] Robert Sklar, *Film*, 26–27, 33–34.

makes effective use of all of the elements at the filmmaker's disposal to create a very evocative film.

Viewers may find a couple of more recent films on the subject more entertaining, but historically interesting as well. In Jean-Pierre Jeunet's *A Very Long Engagement* (2004) Mathilde (Audrey Tatou) is looking for her fiancé, a man whom we see at the beginning of the film court-martialed and condemned to die along with four other men. Mathilde's investigation reveals the fate of all the men and affords the filmmaker the opportunity to investigate different aspects of French life at the time. In Christian Carion's *Joyeux Noël* (2005), French, German, and Scottish soldiers fraternize across enemy lines on Christmas Eve, 1914. At least two other non-French classic films, Lewis Milestone's *All Quiet on the Western Front* (1930) and Stanley Kubrick's *Paths of Glory* (1957), bear comparison to these films.

The trauma of the First World War, in which France at least hung on to contribute to an Allied victory, was superseded by the disaster of 1940, when Anglo-French forces failed to prevent the invading Germans from overrunning the country entirely. Defeat, the subsequent occupation, and the collaboration of France's Vichy government with the Germans, made the experience of the Second World War, in addition to the hardships of the war itself, a shameful period in French history as the ideals of liberty, equality, and fraternity were trampled and the nation became complicit in the murder of a quarter of France's Jewish population. It took some time for filmmakers to begin to explore these traumas, but one must credit two French filmmakers, Alain Resnais and Marcel Ophüls, for "reopening" wounds with their films *Night and Fog* (1955) and *The Sorrow and the Pity* (1969), which helped, eventually and certainly with some resistance, to spark an examination of the past and of the national conscience.

The Sorrow and the Pity helped open the door for cinematic explorations of the Second World War experience in France. Louis Malle's *Lacombe Lucien* (1974) and *Au revoir, les enfants* (1987) both examined issues of collaboration and resistance with particular reference to the persecution and deportation of the Jews. A film that did not win a great deal of critical acclaim, but which takes on the painful subject of France's defeat and capitulation in June 1940, is Jean-Paul Rappeneau's *Bon voyage* (2003). One can scarcely imagine the circumstances in which the French people found themselves as their armed forces collapsed and the Germans advanced on Paris. For a nation that had once dominated Europe and determined much of its politics and culture, the defeat was an incomprehensible and shameful disaster. Yet there is little sense of patriotism among the lead characters in *Bon voyage*, engaged in a complicated but farcical intrigue revolving around the entirely self-absorbed film actress Viviane Denvers (Isabelle Huppert). The fact that a promising cabinet minister, Jean-Etienne Beaufort (Gérard Depardieu) gets caught up in the mess, is a comment on the ineffectiveness of the French government in the face of defeat. A subplot about the attempt to smuggle heavy water, needed for nuclear experimentation, out of France to Britain, weaves in an element of heroism and provides the central male character, Frederic (Grégori Derangère), with an opportunity to redeem himself from his earlier foolish behavior.

One might expect a film set against the historical backdrop of France's defeat in 1940 to be serious, grave, and perhaps suspenseful. But *Bon voyage* does not play the story straight, and the farcical elements remind us that this is a movie. Though one of the cardinal points of the Hollywood style is a seamlessness that draws viewers into the story and tries to make them forget they are watching a movie, the filmmaker here clearly intends to mimic the style in a way that has the opposite effect. The story of France's defeat is therefore a more tangled mess of millions of people looking after themselves and unable to focus on, let alone effectively address, a looming catastrophe.

The third major trauma for France in the twentieth century was that of decolonization. Any sympathy that one can muster for European countries suffering the humiliation of losing territory and national prestige must be tempered by the recognition that colonial rule violated the human rights of the indigenous peoples. But reality proved to be a more complicated business, as in Algeria, for example, about one million European French considered the North African colony their home. France fought two brutal wars to hang on to its colonies, in Indochina from 1946 to 1954, then in Algeria from 1954 to 1962. We have discussed the Gillo Pontecorvo's *The Battle of Algiers* (1966) earlier, and it is perhaps *the* movie to see about decolonization. Yet while it is easy to be judgmental on the topic of colonialism, a film such as Regis Wargnier's *Indochine* (1992), presents a more nuanced picture of the trauma of decolonization. Catherine Deneuve's character Eliane at times seems to be an allegorical figure representing France in the last days of colonial rule—from a French perspective, of course. Cultured but tough, well-intentioned and of course beautiful, Eliane has a complicated and strained relationship with her adopted Vietnamese daughter, Camille (Linh Dan Pham), not unlike France's relationship with Vietnam. The film is highly melodramatic, even a little over the top during the first part, but it settles into a more compelling narrative as it continues. It aspires to grand narrative in its portrayal of fictional events set against a real historical backdrop of France's endgame in Indochina. It does not succeed on that count, but it remains a significant cultural artifact of the 1990s, aiming to reflect and perhaps find closure on the colonial experience.

Germany

Despite the economic challenges facing the country, Germany's Ufa (Universum Film Aktiengesellschaft) company was one of Europe's biggest producers and distributors of films in the 1920s, generating a number of films that are considered classics of world cinema today for their bold visual style known as expressionism, including Fritz Lang's *Metropolis* (1926) and Josef von Sternberg's *The Blue Angel* (1930), which brought Marlene Dietrich to the world's attention. The production, content, and reception of German films in the 1920s and 1930s reveal a great deal about German culture and politics as extreme nationalism gained momentum. While Ufa, which had received financial help from the U.S. studios Paramount and Metro-Goldwyn-Mayer (MGM), had an interest in producing films of broad appeal—*The Blue Angel* was produced in German and English-language versions—the domestic German market appeared to prefer more strongly nationalistic fare. Though initially sponsored by the state, Ufa was a private company, and the government of Germany under the Weimar Republic (1919–1933) did not control its content.

One remarkable cultural artifact of 1920s film is Walter Ruttmann's *Berlin: Symphony of a Great City* (1927). The director would go on to make films for the Nazis, and died while filming military activities on the Eastern Front in July 1941, just weeks after Germany invaded the Soviet Union. This film, however, is politically very neutral: a documentary that films different aspects of Berlin city life from sunup to sundown, starting with a train arriving in the center of the city as it starts its day. There is no real story here beyond the generalities of city life, making this film interesting to watch only for its visual style and the fact that it captured scenes of everyday life in a major European city in the year 1927, though some scenes clearly were more staged than others. Still, for the study of urban history, it provides precious documentation. As a silent film, it had no narration, the titles are minimal and the overall effect is that of a visual poem.

For Germany, as for France, the two world wars dominated the first half of the twentieth century. Defeat in the First World War made that conflict an unpopular topic in German film, and though later German film would explore the Nazi experience in considerable depth, one cannot produce a list of more recent German films that do for 1914–1918 what several French films have done in recent decades to explore that experience. The historian Fritz Fischer had argued in the 1960s that Germany had played a much more aggressive role in the origins of the First World War than was generally accepted up to that time, despite the fact that the Allies had included a "war guilt clause" in the Treaty of Versailles at the end of the war. In the popular conception, Nazism was a terrible aberration in German history, and popular culture explored its terrible impact using that assumption. The experience of the First World War was repressed in the 1920s and suppressed entirely in the Nazi period. Erich Maria Remarque's *All Quiet on the Western Front* appeared in the late 1920s, only to be banned in all forms by the Nazis. Subsequently, the brutality of the Nazi regime and the cataclysm of the war they caused has overshadowed the experience of the earlier conflict in the popular imagination.

German films about the Nazi experience are abundant, and one can effectively trace the history of Germany's dealing with its Nazi past through film. Though obviously all modes of cultural expression should be considered, movies are among the most public of cultural offerings and, along with books, provide evidence of a broad cultural response rather than only that of educated elites. The television miniseries *Holocaust* (1978), though a U.S. production, had a profound impact in Germany. Though certainly a powerful and well-made series, it was also accessible and rather straightforward in its narrative. In examining Germany's own exploration of its Nazi past, the filmmaker Rainer Werner Fassbinder was an important figure who made a series of challenging films in the 1970s and early 1980s that were prominent in what became known as the German New Wave. *The Marriage of Maria Braun* (1979), followed by *Lola* (1981) and *Veronika Voss* (1982), explore the legacy of the Nazi experience, including the war, through the lives of women. Maria Braun (played by Hanna Schygulla), for example, marries an American in the last days of the Second World War, in what is clearly a metaphor for the alliance born between defeated Germany and the victorious United States. At 940 minutes, his *Berlin Alexanderplatz* (1980), an adaptation of the Alfred Döblin novel set in the Weimar period, has been described as one of the longest feature films ever made, though most people who saw it viewed it as a television miniseries. While commenting on the Weimar and Nazi periods, and the Second World War in particular, Fassbinder's films also reflect a deep ambivalence about the relationship between Germany and the United States during that period of the cold war, when many Germans opposed the policies of the United States, especially with respect to nuclear weapons.

Since the end of the cold war, German filmmakers have produced a number of world-acclaimed films on historical subjects. Caroline Link's *Nowhere in Africa* (2001) portrays the challenge that a Jewish refugee family faces after it flees Germany in the 1930s. Though somewhat melodramatic, it also departs from the central narrative of Holocaust history to remind viewers that the experiences of the millions of people affected by Nazi persecution were diverse, and that the stresses created by that persecution profoundly affect family life, as Marion Kaplan describes in her book *Between Dignity and Despair: Jewish Life in Nazi Germany* (1999). Oliver Hirschbiegel's *Downfall* (2004), starring the great actor Bruno Ganz as Hitler, follows the last days of the Nazi regime almost exclusively from within the confines of the bunker where it lived out its last nightmarish days. Other films have taken up this macabre topic, but none has been so effectively illuminating. Especially striking is the portrayal of denial: Hitler and others continue to discuss victory even as bombs pulverize the city above them.

After the end of the cold war, reunification fulfilled a German dream but also introduced many challenges. Wolfgang Becker's *Good Bye Lenin!* (2003) uses an improbable plot to realize a common fantasy in eastern Germany at the time: a desire to go back to the familiar patterns of life under the old communist regime of Erich Honecker. East Berliner Christiane Kerner (Kathrin Sass), apparently a zealous proponent of socialism, suffers a stroke on the eve of the collapse of the regime. When she awakens from her coma months later, her devoted son Alex (Daniel Brühl), to protect her fragile health, takes great pains to conceal the changes that have overtaken the city and the country by restoring her immediate environment to what it was. Historians will appreciate Alex's efforts to reconstruct accurately the period detail, and the film skillfully shows how objects and products of everyday life can powerfully evoke feelings of nostalgia, even if those objects and products are unfamiliar to most viewers. While this aspect of the film is very funny and may indeed have allowed some eastern German viewers to sigh wistfully for the old days, the underlying drama is far more critical of the old regime.

Finally, Florian Henckel von Donnersmarck's *The Lives of Others* (2006) masterfully probes the political realities of life in East Germany by following the workings of a Stasi (secret police) agent assigned to spy on a prominent playwright. From the exposition, the viewer learns that Hauptmann Gerd Wiesler (Ulrich Mühe) is a true believer in the ideals of socialism. However, as he observes the movements of Georg Dreyman (Sebastian Koch) and his live-in girlfriend, the actor Christa-Maria Sieland (Martina Gedeck) and listens in on their conversations and other intimacies, he learns that he is part of a system that is far from ideal. Not unlike the Nazi regime from which it so vehemently distanced itself, the communist regime in East Germany was filled with rivalries and infighting that had very little to do with ideology and that put the lie to the image of unity promoted by those ideologies. At the same time, *The Lives of Others* is very cinematic, drawing the viewer into the story almost as a participant, not unlike Wiesler himself.

Britain

To many Americans, British films hardly count as foreign; the absence of a language barrier gives films from Britain, Canada, Australia, and other English-speaking countries an obvious language advantage. Indeed, many films set in a non-English-speaking environment, if done in English, will have the characters speaking the English you would hear on the BBC (British Broadcasting Corporation), as if the Queen's English somehow remains the standard and will be least distracting to audiences. Occasionally, it can be confusing whether a film is British or American: *Cavalcade*, a 1933 film based on a Noel Coward play, set entirely in England with a British cast, is listed as an American film because an American studio produced it.

The discussion on India already has shown some of Britain's global reach with respect to filmmaking, but British history itself is richly represented in film. British literary classics filter the history somewhat, but their enduring popularity and global audience make Jane Austen's English society of the early nineteenth century and Dickens' London very familiar to audiences today.

Some of the more heralded historical dramas from Britain in recent years have been the works of James Ivory and Ismail Merchant, who often worked with Ruth Prawer Jhabvala, who in 1993 adapted Kazuo Ishiguro's celebrated novel *The Remains of the Day*. None of these people were born in England (United States, India, Germany, and Japan, respectively), yet the film seems quintessentially British, as do many of their collaborations. *The Remains of the Day* follows the life of a devoted British servant, James Stevens (Anthony Hopkins), working at an old country estate, the fictional Darlington, for man who during the course of the story hosts a conference that affirms a policy of appeasement toward Germany, and whose Nazi sympathies extend to dismissing a Jewish employee. Stevens' fellow servant, the housekeeper Miss Kenton (Emma Thompson) takes a stand against her employer and leaves, but Stevens prizes duty above all else.

Stephen Frears is among the best-known of British directors working today, and his work has a more distinct edge than the Merchant–Ivory films. He directed *The Queen* (2006, discussed in Chapter 6), but some of his older films, such as *My Beautiful Laundrette* (1985) and *Sammy and Rosie Get Laid* (1987), portray life in postcolonial London that by now have achieved a level of historical interest that would warrant another look, perhaps in comparison to his own more recent work, such as *Dirty Pretty Things* (2002), about a kind-hearted Nigerian doctor Okwe (Chiwetel Ejiofor) drawn into the grim underworld of contemporary London. Canadian director David Cronenberg's *Eastern Promises* (2007) similarly explores the dark side of the thriving world city.

Italy

The Italian film industry has produced some of the greatest directors in the history of the medium, and among their works are some beautiful works of history. Vittorio De Sica, Roberto Rossellini, Federico Fellini, Michelangelo Antonioni, Luchino Visconti, Bernardo Bertolucci are all directors of global stature, and one might add the name Sergio Leone, director of the great Spaghetti Westerns, and Francis Ford Coppola, an American with Italian roots explored in his work, to the impressive list. Just as post-Second World War Italy has become renowned for excellence in design, from fashion to furniture to automobiles, the visual artistry of Italian films, from the gritty realism of the neorealists to the rich visual beauty of such 1970s films as De Sica's *The Garden of the Finzi-Continis* (1970) and Ermanno Olmi's *The Tree of Wooden Clogs* (1978, discussed in Chapter 2), make them world-class.

Unified as a modern nation state only in the latter half of the nineteenth century, Italy failed to establish a stable and functional political culture. Though the northern part of the country was relatively well-off by European standards, the south remained poor. Though it ended up on the victorious side in the First World War, it had endured humiliating defeat in battle and did not achieve its objectives at the Paris Peace Conference in 1919. The Fascists under Benito Mussolini gained power in 1922, promising stability and strength and redemption through militant nationalism. Mussolini's unrealistic dream of restoring the glory of the Roman Empire led to disaster in the Second World War, with Italy now on the losing Axis side. Though Italy did not produce world-class movies during the Fascist era, the regime did not produce as brutal an environment for the creative arts as did the Nazis in Germany or the communists in the Soviet Union. Coming to terms with the Fascist experience would be a prominent theme in Italian cinema after the war.

But first a group of directors would influence filmmakers all over the world with a phenomenon that became known as neorealism: a style that aimed for a visual truthfulness in exploring the fundamental challenges and struggles of human existence, especially among the poor. The look of these films is often somber, filmed on location amid the poverty and devastation wrought by the war. The frankness and lack of artifice suited the times and, even though the camera was not shooting beautiful subjects and scenes, the visual appeal of these films was nevertheless very strong, and these films became extremely influential worldwide. Visconti's *Ossessione* (1943) an adaptation of *The Postman Always Rings Twice*, was considered the first film in this movement, but Rosselini's *Rome: Open City* (1946) was the first to attract worldwide attention, capturing the drama of the last days of the Second World War almost in the fashion of a documentary. Vittorio De Sica's *Shoeshine* (1946) and *Bicycle Thieves* (1948) are the two films often listed among the greatest ever made. The historical appeal of these films is great, in that they aimed to document contemporary life. No film should be taken entirely at face value, but these films lack the artifice through which we often must sort to get at historical realities.

Perhaps the most pointed film assessment of the Fascist era has come from Bernardo Bertolucci, who in the 1970s made two important films on the subject, *The Conformist* (1970) and *1900* (1976). In *The Conformist*, Marcello Clerici (Jean Louis Trintignant) a man of weak character joins the Fascists in 1938 and agrees to go to Paris to murder his former teacher, a dissident. *1900* is an extraordinarily ambitious film, running over five hours long, chronicling the lives of two men, a poor peasant Olmo (Gérard Depardieu) and the affluent son of a landowner Alfredo (Robert De Niro), from their births in 1900 through the end of the Second World War. Particularly the latter film shows that, away from the scrutiny of the Motion Picture Association of America (MPAA) ratings system, history can be portrayed with much of the sex and violence it contains. Though difficult for some viewers to watch, it shows the brutality of Italy's political struggles, which we can sometimes underestimate when we compare the Fascists to the National Socialists in Germany.

The Garden of the Finzi-Continis was an art-house favorite in the 1970s, a foreign-language film that overcame the challenge of subtitles with a straightforward narrative and great visual beauty. It also won the Academy Award for Best Foreign Language Film in 1971. Dominique Sanda was one of the big international stars of the 1970s, working with many of Europe's leading directors. In this film, she plays Micol Finzi-Contini, who along with her brother Alberto (Helmut Berger) lives a pampered and sheltered life on the beautiful family estate. They are beautiful people concerned primarily with the relatively trivial problems that a life of extreme affluence can present, but in the end, their splendid isolation comes to an end as the world closes in on them and they, because they are Jewish, face deportation to their deaths.

Federico Fellini may be the most celebrated of all Italian film directors. He certainly was an important cultural influence at the height of his career. Though certain of his films would be challenging to analyze historically, such as *8½;* (1963) many serve as important cultural markers, such as *La Dolce Vita* (1960), which captured postwar affluent European life in a significant way and became a major international hit that even made its mark on American popular culture. His *Roma* (1972) would be of interest to anyone studying contemporary Italian history. One of his more popular films, *Amarcord* (1973), is a nostalgic look at life in the village in which he grew up in the 1930s. One probably would not call Fellini a filmmaker-historian, but he was important enough as a director that no historian of the period would want to overlook his work.

Russia/Soviet Union

For much of the twentieth century, film served the aims of the communist regime in the Soviet Union after the end of czarist rule in 1917. While films depicted aspects of the Russian experience before and after the Bolshevik Revolution, the role of the state was a significant factor in the production and content of films. Yet students of history cannot simply dismiss Soviet-made films as propaganda, which itself is worthy of study as a manifestation of the reality the state aims to put forth. And some great talent emerged from these challenging circumstances to make great films.

The Bolshevik Revolution in 1917 aimed to propel Russia forward into the next phase of history, according to the Marxist ideology of its leaders. That same ideology did not predict that underdeveloped Russia would be the place where industrial workers would seize control of the "means of production" from greedy capitalists and build a new society based on the fraternity, or socialism, of the working class. In any case, the revolution quickly devolved into a dictatorship that relied on fear and force to transform Russia into a socialist state. Yet socialism and communism had adherents throughout the world, and as long as its ideals remained alive, they inspired artists, including filmmakers. Lenin, the Bolshevik leader, believed strongly in the power of film to build the revolution. The new regime used agit-trains and other means of transportation to spread the gospel of revolution to the far reaches of the old Russian Empire, and Soviet filmmakers accordingly developed a style of filmmaking conducive to propagandizing masses of people who had no experience of electricity, let alone film. The montage style of filmmaking, where the film's meaning lies less in individual shots than in the way they relate to each other, became a favored tool for indoctrinating the public with brief but powerful films. For example, the films of Lev Kuleshov, who pioneered these techniques, served the propaganda aims of the new regime. For scholars of film, they demonstrate an artistic development of the medium in a particular set of social and political circumstances. His film *The Extraordinary Adventures of Mr. West in the Land of the Bolsheviks* (1924), is a comedy, but it was also propaganda directed against the West and aimed exclusively at domestic audiences.

In contrast, several of the films of Sergei Eisenstein (1898–1948) have been hailed as among the best ever made. The visual style is not dissimilar, but Eisenstein created films that can be watched for their artistry as well as their storytelling power. Many of his works can be described as historical drama. His most famous film was *Battleship Potemkin* (1925), made to commemorate the twentieth anniversary of a mutiny at the port of Odessa on the Black Sea, an episode in the revolution of 1905. A partly fictionalized story about a popular uprising against the oppressive rule of the czar obviously served the propaganda aims of the new regime, but Eisenstein's powerful images and masterful editing turned this silent film into one that international critics have hailed as one of the best, if not *the* best work of cinematic art, ever. Later filmmakers would cite the shot of the runaway baby carriage crashing down the steps as a kind of homage to the film's most famous scene on the steps leading down to the waterfront.

Eisenstein's 1928 film *October*, also known as *Ten Days That Shook the World*, was a reenactment of the Bolshevik Revolution in Russia in the fall of 1917, made to commemorate the events on their tenth anniversary. Though it makes no use of actual footage of those events, footage from *October* would appear in later films as though it were documentary footage. The film was not a success in its day. In Moscow, it played only for a week, and in New York, it received poor reviews. Reception was better in Berlin, though this was not the most popular of Eisenstein's films there, either. Britain banned all Eisenstein's films. Produced by the Soviet government, it aimed to portray the Bolshevik Revolution as a spontaneous popular uprising rather than a coup led by a small group of middle-class revolutionaries. Viewers today may find Eisenstein's visual style interesting, but at the time critics wrote of a lack of story, a criticism typically reserved for works of narrative fiction. One could say therefore that the regime's ideological agenda defeated the film's cinematic agenda. Ironically, one of the frequent points of tension between historical accuracy and the demands of commercial cinema is the tendency to simplify events and to concentrate them in the hands of a few individuals in order to make for a more compelling drama. In this case to have done so would have been more historically accurate than to suggest that the events of November 1917 were the work of countless workers, soldiers, and peasants.

Historians today would approach *October* as a primary source. Though it presents an interpretation of past events, its is not a careful analysis of those events, but rather a commemorative reenactment based on Marxist ideology and Communist party dogma, which maintained that historical change came about through class conflict. Rather than test that belief, the film shapes the past to suit it. The film, therefore, is a document of the early period of Soviet communism, reflecting the belief of the dictators of the 1920s and 1930s that film would play an important role in consolidating their support.

Though not an extremely prolific filmmaker, Eisenstein made several more great films, managing even to work under Joseph Stalin, who effectively drained most of the excitement from the Soviet arts scene as he consolidated his power. Current events likewise could alter dramatically the way audiences viewed the past in film. Eisenstein toured Europe in 1928 and made his way to America, but Hollywood's studio system had its own strictures, and he failed to establish himself there. A filmmaking venture in Mexico involving the celebrated novelist Sinclair Lewis also ended in complete failure. Though under suspicion from his filmmaking colleagues back in the Soviet Union, he managed to achieve success again with *Alexander Nevsky* (1938), recreating the 1242 battle in which the Russian prince of Novgorod defeated the invading Teutonic Knights in a famous battle on the ice of Lake

Peipus. A rousing drama about fighting off a German invasion was not too far from reality in the late 1930s—and a story Russian and Western audiences could embrace—but when Stalin cut a nonaggression pact with Hitler in August 1939, the film became a political embarrassment to the regime, but only until June 1941, when Germany did invade the Soviet Union.

During the cold war, Western audiences did not see much of Soviet cinema until tensions began to diminish after the Cuban missile crisis. Adaptations of literary classics set in the past, such as *War and Peace* (1968), *The Brothers Karamazov* (1969), and a biographical film *Tchaikovsky* (1971), won Best Foreign Language Film Academy Award nominations, and *War and Peace* won. Another nominated film, *The Dawns Here Are Quiet* (1972), based on a novel by Boris Vasilyev, tells the story of five young women serving in an antiaircraft unit in northwestern Russia (Karelia), near Finland, during the Second World War. The film includes a contemporary framing device, in color, as a group of young people prepares to place a memorial plaque at the place where one of the women died, but most of the film is devoted to their story, portrayed in black and white, which includes their remembrances of family and friends back home, again in color, but using stylized, dreamlike settings. The film therefore has an interesting look, contrasting a socialist 1960s "mod" gloss on the flashbacks with the natural beauty of the Russian north. The film itself is a memorial tribute to the women who served in combat during the war. One might hope for a film from Russia that more strongly counters the enduring tendency of people in

A film about a glorious Russian victory over the Teutonic Knights, *Alexander Nevsky* (1938) became an embarrassment for Stalin after he made a pact with the Nazis in 1939. But it regained its propaganda punch after Germany attacked in 1941. *Source:* Corbis/Bettmann.

the West to underestimate the scale and importance of the war in the East, but this is not such a film.[4] One can certainly describe this film as propaganda, but it invites comparison to other war films made in other countries both during and after the war, both for its portrayal of women and for its portrayal of the cause for which they are fighting.

With the collapse of the Soviet Union in 1991, filmmakers presumably were freer to express themselves apart from the watchful eye of the state. Nikita Mikhalkov's *Burnt By the Sun* (1994) won international acclaim, including the Best Foreign Language Film Academy Award, and earned back most of its estimated $2.8 million dollar budget in U.S. box office receipts alone. Set in the summer of 1936, the story is set in the idyllic Russian countryside, at the dacha of Colonel Sergei Petrovich Kotov (played by the director), a "hero of the Revolution," his wife Marusia (Ingeborga Dapkunaite) and young daughter Nadya (Nadezhda Mikhalkova). Cousin Dmitri (Oleg Menshikov) arrives from Moscow and as an unexpected house guest proves to be both charming and talented, but Kotov knows that Dmitri has come "on business." While the viewer is lulled by the sun, breeze, and trees, the film's energy derives from the tension between the loveliness portrayed onscreen and the brutality that lurks. At the end, the fate of the characters is revealed, though the violence takes place mostly off-screen. One might argue for a more graphic depiction of Stalin's terror, but this film is quite effective in portraying what was lost: happy lives, love, families.

SOUTH AMERICA

Movies also can greatly enhance the study of South American history and culture. Two countries in South America, Argentina and Brazil, have global stature as film producers. Though plagued by social, political, and economic instability that certainly had an impact on their film industries, both countries have produced films in recent years that have either shed light on their historical experiences or will become significant historical markers in years to come.

Colonization of the Americas has been the focus of several films, including the British production *The Mission* (1986), directed by Roland Joffé, which very effectively shows the tangle of economic, religious, and political motivations that shaped colonialism. As the title suggests, the film focuses on the work of Spanish Jesuit missionaries with a group of indigenous people during the 1700s. The fate of the mission depends on the disposition of the territory in which it is located, a subject of negotiation between the Spanish and Portuguese crowns. Under Portuguese rule, however, the natives face enslavement and their community faces destruction.

---

[4] The German film *Stalingrad* (Joseph Vilsmaier, 1993) at least shows some sense of the magnitude of that all-important battle. Perhaps it is for the best, but there is no film that attempts a grand narrative on the massive struggle between the Germans and the Soviets during the Second World War.

Brazil

Brazil has aimed, with mixed success, to foster a national film industry in the face of strong U.S. competition. During the 1950s and 1960s, the Brazilian government developed a system whereby the equivalent of a tariff imposed in movies coming into the country for screening would be taxed, with the proceeds going to finance the production of Brazilian films. The system increased Brazilian film production, but had the effect of increasing the cost of tickets to the consumer, and in challenging economic times, movies became too expensive for many people. Economic and political instability had a large impact on Brazilian film production, but in recent years, Brazil has produced a number of widely acclaimed films that candidly portray the grimmer aspects of contemporary urban life.

Made as Brazil prepared to return to democratic civilian rule after twenty years of military leadership, Carlos Diegues' film *Quilombo* (1984) colorfully tells the story of a community of escaped slaves (quilombo) called Palmares, established in the 1650s in northeastern Brazil. The film presents the quilombo as a kind of socialist peaceable kingdom, which may be a twentieth-century idealization, but the historical record does verify that Portuguese colonial officials fought to destroy these communities and that it took a long time for them to do so, against fierce resistance from those who understood that they were more likely to be exterminated than (re-)enslaved. The film is an unabashed tribute to this doomed spirit of resistance. Its intent to celebrate these communities rather than simply reconstruct them possibly costs the film some historical accuracy, but serves the purpose of addressing issues of ethnic diversity and prejudice in contemporary Brazil.

Throughout the world, millions upon millions of people live in slums. Some of the most powerful portrayals of the desperate lives people live in these environments have come from Brazil. São Paulo (population 17 million) and Rio de Janeiro (11 million) are among the world's largest cities. In Hector Babenco's *Pixote* (1980), the title character is a ten-year-old boy who is arrested for living in the streets of São Paulo. He is mistreated in the detention center, and when he finally escapes, he has become hardened and seems destined for a life of crime, however long that may last. This is a film that cannot be enjoyed in any conventional sense, but it raised awareness about the terrible lot of millions of people. Adding to the tragic sense of the film is the knowledge that the boy who played Pixote, Fernando Ramos da Silva, himself came from the streets, and his experience making this film did not turn his life around. Returning to the streets, he was murdered before his twentieth birthday, in 1987.

In Fernando Meirelles and Kátia Lund's *City of God* (2002), Rocket (Alexandre Rodrigues) and Li'l Zé (Leandro Firmino) come from the same dangerous part of Rio de Janeiro, ironically called the "City of God." Li'l Zé is a fierce and ruthless gang warrior, but Rocket uses a discovered gift for photography to escape becoming a warrior himself, though he powerfully documents the brutality in his work. This film has a more suspenseful story than does *Pixote*, and it also makes a powerful impression visually. It earned Academy Award nominations for Best Director, Editing, Adapted Screenplay, and Cinematography. The film does portray the past to some extent, but focuses primarily on the present. The film has been compared to the work of Martin Scorsese and Quentin Tarantino. While the historical perspective is perhaps not quite there yet, this film would bear comparison to other portrayals of violence in urban life in other countries by those and other directors.

Argentina

With a population made up mostly of Spanish, Italian, and German immigrants, Argentina was one of the world's richest countries a century ago, but social and political instability led to decades of dictatorship and economic hardship in the twentieth century. Juan Perón, who earlier ruled with his second wife Eva and was later succeeded by his third wife Isabel, was the predominant political figure of the century. Eva, however, is the only Argentine to be featured in a major Hollywood movie, Alan Parker's adaptation of Andrew Lloyd Webber's musical, *Evita* (1996), starring Madonna in the title role. As an introduction to Argentine history, it is an entertaining and well-made film, and at least partially shot in Argentina itself, though Budapest also sometimes stands for Buenos Aires. For the historically minded, it should inspire further exploration and study. Ironically, though Juan Perón married a film star, his censorship diminished Argentine cinema both in terms of quality and commercial success, and, as with so many other aspects of Argentine life, it would take decades to repair the damage.

During the 1970s, Isabel Perón became the first woman head of state in the Western Hemisphere, but she was overthrown in a 1976 coup that led to a military dictatorship that murdered an estimated 30,000 people deemed enemies of the state. This "dirty war" provided the historical backdrop for Luis Puenzo's *The Official Story* (1985), which won the Academy Award for Best Foreign Language Film. A high school history teacher (Norma Aleandro), married to a lawyer (Hector Alterio), gradually learns where her adopted daughter came from. Made just a few years after the brutal military regime in Argentina gave way to restored democracy, the film explores one woman's awakening to the political circumstances in which she has been living, and how those around her have been affected by it. Of two films by Héctor Olivera about the dirty war, *Funny Dirty Little War* (1983) is available for viewing in the United States, but *Night of the Pencils* (1986) is not. An American film, Constantine Costa-Gavras' *Missing* (1982), portrays the true story of the efforts of American Ed Harmon (Jack Lemmon) and his daughter-in-law Beth (Sissy Spacek) to find their son/husband, the journalist Charles Horman (John Shea), who has disappeared in an unnamed South American country. Circumstances are similar to those in Argentina, but the actual setting for this drama is Chile, where from 1973 to 1990, Augusto Pinochet led a military dictatorship that treated its opponents with similar brutality.

A relatively recent film, Walter Salles' *The Motorcycle Diaries* (1984), demonstrates the limits of the term *national cinema*. Salles is Brazilian, and the film was therefore presented as a Brazilian entry in film festivals worldwide, but it actually had almost nothing to do with Brazil aside from the director's national origin. Set during the 1950s, it chronicles a journey through South America by the young Che Guevara (played by the Mexican actor Gael García Bernal) and his friend Alberto Granado (Roberto De la Serna, an Argentine actor). The two set out from Buenos Aires and travel through Argentina, Chile, Peru, Colombia, and Venezuela before parting ways. Guevara, who had studied medicine, went on to become a revolutionary. He figured prominently in the Cuban Revolution in 1959 and later traveled to Bolivia to foment revolution there, but he was killed there in 1967 at the age of 39. This film, however, is limited to the time the two men spent traveling together. The viewer sees the oppression and misery that would radicalize Guevara, and whatever one may make of his later activities, this film shows that they at least had humanitarian roots. This is a beautiful visual introduction to diverse parts of Spanish-speaking South America, and it has great heart as well.

NORTH AMERICA

Neighbors to the United States, and overshadowed by Hollywood, Canada and Mexico nevertheless have substantial cinematic traditions of their own. Though Canada has struggled to define, with some success, a culture distinct from that of its southern neighbor, Mexico has the advantage of a different language and a more distinctive heritage, though the Hispanic presence in the United States is now larger than that of African Americans, and of the ten largest cities in the country, all except Philadelphia have a 25 percent or greater Hispanic population. Though Canada has been called the Great White North, it too has a great deal of ethnic diversity that is reflected to a degree in its film industry.

Canada

With a population only about one-tenth that of the United States, spread across a country of about the same size, Canada has tended to export its filmmaking talent to Hollywood, where the money is bigger and the potential audience far greater. In recent years, a relatively weak Canadian dollar has drawn U.S. filmmakers to Canada for shooting, making Vancouver in particular a moviemaking center. The fact that Vancouver therefore provides a generic backdrop for many movies and TV shows is unfortunate for those, including historians, who prefer authentic settings and a strong sense of place.

Though Canadian writers have done well throughout the English-reading world, Canadians by and large are very much like Americans in what they watch, and it has been difficult to establish a strong Canadian film industry for feature films. To the chagrin of those who would see this as an example of Canada losing out to a more vulgar American culture, the all-time top-grossing Canadian film worldwide is the decidedly low brow *Porky's* (1982), a teen sex comedy set in Florida in the 1950s. Historical accuracy was not high on the agenda of the filmmakers, nor was it the key to their financial success.

The Canadian government has aimed to cultivate a distinct cultural identity through subsidies for the arts and the sponsoring of a national television and radio network, the Canadian Broadcasting Corporation. In filmmaking, the emphasis has been on the documentary film, and the National Film Board of Canada, despite struggles over the years, has cultivated a reputation for excellence in that realm, though it has received more acclaim for its strong tradition in animated films.

Canadian history, therefore, remains largely unknown to movie audiences. Within Canada, Quebec has done relatively well because of its distinctive language and culture. Denys Arcand's films *The Decline of the American Empire* (1986) and *The Barbarian Invasions* (2003) gained international attention, and the latter film won the Best Foreign Language Film Academy Award in 2004. Though both films were set in the present, they portrayed the lives of Montreal intellectuals and professionals who engage, among other things, in discussions about the state of the world, casting a jaded and critical eye in the direction of America.

Mexico

The Mexican film industry also has gained increasing recognition over the years, and Alfonso Arau's historical drama *Like Water for Chocolate* (1992) became one of the most commercially successful foreign language films in the United States. Adapted by Laura Esquivel from her own novel, the film is a love story that begins in early twentieth-century Mexico, about to erupt in revolution. The title of the film refers to water near the boiling point, and describes both the frustrated love of the central character Tita (Lumi Cavazos) and Pedro (Marco Leonardi) and the broader sociopolitical context of their lives. Tita's mother (Regina Torné) is a harsh and cruel woman who insists that Tita, her youngest, will follow family tradition by not marrying and taking care of her instead. She marries off her daughter Rosaura (Yareli Arizmendi) to Tita's beloved Pedro. But modern ideas and magical powers exercised through cooking enable Tita to break free of the shackles her mother has imposed. John (Mario Ivan Martinez), a goodhearted doctor from Texas, helps also: he hopes to marry Tita but is a terribly good sport about her love for Pedro, who may stir Tita's soul but is not the modern soul that John is. The history here is more symbolic than specific, but the revolution (1911–1917) promises freedom from the strictures of traditional Mexican society, most obviously for Tita's sister Gertrudis (Claudette Maillé), who rushes naked from the shower to ride off with a revolutionary. She returns years later as a general—at least that is what her lover calls her.

Movies cannot be our sole source of information, but they provide a means of traveling vicariously through time and space to just about every part of the world. Host Ellen de Generes suggested that the 2007 Academy Awards ceremony was the most international ever: Mexico made a particularly strong showing with Alejandro González Iñárritu's *Babel* (2006), a film connecting stories in Morocco, Japan, Mexico, and the United States, and Guillermo del Toro's powerful *Pan's Labyrinth* (2006), a horror fantasy film set in Spain in 1944. Germany took the Best Foreign Language Film prize for *The Lives of Others* (2006) and a U.S. film almost entirely in Japanese, *Letters*

In *Like Water for Chocolate* (1992), Tita (Lumi Cavazos) lives within the strictures of a Mexican society on the brink of revolution, but finds power in the kitchen. *Source:* Miramax Pictures/Everett Collection.

from Iwo Jima (2006), contended for Best Picture. However, almost as if by way of apology, a collage of films portraying the American experience ran toward the end of the ceremony, ending with a big American flag, almost as if to ward off criticism from those who would see foreign as a negative, further evidence of an ongoing culture war within the United States.

While Hollywood continues to take heat from conservative critics in America, the movies it produces reach worldwide audiences and not infrequently account for more than half of a movie's box office revenue. Yet as consumers we usually do not reciprocate. This survey has identified several of the key national film industries around the world, but I could go on. Israel in recent years has produced quite a few fine movies, as has Iran: Majid Majidi's *Children of Heaven* (1999) is a lovely film that shows the patterns of daily life in modern Teheran, a film I believe most people could enjoy or at least appreciate. In some ways, we are prisoners of our high-end production values and slick storytelling. Many of these films ask us to slow down and appreciate other aspects of good filmmaking and other traditions as well.

Questions for Discussion

1. Film is sometimes described as a universal language. What does that mean?

2. If film is a universal language, how can it also teach us about diverse cultures and histories?

3. How does the filmmaking industry fit into the global marketplace?

10

■ ■ ■

Your Turn: Writing About History in Film

If you are reading this book for a course, you probably also have a writing assignment to complete. As a professor, I know that it is difficult to guide a large class through the process of research, analysis, and writing a paper, but the exercise deepens your understanding of a topic and expands your critical thinking and writing skills. Developing those skills is one of the most important aspects of your college career, and the purpose of this chapter is to support your professor's efforts to make the writing assignment an integral part of the course experience and to help you to get the most out of this assignment. If you are in a large class, chances are you are viewing quite a number of films and discussing them in class. Your own research topic may not come up. But you should be making as many meaningful connections as you can, thinking about how your own research is deepening your understanding of the human experience, and how film and specific films are helping you to do that.

Let us admit first of all that there may be a few of you to there who chose this class with not necessarily the loftiest of motives: I've run into a few seniors, for example, looking for a fun class in that last semester, looking to catch a wave toward graduation. We can work with that. Film is an enjoyable medium, as you all know. But writing a worthwhile paper is also going to involve a significant commitment of your time and effort to research, analysis, and writing—that is, work—which, if you choose your topic well, will also be enjoyable. The popularity and availability of film makes writing about history and film a good way for students to develop original historical insights. This chapter provides

- guidelines for choosing a topic carefully;
- guidelines for designing your analytical framework; and
- reasons to explore the research portal that follows.

These guidelines are not meant to restrict your historical imagination, but rather to stimulate it.

The essential elements in choosing a topic are to ensure that the issues to be dealt with are historical in nature and that film material is a major, though never sole, source of evidence. History is a very broad and multifaceted discipline, and the principal issue in defining a topic is to ensure that it deals with the past in some significant way. Students often want to write about their favorite films, and that certainly can help motivate them to be diligent and meticulous in their research. But recent films set in the present tend to explore contemporary issues, and generally speaking, not enough time has passed for a historical perspective to take shape. But if you thought *Crash* (2004) was brilliant, you may wish to channel the interest and engagement that you felt with that movie to explore films from an earlier era that attempted to do something similar. It is much easier to think historically about less recent experience, and therefore, older films and films set in the past provide more suitable material for this kind of analysis and writing. The project should be an exercise in thinking historically: to explore aspects of the human experience with a particular sensitivity to change over time. For example, movies such as Spike Lee's *Do the Right Thing* (1989) and Lawrence Kasdan's *Grand Canyon* (1991), discussed in Chapter 8, made with similar aspirations—to capture the spirit of the times in contemporary urban America—are now old enough for us to have gained some historical perspective on them. Within a carefully defined time frame, you could examine the content, production, and reception of these films within a broader historical context that would include significant events such as the 1987 Tawana Brawley controversy, the 1991 Rodney King beating, and the 1992 violence in Los Angeles that followed the acquittal of his police assailants, whose actions had been caught on tape.

This chapter serves in part as a review of some of the films discussed earlier, but it is meant to make you start thinking of those and other movies as potential research topics. Getting started is one of the hardest parts of the process, and the following discussion sets out a number of ideas for the kind of project you can undertake. You may wish to begin with a theme, a particular film, or a genre of film. The themes one can explore are endless, but portrayal of particular groups in society is one for which there is an abundance of evidence in film. Just taking the Western genre, for example, one could examine the portrayal of and attitudes toward Native Americans, Mexicans, women, men, or any combination of those. You need to acquire some understanding of the genre itself, especially the basic structure on which most Westerns are built. Westerns generally adhere to the structure or deliberately challenge them, but the consistencies in most Western films make the differences among them stand out. Compare a Western from the 1930s with a Western from the 1970s or more recently, and you will find consistent patterns in storytelling, but you will see differences in how Indians, Mexicans, women, and even white male heroes are portrayed.

Continuing with the possibilities of the Western genre, one could explore the fact that most Westerns are set in the time period following the

Civil War through the end of the nineteenth century. Their formulaic nature makes them more significant as *myth* than as history, which actually does not diminish their historical interest; they become rather an exploration of preoccupations and values rather than an attempt to understand the past as it actually was. But most Westerns do place themselves in some kind of real historical context, and to the extent that they present a certain interpretation of the past, they can also be examined as historical interpretations of expansion across the West, the displacement of the Native Americans in that process, interactions with nature, and the environment and the impact of all these developments on American identity and culture. Even if these interpretations are not the primary focus of the film, and usually they are not, they can nevertheless reveal quite a lot about our general understanding of the past, including, for example, varying degrees of indifference to the fate of Native Americans.

Continuing in the Western vein, a student could also explore the historical significance of a particular film. This probably should be a film of some significance, either by virtue of its having been seen by a large number of people or having achieved great critical acclaim or the status of a classic. *High Noon* (1952), rated among highest (#33 in 1997, #27 in 2007, but *The Searchers*, 1956, shot past it in the later survey) of all Westerns among the American Film Institute's "100 Best American Films of All Time," was made at the height of Senator Joseph McCarthy's hysterical anticommunist crusade. Whether or not the filmmakers *intended* it to be a cold war allegory, many viewers took it that way. For in-depth examination of a film's historical significance, John E. O'Connor's categories of production, content, and reception serve as an excellent basic outline, and in establishing your analytical framework, you would want to set these elements into a contextual model such as we developed for *That Hamilton Woman* in Chapter 4.

The time period in which most Westerns are set predates the emergence of film as a popular medium, meaning that for the most part film does not serve as an archival source in the same way that it can for twentieth century history. Narrative or documentary films about the period before film are almost by definition going to be secondary sources—interpretations of the past based on nonfilm sources. Twentieth century topics offer more options with respect to the ways film can be used, since so much of the twentieth century experience has been captured on film. Film footage documenting events may be used as a primary source, and films from a particular place or era may be interpreted as an artifact of that place or era. Though the United States would come to dominate the world film industry in a way no other nation would, all developed and some underdeveloped countries had their own film industries. The availability of film material from other countries may limit research conducted on North American campuses, but in theory, the research possibilities are global in scope.

The cost of making and distributing film is high, however, and as a result, some events are more thoroughly documented than others. Material from the silent era (to the later 1920s) will be of limited availability, though what is available can be surprising. The cable channel Turner Classic Movies shows a tremendous variety of material, including silent films, and it is always worth checking the Web site, www.turnerclassicmovies.com, for titles. While many students like to examine more films with which they are already familiar, a project that will familiarize them with the film of a different era will be both easier to pull off and more beneficial as an exercise in writing history. What follows, therefore, is a survey of possible themes that appear from a brief survey of film history.

Film from the silent era is less readily available than later films, but the films of figures such as D. W. Griffith, Charlie Chaplin, Harold Lloyd, and Buster Keaton have been preserved and could be used for research. D.W. Griffith considered himself a historian, and two of his most famous films, *The Birth of a Nation* (1915) and *Intolerance* (1916) are historical films made on a grand scale. Both of these films remind us that we should never take a film's historical interpretation at face value. *The Birth of a Nation* helped to establish many of the conventions of narrative film, and its innovations do not leap out at today's audiences, who are steeped in those conventions. Rather, its racial views, which seemed to bother few of the millions who made it the most commercially successful film ever (until 1939), are most striking. Discussed in Chapter 8, *The Freshman* (1925) might be of particular interest to college students: though the films of Chaplin, Keaton, and Lloyd are about physical comedy, they also capture their times in interesting ways. The state-of-the-art restoration of the Harold Lloyd films gives them a freshness, vitality, and immediacy that allow the viewer to connect with the past in an extraordinary way. The early days of the film industry, prior to the evolution of the male-dominated major studios, were an early golden age for women in filmmaking, as the research of Jane Gaines and others demonstrates.

When sound emerged in the later 1920s, the First World War was a significant subject for serious films. *Wings* (1927) won the first Academy Award for Best Picture, the only silent picture to win that award. Films of the later 1920s and 1930s about the First World War reflected contemporary feeling about the significance of that conflict, but reflected also a growing antiwar sentiment in democratic societies at large. As discussed in Chapter 8, *All Quiet on the Western Front* (1930) and *Cavalcade* (1933), both Best Picture winners, also dealt with the experience of war. *All Quiet* was based on the celebrated German novel (both the book and film were later banned by the Nazis), whereas *Cavalcade* was based on a Noel Coward play. The terrible toll of the First World War and its lack of tangible positive results even for the victors had bred a strong antiwar sentiment in Britain and Western Europe, and these films document the ambivalence people felt as they reconciled patriotic sentiment with a deep sense of the futility of war.

The Academy Awards are the most prestigious awards given in America for filmmaking, a product of the late 1920s when, at the end of a decade in which the "culture wars" were particularly intense, Hollywood studio heads were looking to improve the image of film in American society.

By rewarding excellence in filmmaking, the Academy of Motion Picture Arts and Sciences (AMPAS) encouraged the making of films that would be taken seriously. One cannot know how the history of Hollywood would have been different without Academy Awards, but they have become a significant aspect of film culture. Looking at the films of the 1930s that garnered Academy Awards and nominations, one can get a sense of what the studios identified as "prestige pictures," films that would bring respect and acclaim to them and to the industry. Literary adaptations and historical dramas loom large among these. While Hollywood still cultivates that respectability today, it is difficult to imagine a biopic of Emile Zola or Louis Pasteur being made today. The desire of filmmakers and the filmmaking industry to be taken seriously as a social and cultural force was one of the incentives that drew them to history, and story of the "prestige picture" is therefore an interesting one to explore.

Over the decades, one can see patterns in award giving that tend to favor Hollywood's more ponderous fare, but among all the dramas honored over the years are a significant number of comedies as well. Film comedy during the Great Depression makes a great research subject, though the paper topic would need a more specific focus. With hard times awaiting many Americans outside the movie theater in the 1930s, comedies helped to buoy spirits inside, and not always at the expense of a critical edge. Frank Capra's *It Happened One Night* (1934) and *You Can't Take It with You* (1938) took top honors in their respective years. In the 1940s, he went on to make the important *Why We Fight* documentary series (1943–1945, see Chapter 5) and *It's a Wonderful Life* (1946). Even as escapism they could yield insights, but there is more going on in these films than that. The same is true of *My Man Godfrey* (1936, see Chapter 8), which, though an over-the-top screwball comedy nevertheless comments incisively on American society during the Great Depression. Later, Preston Sturges would continue the tradition of providing social criticism through comedy with films like *The Great McGinty* (1940), *Sullivan's Travels* (1941), *The Lady Eve* (1941), and *The Palm Beach Story* (1942). *Sullivan's Travels*, in particular, explores the tension between film's potential to serve society and its imperative to entertain.

Almost any topic of interest in the history of America in the 1930s can be explored through film, including the experience and portrayal of women, ethnic minorities, and class differences, the latter being of particular interest in an era of economic crisis. John Stahl's *Imitation of Life* (1934), based on the novel by Fanny Hurst, is a good place to start your investigation. Several films dealing with themes of crime and punishment also have become classics, for example Mervyn Le Roy's *I Am a Fugitive from a Chain Gang* (1932) and Fritz Lang's *Fury* (1936). William Keighley's *G-Men* (1936) was among the first films to promote the image of the newly formed Federal Bureau of Investigation (FBI). Popular gangster films, such as William Wellman's *The Public Enemy* (1931) and Howard Hawks' and Richard Rosson's *Scarface* (1932) also make compelling documents as well, all the more so for the enduring popularity of the genre both in television and film.

The 1930s also produced films that revisited characters that had appeared before on the screen and would continue to appear into our own time. Long before Judi Dench (*Shakespeare in Love*, 1998), Cate Blanchett (*Elizabeth*, 1998), and Helen Mirren (*Elizabeth I*, 2005) played her, England's first Queen Elizabeth was a popular screen character, portrayed twice by Flora Robson, in *Fire Over England* (1936) and *The Sea Hawk* (1940), and by Bette Davis in *The Private Lives of Elizabeth and Essex* (1939). An interesting theme to explore is the portrayal of the revered queen, and England in general, as a great crisis loomed once again. A costar in the latter two films, Errol Flynn became very popular for his many swashbuckling roles in this era, and his *The Adventures of Robin Hood* (1938) remains the greatest portrayal of that legendary figure. Elizabeth I and Robin Hood are examples of characters that appear again and again as subjects in the movies. Elizabeth, of course, was one of England's greatest monarchs, ruling at a time when her country was emerging as a world power. If sources permitted, we might be able to trace Robin Hood back to a real person, but of greater historical interest is what people have done with the story over the years. He should be considered a mythical figure, the archetypal outlaw who challenges the injustices of the legal authorities and is therefore an agent of reform. A worthwhile research topic would be to examine different portrayals over time: what does each generation have to say about the character, how does it correspond to the historical record, and what do these portrayals say about the time in which they were made?

In the later 1930s, Hollywood paid relatively little attention to the "gathering storm" in Europe, with a few very interesting exceptions, such as *Confessions of a Nazi Spy* (1939) and Alfred Hitchcock's *Foreign Correspondent* (1940); both films are worthy of exploration as documents challenging America's prevailing isolationism. Another interesting phenomenon of this period and related to these films is the changing of endings to suit the rapidly changing times and politics of the early 1940s.

Perhaps a Technicolor escape into the romanticized Old South was more in line, therefore, with popular sentiment before 1941. As intended by its producer David O. Selznick, *Gone with the Wind* became a film event that remains unsurpassed in American culture. Margaret Mitchell's 1000-plus-page novel, published in 1936, had been a phenomenon in itself. Students today still express an interest in writing on it, and there is voluminous material on its content, production, and reception. It became the all-time box office champion and would retain that distinction until *The Sound of Music*, with the help of inflated 1965 dollars, surpassed it. In the novel and on the screen, *Gone with the Wind* is historical fiction, but as a cultural icon, it has more to do with the 1930s than with the Civil War. While audiences today may flinch at some of the depictions of politics and ethnicity, the film did poke at racial barriers. Hattie McDaniel's character Mammy is a faithful servant but also a pistol who enlivens the story and helps carry the film, and her Academy Award (for Best Supporting Actress) drew attention to African American actors in Hollywood. The film may not resonate with audiences that same way that it did for decades after its release, but it was and remains a phenomenal film: its portrayal of history, for good *and* ill, and its own significance as a cultural artifact make it a film of multifaceted historical significance.[1]

The remarkable consensus on America's intervention in the Second World War after the attack on Pearl Harbor made Hollywood every bit as patriotic as Peoria, and the films of the war era tend to be efforts to build morale and wave the flag. After two decades of ambiguity, the First World War was now a good thing: *Sergeant York* (1941), telling the story of pacifist-turned war hero Alvin York, was made prior to U.S. entry into the war, and succeeded rather brilliantly: it captured both the ambivalence of American public opinion about war in general but hailed York's heroism as the country entered the war. Unfortunately for you, Robert Brent Toplin already has written a great essay on *Sergeant York*, but it serves as a good model for its exploration of the film's content, production, and reception, and the theme of how historical and contemporary films correspond to the rapidly changing world situation can be studied for many films of the early 1940s.[2]

By 1942, however, the time for subtlety was over, and Hollywood films strongly promoted the war effort. History was enlisted in the effort, as the biopic *Yankee Doodle Dandy* (1942) demonstrated. George M. Cohan (1878–1942, played by James Cagney in an Oscar-winning performance), a major figure in the history of Broadway and American entertainment, composed a number of patriotic songs still well-known today, such as *You're a Grand Old Flag* and *Over There*, the song that accompanies every documentary narrative about U.S. involvement in the First World War. *The Great Ziegfeld* (1936) about another legendary figure in the history of Broadway completely ignored the First World War, focusing instead on the glamorous productions Ziegfeld created and portraying somewhat indulgently his personal infidelities and spendthrift ways. Cohan was a different person, obviously, but *Yankee Doodle Dandy* completely ignores his divorce, which would still have been a big deal for audiences then, and portrays him instead as a straight-on patriot. In both cases, the production numbers are anachronistic, deigned to suit the tastes and purposes of their own time rather than render accurately the entertainments of a bygone era.

The Second World War made demands of the American people that challenged assumptions about the roles of women, African Americans, and other minorities. Hollywood did not necessarily pick up on these during the war itself, but to the extent that attitudes toward women and minorities had to change, Hollywood's propaganda machine was ready. Connie Fields' film *The Life and Times of Rosie the Riveter* (1980) includes a lot of archival footage

---

[1] On Hattie McDaniel and other African American actors in *GWTW*, see Donald Bogle, *Toms, Coons, Mulattoes, Mammies and Bucks: An Interpretive History of Blacks in American Films* (New York: Continuum, 2003), 82–94.
[2] Robert Brent Toplin, *History by Hollywood: The Use and Abuse of the American Past*. Urbana: University of Illinois Press, 1996, 82–101.

presenting contemporary attitudes toward women in the workplace, first prodding women to work, then, as the war neared its end, prodding them back home. Fields' film also very effectively addresses questions of race in ways that films at the time mostly did not. For films from the time looking at women and the war, Mark Sandrich's *So Proudly We Hail* (1943) and Richard Thorpe's *Cry Havoc* (1943) both present the story of the nurses in the Philippines, women who served near the front lines and whose story was meant to inspire the public when the end still seemed a long way off and the outcome somewhat uncertain.

Many topics relating to the Second World War can be explored through movies, both from the time and made since. After more than sixty years, the Second World War continues to inspire filmmakers. Changing perspectives on the war and changing sensibilities in the population at large mean that the subject never stagnates. Because the justice of the cause has never been in dispute, unlike Vietnam or more recent engagements, movies about the Second World War are not as vulnerable to the kind of ideological pillorying that greets other films. And it was a very significant time in the U.S. and world history and can still be explored on many fronts.

During the war itself, the artistry and effectiveness of movies about the war varied greatly, but *Casablanca* (1942) is by another remarkable consensus the best of them all, perhaps because the American hero is suave and cosmopolitan, comfortable in an international milieu. *The More the Merrier* (1943) is a delightful comedy that captures life on the home front, in this case a crowded Washington, DC, bustling with wartime activity. Even the propaganda was pretty good, and Frank Capra's *Why We Fight* series is a good point of departure for an examination of propaganda that promoted the cause without insulting the intelligence.

Though Americans could feel good about fighting a war against dictators and not of their own making, it also brought out and in some cases challenged the prejudices that continued to affect American society, and one can explore wartime films for evidence of segregation and prejudice in that society and also ways in which racism shaped people's views of the conflict itself. Exploring this subject is not unpatriotic, but rather a vote of confidence in American values of free thought and free expression. It is also important to recognize that the internment of Japanese-Americans, the racial tensions that affected the wartime workplace, and the segregation of the armed forces, while inexcusable from today's perspective, paled in comparison to the racist world view and actions of the Nazis and the other Axis powers.

Students wanting to explore these topics should narrow the scope of the study to achieve the necessary depth of analysis. A student of mine wrote a very good paper about the portrayal of the Battle of the Bulge, one of the darkest moments for Americans fighting in Europe, in a series of films dating from the 1940s up to the present, the most recent being HBO's *Band of Brothers* (2001), an eight-part series on which Tom Hanks and Steven Spielberg worked with Stephen Ambrose. One of the more obvious differences among the films is the way in which violence has been portrayed over the years.

The discussion should focus not so much on whether *Saving Private Ryan* (1998) is a better film than *The Longest Day* (1962) as on what makes them different and how each is a product of its own time and a document of society's "memory" of the war at different points in time.

In the postwar period, a series of serious social issue films garnered much attention and praise; *The Lost Weekend* (1945), *The Best Years of Our Lives* (1946), and *Gentleman's Agreement* (1947), all of whom won the Academy Award for Best Picture, tackled alcoholism, war veterans returning to civilian life, and anti-Semitism, respectively. Film noir (literally French for black film but better translated as dark film) seemed to reflect a more cosmopolitan, worldly wise America, with its unsentimental approach to the darker side of life. Billy Wilder's *Double Indemnity* (1944) and Otto Preminger's *Laura* (1944) helped to kick off the trend in the United States, but like the term, the style emerged in France with films such as Marcel Carné's *Quai des Brumes* (1938) and *Le Jour se lève* (1939).

Hollywood, with varying degrees of candor, has turned the camera on itself and the entertainment industry in general, throughout its history. One of the more incisive treatments, Billy Wilder's *Sunset Boulevard* (1950), fits the film noir genre—snappy dialogue, dark tone, albeit with a little more humor than usual. It explored the film industry as it entered a period of decline. For the historian, it offers a retrospective glimpse at Hollywood's golden age, personified by the almost forgotten silent film star Norma Desmond (Gloria Swanson), and Hollywood's emerging sense of its own history. Its jaded and cynical look at "the biz" drew cries of treason from some of the studio bosses.

As the cold war set in, the studios became extremely skittish about controversy, especially as the House Un-American Activities Committee (HUAC) took on Hollywood. The blacklist damaged and destroyed careers of the Hollywood Ten and other individuals denounced as "red." Fearful of writers and directors with a critical perspective on contemporary life, the studios also were looking for ways to get Americans away from their new television sets and back into the theaters. The Bible was an uncontroversial source for several big-budget spectacles that drew upon special effects to recreate miracles, such as in *The Ten Commandments* (1956). It also could provide respectable cover for some pretty sexy stories as well, such as *Samson and Delilah* (1949), *David and Bathsheba* (1951), and *Solomon and Sheba* (1959), though the treatment depended a great deal on the director and the studio.

The atomic bomb, of course, intensified the rivalry between the United States and the Soviet Union and made the cold war that much more frightening for everyone. The McCarthy era did not lend itself to exploration of these fears directly, but fear in other forms could generate good box office, helping to explain the relationship between science fiction and the cold war. Robert Wise's *The Day the Earth Stood Still* (1951), discussed earlier, is a marvelous cold war document, but one needs to look further into the "B" movies to find the movies about werewolves and aliens that are so bad they are good.

Among the films taken most seriously today are Don Siegel's *Invasion of the Body Snatchers* (1956) and Fred Wilcox's *Forbidden Planet* (1956).

Both acclaimed and controversial, the director Elia Kazan (1909–2003) and his work are pivotal to the study of the cold war and the film industry in the late 1940s and early 1950s. He won his first Best Director Academy Award for *Gentleman's Agreement* (1947), and his second for *On the Waterfront* (1954), a film widely viewed as one of the best American films ever (American Film Institute ranked it #8) that plays out on one level as Kazan's defense for having cooperated with the HUAC. Hollywood was not entirely forgiving when the Academy honored Kazan with a lifetime achievement award in 1999. Few would dispute his talent and importance as a director though, and the fact that he made serious and challenging films in an era when courage was not in great supply in Hollywood. Irwin Winkler's *Guilty by Suspicion* (1991) recreated this era in a well-done but somewhat obvious film. An examination of Kazan, in contrast, brings out a more complex story, even if its central figure is less than heroic.

The 1950s were not all about avoiding issues, however. Films such as Sidney Lumet's *Twelve Angry Men* (1957) looked insightfully at the justice system and how it is supposed to work. Nicolas Ray's *Rebel Without a Cause* (1955) and Richard Brooks' *Blackboard Jungle* (1955) looked at youth culture and juvenile delinquency, and the latter film starred Sidney Poitier, whose career and story are integral to the history of blacks in American film. The Academy honored him in 1963 for a relatively gentle film, Ralph Nelson's *Lilies of the Field* (1963), but in the meantime he had made powerful films such as Stanley Kramer's *The Defiant Ones* (1958) and Daniel Petrie's *A Raisin in the Sun* (1961), and would go on to make important films such as Stanley Kramer's *Guess Who's Coming to Dinner* (1967) and Norman Jewison's *In the Heat of the Night* (1967) later in the 1960s.[3] Later stars such as Denzel Washington cite Poitier as the man who made their careers possible.

A number of films from the early 1960s make for interesting viewing today as manifestations of the progressive, liberal spirit that animated the Civil Rights Movement. Sidney Lumet, Stanley Kramer, John Frankenheimer, and other directors made a number of political dramas, even thrillers, that showed how government could become corrupted or even overtaken by undemocratic interests. No longer cowed by HUAC or McCarthyism, these directors through their films attempted to bring the discussion back around to the U.S. Constitution. Otto Preminger drew directly from the Constitution for the title of his 1962 film *Advise and Consent*, a look at the confirmation process that includes a surprising subject for a film of that era.

John Frankenheimer's *The Manchurian Candidate* (1962) was based on Richard Condon's novel of the same name. The novel, written in an over-the-top style that now seems dated, is still in print; it was reissued at the time of

---

[3] See Donald Bogle, *Toms, Coons, Mulattoes, Mammies and Bucks*, 175–183; 215–219.

211 Chapter 10 • Your Turn: Writing About History in Film **211**

the 2004 remake of the film, which shifted the story to the near future, looking back on the first Gulf War. The 1962 film was a closer adaptation, telling the story of a group of Americans captured in the Korean War and brainwashed to become killers. At the time, apocryphal stories of brainwashing circulated in American culture. In the film, one of the men, Raymond Shaw (Lawrence Harvey), has become a remote-controlled killer. As we observe the actions of his domineering mother (Angela Lansbury) and his McCarthy-like dolt of a stepfather, Senator Iselin (James Gregory), our assumption that Russian and Chinese communists control Raymond is challenged: while the "Commies" come off as friends, in the end, the greater menace comes from the lunatic enemies within. While the plot is clearly over the top, as is Frank Sinatra's performance as Bennett Marco, the man who figures everything out, the film nevertheless captures some of the essentials of cold war politics, with all its viciousness and opportunism. Frankenheimer directed another political thriller two years later, *Seven Days in May* (1964), that took the notion of a coup d'état a step further. Burt Lancaster plays General Scott, who leads a plot within the Pentagon to overthrow a cardigan-wearing President (Fredric March), preparing to sign a nuclear disarmament treaty with the Soviets, setting up the classic cold war dilemma of détente versus a hard-line approach to the Soviets. The screenplay, by Rod Serling, is an interesting exploration of cold war issues, as indeed were many episodes of his CBS television series *The Twilight Zone* (1959–1964). "Rod Serling's cold war" would make very good research topic.

The 1962, Cuban Missile Crisis brought the world to the brink of nuclear war, and a pair of films that appeared in 1964 confronted the fear that much of the world hard lived with since the advent of the nuclear arms race. The first of the two to appear, Stanley Kubrick's *Dr Strangelove or: How I Learned to Stop Worrying and Love the Bomb*, took a darkly comic approach to the portrayal of a nuclear Armageddon. Filmed in the early months of 1963 and released in January 1964, it won acclaim for Kubrick and its star Peter Sellers, in a brilliant triple role. *Fail-Safe*, in contrast, takes a grimly serious look at a situation in which a technological malfunction creates a situation where the United States and Soviet Union find themselves on an unstoppable course toward nuclear war. *Dr. Strangelove* was the greater commercial and critical success, but the similarities between the plots and the appearance of these films so soon after the Cuban Missile Crisis makes a study of the films together a good paper topic.

While *The Graduate* (1967) was hippie-free, the counterculture did show up in films of the later 1960s, and Dennis Hopper's *Easy Rider* (1969) is its iconic film. A couple of documentaries featuring the Rolling Stones, Jean-Luc Godard's *Sympathy for the Devil* (1968), and Albert and David Maysles and Charlotte Zwerin's *Gimme Shelter* (1970), provide another look. The Sixties, as we think of them, actually continued into the 1970s and lasted until the end of the Vietnam War.

The critical and commercial success of Arthur Penn's *Bonnie and Clyde* (1967) certainly owed something to its having captured something of its own

time, perhaps more so than the 1930s in which the film was actually set.[4]
Bonnie and Clyde also adopted to a degree the cool new look of the French
New Wave, a group of French filmmakers who aimed for a rougher look,
including jarring cuts, to remind viewers that they were watching film.
Many subsequent films would explore the underside of American life by
focusing on an antihero, a flawed if not downright criminal central character.
In William Friedkin's *The French Connection* (1971), Gene Hackman plays a
New York cop who plays almost as dirty as the drug dealers he is hunting
down. This award-winning film (Academy Awards for Best Picture,
Director, Actor, and Adapted Screenplay), also portrayed New York in a
harsh, gritty light, though John Schlesinger's *Midnight Cowboy* (1969) might
be cited as the first of a host of films to focus on the mean streets of that city.
Martin Scorsese, with films like *Mean Streets* (1973) and *Taxi Driver* (1976),
became the master of what almost be considered a subgenre of films about
decay, alienation, and crime in contemporary urban life. Sidney Lumet's *Dog
Day Afternoon* (1975)—based on a true story!—also bears mentioning in this
general category; it also drew large audiences and critical acclaim.

The Civil Rights Movement, aided by an unusually progressive U.S.
Supreme Court under Chief Justice Earl Warren, and Lyndon Johnson's
Great Society marked the apex of a wave of liberal reform in the 1960s, and
many films from the time reflect that liberal sentiment. Regardless of era,
few filmmakers share the outlook of America's most conservative people,
though they often are not as liberal as opponents make them out to be. The
money factor, meanwhile, also pushes the film industry toward the mainstream, as producers seek fare that will not alienate or offend audiences, at
least not in ways that will harm their moneymaking potential.

The cold war certainly had an impact on this era of liberal reform, and
in the form of the Vietnam War, helped to do it in. The Vietnam War itself did
not get a great deal of cinematic attention in its own time, except for John
Wayne and Ray Kellogg's *The Green Berets* (1968), which used John Wayne to
get audiences to associate it with a more popular war, namely the Second
World War. It also showed up in the background, on TV, in Richard Lester's
Petulia (1968). But the later 1970s brought on a relative rush of Vietnam-
themed movies, many of which were highly acclaimed: Michael Cimino's
The Deer Hunter (1978), Hal Ashby's *Coming Home* (1978), and Francis Ford
Coppola's *Apocalypse Now* (1979), followed in the 1980s by Oliver Stone's
Platoon (1986) and John Irvin's *Hamburger Hill* (1987) and Stanley Kubrick's
Full Metal Jacket (1987).

Political films from the 1970s included Alan J. Pakula's *The Parallax
View* (1974) and Sydney Pollack's *Three Days of the Condor* (1975), fictional
thrillers that interacted with the social and political realities of the time. The
biggest political film of the decade, however, was about a real-life political
scandal that undid a presidency. Pakula's *All the President's Men* (1976),

---

[4] Toplin has a chapter on this film in *History by Hollywood*, 128–153.

Francis Ford Coppola's *Apocalypse Now* (1979) presented a film about
Vietnam that was more metaphoric than historically specific, drawing upon
Joseph Conrad's *Heart of Darkness* to make his statement.
Source: Zoetrope/United Artists/The Kobal Collection.

starred Robert Redford as Bob Woodward and Dustin Hoffman as Carl
Bernstein, the *Washington Post* reporters who "followed the money" to
uncover the truth about the break-in at the Watergate Hotel in June 1972,
ultimately forcing the resignation of President Richard Nixon in August
1974. Appearing in April 1976, the film won the admiration of critics and did
well at the box office, making it a very significant cultural marker for the
decade and a remarkable success in presenting the history of the scandal so
soon after the fact. Nevertheless the film does sacrifice some facts for the
sake of creating a suspenseful and exciting film: how else would the film
have succeeded, given that everyone knew the end of the story? While some
good essays exist on this film's historical significance, it is still worthy of
study more than thirty years later.[5]

The 1970s also produced the summer blockbuster, movies made to draw
bored adolescents to theaters to see big-budget spectacles over and over. The
ones that became phenomenally successful proved to be more than just a two-
hour thrill ride, and the concept of the blockbuster itself is historically significant. These films made big money: while *Gone with the Wind* held the box
office record for 25 years until *The Sound of Music* took over, followed by *The
Godfather* (1972), the all-time box office champion would now change every
few years. Steven Spielberg's *Jaws* (1975) started the trend, becoming an

---

[5] See Toplin, *History by Hollywood*, 179–201, and William Leuchtenberg in Carnes, *Past Imperfect*,
288–291.

inextricable part of American (and world) culture in the summer of 1975. Two years later George Lucas' *Star Wars* (1977) overtook it, the first of a trilogy that audiences would flock to, dominating the box office again in 1980 and 1983. *Star Wars* also took the marketing of tie-in merchandise to an extraordinary level: children and their parents demonstrated an insatiable and enduring consumer appetite for *Star Wars* lunch kits, bed sheets, Halloween costumes, Lego, action figures, video games, clothing, and on and on. The release of the second trilogy (1999, 2002, and 2005) was also a huge commercial success on all fronts and included the revival of the original trilogy.

In the meantime, the Spielberg's Indiana Jones series (1981, 1984, and 1989), like *Star Wars*, revived the spirit of the adventure movies kids used to see in the 1930s, 1940s, and 1950s. The Indiana Jones movies were set in the past, with the bad guys being Nazis and their collaborators. The history was pretty cartoon-like, however, and clearly the films are not trying to make a historical statement. In general, these summer blockbusters are not easy to work with as historically significant, but it is not impossible. If you have seen *Star Wars* eighty times, you may in fact have a more difficult time than a less avid fan in teasing out its historical significance, which would lie in the nature of the fantasy world being created. Amid all the special effects, and sometimes encumbered by weak writing, *Star Wars* presents itself as myth, and the degree to which that myth reflects the time in which it was spun is where you would want to direct your scholarly attention.

The Reagan presidency and the (final, as it turned out) intensification of the cold war helped to define America in the 1980s. John Milius' *Red Dawn* (1984) and George Cosmatos' *Rambo: First Blood Part II* (1985) were violent right-wing cold war fantasies. *Red Dawn* was about an invasion of the United States by the Soviet Union and its allies, resulting in the occupation of a community in Colorado. Though panned by critics, it did fairly well financially and starred a group of young actors playing teenagers that form a guerilla group. Sylvester Stallone, taking a break from his successful *Rocky* series, played muscle-bound ex-Green Beret John Rambo, who pulls off a daring rescue of soldiers missing in action in Vietnam. *Rambo* played out a simplistic fantasy in which complicated international problems could be resolved through brute force or by a single hero. Critics derided both films, but both films did well commercially. Complexity was out, and one film that commented on this more thoughtfully was Hal Ashby's *Being There* (1979), the story of a simpleton elevated to greatness. Tony Scott's *Top Gun* (1986), another big moneymaker, starred Tom Cruise in an extended advertisement for the F-14 and the Navy's Fighter Weapons School. Oliver Stone's *Wall Street* (1987) explored the men at the top of the era's vaunted trickle-down economics. Another very 1980s movie, Mike Nichols' *Working Girl* (1988), showed that an ordinary woman (Melanie Griffith) could achieve the corporate success of her socioeconomic "betters" both on and off the job. As discussed earlier, the movie that might have become an iconic representation of the era was the adaptation of Tom Wolfe's *Bonfire of the Vanities* (1990), directed by Brian De Palma, worth studying as a prime example of a bomb.

In addition to *Grand Canyon*, other films from the early 1990s have begun to bear the marks of their times as separate from our own, a critical factor in using film to document the past. Jonathan Demme's film *Philadelphia* (1993) took a look at the AIDS crisis and the stigmas associated with AIDS and with homosexuality. Tom Hanks plays the lead role of Andrew Beckett, a lawyer who is fired by his firm when his colleagues learn of his illness. In the fine tradition of earlier social issue films, this film also can be examined as a cultural marker.

Today we are beginning to see movies that take up the war in Iraq directly or indirectly. For example, as Paul Haggis' *In the Valley of Elah* (2007) deals with the murder of an Iraq war veteran, and Brian De Palma's *Redacted* (2007) is about the brutality of the war itself. Stephen Gaghan's *Syriana* (2005) examines the worldwide oil industry. While Ridley Scott's *Black Hawk Down* (2001) is about Somalia in 1993, it is worth reviewing in light of more recent events, especially for its portrayal of the experiences of soldiers. A few films have taken up the events of September 11, 2001, most notably Paul Greengrass' *United 93* (2006), which manages to be suspenseful despite, or because, we know how it ends, and Oliver Stone's *World Trade Center* (2006), which focuses on the experiences of ordinary people directly affected by the attacks.

These are all potentially workable paper topics, and of course there are many more. The key is to identify a topic of interest, view one or more of the relevant movies, and begin your research in the relevant literature. Be sure to discuss your topic with your professor as well, to ensure that your research will deepen your understanding of the topic being explored in the course. Early on, it may be helpful to develop a contextual model for your project, a time line that maps the content, production, and reception of your films into a broader historical context. Regarding production, you should look at the artists and producers who made the film to determine as best you can their reasons for making the film. One of the most important questions to answer as a historian is how you can link the production of the film to the time and the environment in which it was made. In the case of *Philadelphia* (1993), for example, was this the first "major motion picture" about AIDS in America, which came to public awareness in the early 1980s? Why was Hollywood slow to respond, particularly since AIDS so strongly affected the arts community?

Regarding content, how does the film portray the issues of the time? What are the chief characteristics of the issues as they are presented? How do the characters and the story represent the realities that the film seeks to portray? How does the portrayal of the story and contemporary life differ from your own understanding of how these issues are understood or would be portrayed today? In other words, how realistic was the film, then and now? If it aims to be realistic and relevant, are there realities that it avoids or ignores?

Regarding reception, how did critics and audiences respond to the film? How did the film raise public awareness of the issues the film sought to portray? Did the film have any discernible impact on public awareness or attitudes toward the issue it portrayed? What is the historical significance of this film today? What events or developments have occurred since the film's making and initial reception that shape the way we look at them now?

Films about the past require a slightly different take on production, content, and reception, but again they are all critical to assessing the historical content of the film. Again, you will want to learn as much as you can about the producers' and filmmakers' intentions for the project, and specifically why this historical subject was chosen. It may well be that the right people shared an interest in a particular topic, but a good question to ask is whether the choice of a particular topic reflects in any way the spirit of the times. As noted above, the popularity of Elizabeth I in the films of the later 1930s may have had something to do with the need for a great leader as Britain faced another grave crisis. She seems to have enjoyed another revival in recent times. Even *The Lord of the Rings*, which of course is not history at all but fantasy, does bear links both to the time in which J. R. R. Tolkien wrote the books and in which Peter Jackson made the films. It may not be straight-out allegory in which the character and story actually represent people and events in real life, but it certainly captures a sense of the crisis and what the proper response to it looks like. No doubt Tolkien's conception of evil was shaped by the menace of National Socialism and other totalitarian ideologies in his own time, and more recently the films seemed to fit a time when the September 11 attacks and other crises in the post-cold war world contributed to a sense of malaise and menace in the world.

Even with extensive knowledge of the production process of a movie, you have to assess what appears on the screen on its own. This can be challenging. From various resources, you can learn a lot, for example, about the production of the *Godfather* movies, the first two of which are brilliant. The third film, *The Godfather: Part III* (1990), however, had some serious flaws that could be traced to the production process: the studio keeping Francis Ford Coppola on a short leash financially, the sudden departure of an actor set to play an important role; the substitution of a family member with virtually no acting experience in that role; and the elimination of Robert Duvall's character in favor of a lackluster substitute because Duvall was too expensive for the limited budget. The result was a movie unworthy of its two predecessors. Understanding the reasons for the film's relative weakness does not change the irrevocable fact of its cinematic inferiority.

Being able to assess the production and content of a movie both separately and together is important to understanding and assessing its reception. Regardless of all the information available to viewers about a movie before they ever see it, a movie cannot rely on that information to make its impact: the content must stand alone as a work of cinematic art. Nevertheless, viewers have the option to learn a great deal about a movie before they ever see it. We also must distinguish more and more between the release of the theatrical version of a movie and its DVD release. Entertainment magazines evaluate the feature separately from the additional materials included in the DVD release, and the content of the feature itself may not be exactly the same. Common features include a commentary track, allowing viewers to watch the film with the director and/or other key participants in the film's making, including actors. Normally a viewer would not first see a movie this way, since it interferes with the auditory experience of the movie itself. But often it is surprisingly interesting, and of course, it provides a lot of information about the production. DVDs also often include a documentary on the making of the movie, which vary greatly in length and quality. A "deleted scenes" feature allows viewers to extend the experience of watching a movie by seeing those scenes or parts of scenes that were cut out in the editing process to get the movie down to its desired length. These do not include *all* the footage edited out, but passages that the editor reluctantly had to cut out. One might also get "bloopers," footage that captures actors messing up their lines and other funny moments. A DVD release can get bad reviews for skimping on these extra features, which can extend the enjoyment of a film until everyone is too exhausted to go on.

You will want to view any film under discussion, probably several times, and take notes. The Internet generally contains an abundance of information about the production, content, and reception of all but the most obscure films. The "Sources" section that follows identifies a number of sites that will be helpful to you as you pursue your research. It also provides a strategy for identifying the print sources most relevant to your topic, both journal articles and books. While it cannot provide an exhaustive list of titles, it should serve as a research portal that will allow you to identify many of the resources you will need. This book has provided you with many issues and questions to explore as you pursue your study of history using film as a resource. Now you should be ready to put your knowledge to active use through your own research, analysis and writing.

11

■ ■ ■

Your Research Portal: Sources on History in Film

By now you realize that your own study of history in film will require substantial research in print and electronic materials. What follows is a guide to both primary and secondary materials that will help you to explore the production, content, and reception of the film material you are studying, as well as its historical context. You should identify and examine enough primary sources to make them the basis of an original work of scholarship. You also will want to find as many relevant secondary sources as you can to support your own insights with the work of those who have worked on your topic or related topics. The discovery of an article or book on *exactly* the same topic can be dismaying, but you may not have to start over: changing the focus of your research may still allow you to make use of the resources you have identified and studied.

HISTORY AND HISTORICAL CONTEXT

Almost any topic that you may choose to research will require an understanding of the relevant history, and the history that is relevant may be more or less obvious, depending on your topic. To state the obvious, you cannot rely on the film alone as your sole source of historical information, just as you cannot rely on any other single source. Generally speaking, you will need to know more both about the time and place being presented in the film and the historical context in which the film was made. To determine whether your topic is viable, you should scope out the resources that are relevant and available. Assuming that the scope of your paper will be limited to what you can discuss thoroughly and substantively in a shorter research paper, as opposed to a longer thesis, you do not want your topic to be so huge that doing a good job would require several months' worth of research; nor do you want a topic so slight or obscure that you will not be able to do adequate research to support your study.

In general, you want the topic of your paper to correspond to the subject of the course for which you are writing the paper, though in some cases that will still give you a wide variety of choice. For a course on the Second World War, you could explore films made about the war, as a way of exploring how the war is portrayed and remembered. You could explore films made during the war, as a way of exploring wartime society and culture. In theory, you could even explore films made during the war, but on a different historical subject, if that subject was somehow relevant to wartime society and culture—stirring the masses by making an appeal to a glorious past, for instance—though clearly that can get a little more complicated and would work better in some cases than in others.

If you choose to write on a single or several different portrayals of a historical event, you probably would not need to conduct primary research on the event itself. If you are writing about different film treatments of the D-Day invasion, for example, you will quickly find that many historians have written on the topic already: for example, John Keegan, Cornelius Ryan, and Stephen Ambrose. Indeed you would not need to look far to find works on the films themselves that comment on their historical accuracy: film reviews and journal articles, perhaps even books. So what can you contribute to the discussion? Of course, there is much more to discuss than a film's historical accuracy. Filmmakers have had different reasons to make films on the subject over the decades, and their portrayals in turn have marked the times in which their films were made. The 1962 film, *The Longest Day*, looks at how the Germans are portrayed, bearing in mind that they were our cold war allies at the time; when Steven Spielberg made *Saving Private Ryan* (1998) thirty-five years later, the cold war was over and, while Germany was still our NATO ally, the Holocaust had become a much more openly discussed and thoroughly explored subject.

GREAT WEB SITES

A research paper that draws entirely on Internet sources is probably not going to be very good. A student would have to make a pretty good case for neglecting print sources altogether, and the instructor may wonder if the whole project had not been pulled together the night before the due date, without so much as a trip to a library. But that would not be the Internet's fault, right? The Internet is in fact a tremendous help to scholars: in addition to helpful and reliable Web sites, it can give you access to your own library's resources: for example, without leaving my office, I can search for and read articles from a large variety of scholarly journals on JSTOR. Even some books can be read online: in writing about the Orson Welles film *The Magnificent Ambersons* (1942), I found a version of the Booth Tarkington novel online. You can also watch movies online with Netflix or similar services.

For scholarly purposes, any discussion of your topic that you find on the Internet should have undergone a process of peer review: that is, other scholars have assessed the material and found it to be of good quality: compelling analysis informed by research in the appropriate sources. Below are a number of Web sites that may be especially helpful, but first a cautionary note about a Web site that often shows up in student papers should be avoided: Wikipedia is a remarkable phenomenon, and you may find it very useful for other purposes, and you may even find it helpful in orienting yourself to a research topic, or filling gaps in your general knowledge that are tangential to your topic; but you should not rely on it as a secondary source, because it is not peer-reviewed and because you cannot attribute its information or arguments to a particular author or scholar.

The American Film Institute (www.afi.com) is a national institute dedicated, among other things, to preserving the heritage of American film. Periodically it complies *100 Best* lists that help document the reception of different movies as classics. A 2007 list of the greatest American films showed some changes from a similar survey done ten years. American Film Institute (AFI) also has its own research facility, the Louis B. Mayer Library, in Los Angeles and a theater and cultural center in Silver Spring, Maryland.

Academy of Motion Pictures Arts and Sciences (www.oscars.org). Best known as the people who give out the Oscars, the Academy also has its own research library, The Margaret Herrick Library in Beverly Hills, California. For research into the content, production, and reception of films, it is a gold mine, but it would require travel to the library itself to study its extensive collection of scripts, photographs, and magazines. It also has the records of the Production Code Administration of the Motion Picture Association of America, which documents the interaction of the film industry with contemporary social and political currents.

Box Office Mojo (www.boxofficemojo.com): A good source of factual information on the commercial success of movies both domestically and internationally, a significant factor in your assessment of a film's reception. This Web site, to a limited extent for older films, would enable you to compare how well the film you are researching performed compared to other movies in release at the time. More detailed information may be hard to attain, especially for older films.

Film and History (www.uwosh.edu/filmandhistory): In 1970, John E. O'Connor and Martin Jackson formed the Historians Film Committee, and O'Connor he subsequently founded the journal *Film and History*, which he edited for many years. He was followed in that role by Peter C. Rollins. The journal is now edited out of the University of Wisconsin–Osk Kosh, where Loren Baybrook is editor in chief. The journal takes up different themes in its issues, including war, sports, and science, so you may find that a particular issue helps you to orient yourself to your own research topic and point you toward many useful primary and secondary sources. The *Film and History* Web site contains many links that also will be useful in your research. The organization also sponsors a Film and History conference every other year, focusing on different themes that subsequently appear in the journal.

Film archive Web sites (http://academic.csuohio.edu/kneuendorf/content/archives/fa.htm): This page lists, with links, the principal film archives in the United States and Great Britain, mostly associated with major research universities across the country, though of course the Los Angeles area has the greatest concentration of materials. The Web sites for the different archives give researchers information about their collections, but making use of the resources most often requires a visit to the archive itself.

Film Reference (http://www.filmreference.com/index.html) is a very helpful Web site for researchers. The first link, movie reviews (http://www.movierevie.ws/) is one quick way to find reviews, but also to see if a film is available on DVD or VHS. Film Reference allows you to look up titles, directors, actors, and actresses and a wide range of topics, with many references to print sources.

The International Association for Media and History (IAMHIST; http://www.iamhist.org/) has a Web site that serves as a portal to many valuable resources, particularly from the United States, the United Kingdom, and Western Europe. IAMHIST is a major scholarly organization in the field of media and history, and that fact adds credibility to the resources referred to in the Web site. For more advanced scholars, the site also is a good source on scholarly conferences.

The Internet Archive Moving Image Archive (http://www.archive.org/details/movies): Researchers will find a vast trove of film materials of all kinds here, including some feature films, but mostly instructional films, propaganda, and other documentary material. Other parts of the Internet Archive may have useful materials as well. You could easily get sidetracked here with all the materials available, so be careful.

The Internet Movie Database (www.imdb.com) is a great resource for personal use. While it is not a scholarly reference, it is very useful as a source of information on the production, content, and reception of films. It includes information on pretty much any film or television show you can imagine, as well as any people involved directly or indirectly in moviemaking. You can also establish an account for free that gives you access to discussions about films. In a limited way, these provide evidence about a film's reception; unfortunately, some contributions are rude and, frankly, stupid, diminishing the quality of the discussion. The Web site also has more detailed information available in a section accessible with a paid account, but that is unnecessary for your purposes.

Metacritic (www.metacritic.com) is a great place to go for full-text reviews of films and data that summarize the critical reception of movies, television shows, and other media productions. There are other sources, such as *Rotten Tomatoes* (www.rottentomatoes.com) that provide much of the same information, but Metacritic is a little calmer in its approach and look than some of the others.

Turner Classic Movies (www.tcm.com), which runs classic movies of all kinds on a commercial-free cable network, has a Web site that contains a lot of useful information, including, of course, upcoming broadcasts.

FILM MATERIALS

The availability of the film for research has improved spectacularly with the advent of video, DVD, and the Internet. Virtually every film referred to in this text is available for you to watch at your convenience, resources permitting. Some foreign titles may be a little harder to find, and some older titles may be available only on VHS, or perhaps not at all. But what is available is amazing, certainly to those of us who remember the days before video. If your research involves viewing many films, a Netflix or similar kind of account is an invaluable resource. Otherwise your library or local video stores will have a wide selection of titles available for borrowing or rental. Though some titles are expensive to purchase, online retailers such as Amazon or Barnes and Noble, or local retailers can get you whatever you might like to have in your collection.

You can also do research using film in archives, and of course what you do will depend heavily on the availability of materials and how much time you have. Living near Hollywood in the Los Angeles area might appear to be an advantage, but the studios themselves are probably not the place to go. I have already mentioned AMPAS's Margaret Herrick Library in Beverly Hills. Additionally, the University of Southern California and the University of California Los Angeles have major film archives, and across the country, university libraries and state archives are worth checking out. In Washington, DC, the National Archives has a Motion Picture, Sound and Video Research Room. In general, to do archival research, it is helpful to have a letter of introduction from your professor and to do as much as you can beforehand to determine what the collection holds and what you need to do to get access to the materials. Archival research can be very time-consuming, so it is important to have a clear sense of direction and purpose if you choose this route. Another option is to explore what the archival film collections hold and see what topics the materials themselves might suggest. The potential reward of archival research is a project that is likely to be original and innovative. If you go on to do graduate work in history, archival research will become a vital part of your training and development as a historian, and undergraduate experience in the archives will be valuable both in and of itself and as something to cite on your graduate school applications.

The Internet has made archival research possible from your own desktop or laptop. The Internet Archive has an extensive moving images collection (http://www.archive.org/details/movies) that includes all kinds of nonfeature films, including what it calls *ephemeral films*, or films made for educational, instructional, or industrial purposes. It includes the Prelinger Archive and A/V Geeks, two large collections of ephemeral films on a wide variety of topics. As is the case with many primary sources, you may need to do additional research to determine both the provenance and significance of these film documents.

SECONDARY SOURCES

Whatever disdain scholars may once have had for commercial movies as a source of historical information and insight, today the study of film and history is a thriving field within the discipline. While political and military history once dominated the field, on the assumption that the exercise of power shaped the lives of people more than any other factor, today historians study all aspects of human experience. The first portion of this list is annotated, describing a number of *books* that are especially useful to understanding film and history in film. Following is a list of books that examine more specific topics; it is far from exhaustive, but gives you a sense of the literature. I have also listed two series that cover decades in American cinema by two different U.S. university presses; these may be helpful in considering the films you study against the larger body of work from that era. Finally, I have included a list of *journals* in which you can find scholarly articles relevant to your research. Databases such as JSTOR are very helpful for searching many journals at once for articles that are more than a few years old. Recently published materials may not yet be available, however, so you would need to check the most recent issues or indexes for recent years to complete your search. Journals listed here are film-related or general historical journals. Your topic may direct you to more specialized historical journals, which are numerous.

Reference and Methodology

Bordwell, David and Kristin Thompson, *Film Art: An Introduction*, 8th ed. New York: McGraw Hill, 2006. This book is the place to go for more detailed discussion of the elements of film discussed in Chapter 3.

Braudy, Leo and Marshall Cohen, editors. *Film Theory and Criticism: Introductory Readings*, 6th ed. New York: Oxford University Press, 2004. This book is one of many places to begin if your research agenda includes developing some familiarity with theory. If you were researching film portrayals of the West, for example, some genre theory, introduced here with readings, might stimulate your thinking. Or if you are examining the historical vision of a particular director celebrated for his or her distinctive style, for example, you may wish to explore what *auteur* theory has to say.

Carnes, Mark C., editor. *Past Imperfect: History According to the Movies*. New York: Henry Holt and Company, 1995. This book features sixty short essays on prominent historical films by well-known historians. The emphasis is strongly on American films on American history, but the book includes discussions of everything from *Jurassic Park* by Stephen Jay Gould to *Apocalypse Now* by Frances FitzGerald. Films discussed are too numerous to list here, but this book is worth looking up if a film you are studying might be in here, or if you are looking for films on a specific historical topic. It includes bibliographical references and a transcript of a conversation between historian Eric Foner and filmmaker John Sayles.

Cannadine, David, editor. *History and the Media*. New York: Palgrave Macmillan, 2004. Includes essays by Taylor Downing, Simon Schama, Jeremy Isaacs, Roger Smither, Melvyn Bragg, Tristram Hunt, Max Hastings, Ian Kershaw, John Tusa, Jean Seaton, and David Putnam. This book explores general issues of exploring history in film, but focuses on a particularly British phenomenon of presenting history on television. In recent years, some historians have become television stars in Britain with slickly presented documentary series. While no doubt this has fostered some jealousy among other historians, either less telegenic, brilliant, or shamelessly self-promoting, depending on one's point of view, the popularity of history on television raises significant questions for the future of the discipline.

Ellis, Jack. C and Betsy A. Mclane, *A New History of Documentary Film*. New York: Continuum, 2005. By no means the only book of this kind, this is a recent work that, if your research focuses on a particular documentary film or filmmaker, would help you understand and place your topic into a broader context.

Landy, Marcia C., editor. *The Historical Film: History and Memory in Media*. New Brunswick, NJ, 2001. Essays are divided into four sections. The first, "Regarding History," includes essays by Pierre Sorlin, Robert Rosenstone, George Custen, and Sue Harper. Custen's essay is an excerpt from his book on the biographical picture, or biopic. The section "History as Trauma" includes, among others, essays on the films *The Marriage of Maria Braun, Schindler's List, Walker*, and *Mississippi Burning*. The third section deals with postcolonialism in film, and includes an essay on Senegalese filmmaker Ousmane Sembene. The final section is on history and television and includes essays on the 1998 CNN *Cold War* series, Ken Burns' *Civil War*, and the impact of Errol Morris' work, particularly the *Thin Blue Line*.

Lewis, Jon, and Eric Smoodin, editors. *Looking Past the Screen: Case Studies in American Film History and Method*. Durham, NC: Duke University Press, 2007. This volume includes a series of essays on specific topics that serve as models of film scholars' approaches to the history of the medium. If you are examining a historical topic using film, your focus and emphases may be different, but the methodologies demonstrated here may be helpful.

O'Connor, John E., editor. *Image as Artifact: The Historical Analysis of Film and Television*. Malabar, Florida: Krieger, 1990. Including essays by leading film scholars, this book sets forth O'Connor's highly influential approach to studying history in film, focusing on content, production and reception.

Rollins, Peter C., editor. *The Columbia Companion to American History on Film: How the Movies Have Portrayed the American Past*. New York, Columbia University Press, 2003. Rollins, who for many years edited *Film and History*, describes this work in the introduction as "a collection of essays that explore how major eras, institutions, peoples, wars, leaders, social groups and myths of our national culture have been portrayed on film" (xi). The book is made up of more than seventy-five essays that discuss eras, regions, wars and other major events, famous people, ethnic and other groups, institutions and movements, places, themes and topics, and myths and heroes. Each essay includes a filmography and bibliography.

Sklar, Robert. *Film: An International History of the Medium*, 2nd ed. Upper Saddle River, NJ: Prentice Hall, 2002. People have described film as a universal language, and this is a great tool for beginning to understand movies as a global phenomenon. Lavishly illustrated, this book describes the development of the medium, the technological changes that have occurred over time, film milestones, movements, and "waves" in the industry worldwide, all in a single comprehensive volume.

_____. *Movie-Made America: A Cultural History of the American Movies*. New York: Vintage, 1994.

Tibbetts, John C., and Welsh, James M. *The Encyclopedia of Novels into Film*. Second Edition. New York: Checkmark Books, 2005. Literary adaptation is often the means by which history appears on screen, so this work is a very helpful place to begin to understand the relationship between the literary and the historical, in general and in specific works.

SCHOLARLY MONOGRAPHS AND COLLECTIONS OF ARTICLES ON FILM IN HISTORY

Though one need not be a cultural historian to make use of moving images as a historical resource, cultural historians can tell us a great deal about the presence and significance of moving images in American society over time. The following is a select list—short enough to be browsed—of scholarly monographs. The publishers of these works are mostly U.S. university presses. For obvious reasons, the University of California Press predominates, but almost all university presses publish historical works in which film is a significant factor.

Abel, Richard. *Americanizing the Movies and "Movie-Mad" Audiences, 1910–1914*. Berkeley and Los Angeles: University of California Press, 2006.

_____. *The Ciné Goes to Town: French Cinema, 1896–1914*. Berkeley and Los Angeles: University of California Press, 1998.

_____. *The Red Rooster Scare: Making Cinema American, 1900–1910*. Berkeley and Los Angeles: University of California Press, 1999.

Andrew, Dudley and Ungar, Steven. *Popular Front Paris and the Poetics of Culture*. Cambridge, MA: Belknap Press of Harvard University Press, 2005.

Bartov, Omer. *The "Jew" in Cinema: From the Golem to Don't Touch My Holocaust*. Bloomington: Indiana University Press, 2005.

Basinger, Jeanine. *The Star Machine*. New York: Knopf, 2007.

_____. *A Woman's View: How Hollywood Spoke to Women, 1930–1960*. New York: Knopf, 1993.

_____ and Jeremy Arnold. *The World War II Combat Film: Anatomy of a Genre*. Middletown, CT: Wesleyan University Press, 2003.

Benshoff, Harry M. and Sean Griffin. *America on Film: Representing Race, Class and Gender and Sexuality in the Movies*. Oxford: Blackwell, 2004.

Berger, Martin A. *Sight Unseen: Whiteness and American Visual Culture*. Berkeley and Los Angeles: University of California Press, 2005.

Bickford-Smith, Vivian and Richard Mendelsohn, editors. *Black and White in Colour: African History on Screen*. Athens: Ohio University Press, 2007.

Biesen, Sheri Chenin. *Blackout: World War II and the Origins of Film Noir*. Baltimore, MD: Johns Hopkins University Press, 2005.

Bodnar, John. *Blue-Collar Hollywood: Liberalism, Democracy and Working People in American Film*. Baltimore: Johns Hopkins University Press, 2003.

Bogle, Donald. *Toms, Coons, Mulattoes, Mammies and Bucks: An Interpretive History of Blacks in American Films*. New York: Continuum, 2003.

Braester, Yomi. *Witness Against History: Literature, Film and Public Discourse in Twentieth-Century China*. Stanford, CA: Stanford University Press, 2003.

Buscombe, Edward. *"Injuns!" Native Americans in the Movies*. London: Reaktion Books, 2006.

Decherney, Peter. *Hollywood and the Cultural Elite: How the Movies Became American*. New York: Columbia University Press, 2005.

Dittmar, Linda and Gene Michaud, editors. *From Hanoi to Hollywood: The Vietnam War in American Film*. New Brunswick, NJ: Rutgers University Press, 1990.

Doherty, Thomas. *Hollywood's Censor: Joseph I. Breen and the Production Code Administration*. New York: Columbia University Press, 2007.

_____. *Cold War, Cool Medium: Television, McCarthyism, and American Culture*. New York: Columbia University Press, 2003.

Dunaway, Finis. *Natural Visions: The Power of Images in American Environmental Reform*. Chicago, IL: University of Chicago Press, 2005.

Gerstner, David A. *Manly Arts: Masculinity and Nation in Early American Cinema*. Durham, NC: Duke University Press, 2006.

Graham, Allison. *Framing the South: Hollywood, Television and Race during the Civil Rights Struggle*. Baltimore, MD: The Johns Hopkins University Press, 2003.

Grieveson, Lee. *Policing Cinema: Movies and Censorship in Early Twentieth Century America*. Berkeley and Los Angeles: University of California Press, 2004.

Haskell, Molly. *From Reverence to Rape: The Treatment of Women in the Movies*. Chicago, IL: University of Chicago Press, 1987.

Heffernan, Kevin. *Ghouls, Gimmicks, and Gold: Horror Films and the American Movie Business, 1953–1968*. Durham, NC: Duke University Press, 2005.

Higashi, Sumiko. *Cecil B. de Mille and American Culture: The Silent Era*. Berkeley and Los Angeles: University of California Press, 1994.

Jelavich, Peter and Berlin Alexanderplatz. *Radio, Film and the Death of Weimar Culture*. Berkeley and Los Angeles: University of California Press, 2006.

Koepnick, Lutz. *The Dark Mirror: German Cinema between Hitler and Hollywood* Berkeley and Los Angeles: University of California Press, 2002.

May, Lary. *The Big Tomorrow: Hollywood and the Politics of the American Way*. Chicago, IL: University of Chicago Press, 2002.

_____. *Screening Out the Past: The Birth of Mass Culture and the Motion Picture Industry*. Chicago, IL: University of Chicago Press, 1983.

Mintz, Steven and Randy Roberts. *Hollywood's America: United States History through its Films*, 3rd ed. Boston, MA: Wiley Blackwell, 2001.

Nowell-Smith, Geoffrey. *The Oxford History of World Cinema*. New York: Oxford University Press, 1999.

Poshek Fu. *Between Shanghai and Hong Kong: The Politics of Chinese Cinemas*. Stanford: Stanford University Press, 2003.

Quart, Leonard and Albert Auster. *American Film and Society Since 1945*, 3rd ed. New York: Praeger, 2001.

Rollins, Peter C. *Hollywood as Historian: American Film in a Cultural Context*. Lexington: University Press of Kentucky, 1997.

Rollins, Peter C. and John E. O'Connor. *Hollywood's Indian: the Portrayal of the Native American in Film*. Lexington: University Press of Kentucky, 1998.

Rollins, Peter C. and John E. O'Connor. *Hollywood's West: The American Frontier in Film, Television and History*. Lexington: University Press of Kentucky, 2005.

Rollins, Peter C. and John E. O'Connor. *Hollywood's White House. The American Presidency in Film and History*. Lexington: University Press of Kentucky, 2005.

Rollins, Peter C. and John E. O'Connor. *Hollywood's World War I: Motion Picture Images*. Bowling Green: Bowling Green University Popular Press, 1997.

Rollins, Peter C. and John E. O'Connor. *Why We Fought: America's Wars in Film and History*. Lexington: University Press of Kentucky, 2008.

Rosenstone, Robert. *Visions of the Past: The Challenge of Film to Our Idea of History*. Cambridge: Harvard University Press, 1995.

Ross, Steven J. *Working-Class Hollywood: Silent Film and the Shaping of Class in America*. Princeton: Princeton University Press, 1999.

Sachsman, David B., Kittrell S. Rushing, and Roy Morris, Jr., editors. *Memory and Myth: The Civil War in Fiction and Film from* Uncle Tom's Cabin *to* Cold Mountain. West Lafayette, CT: Purdue University Press, 2007.

Smoodin, Eric. *Regarding Frank Capra: Audience, Celebrity and American Film Studies*. Durham, NC: Duke University Press, 2004.

Smyth, J.E. *Reconstructing American Historical Cinema: From* Cimarron *to* Citizen Kane. Lexington: University of Kentucky Press, 2006.

Sobchak, Vivian, editor. *The Persistence of History: Cinema, Television and the Modern Event*. New York: Routledge, 1995.

Toplin, Robert Brent. *History by Hollywood: The Use and Abuse of the American Past*. Champaign: University of Illinois Press, 1996.

_____. *Reel History: In Defense of Hollywood*. Lawrence: University Press of Kansas, 2002.

Wasson, Haidee. *Museum Movies: The Museum of Modern Art and the Birth of Art Cinema*. Berkeley and Los Angeles: University of California Press, 2005.

FILM HISTORY SERIES

Both Rutgers University Press and the University of California Press have produced series of books that explore decades or periods in American film.

History of the American Cinema. Berkeley and Los Angeles: University of California Press, 1994–2006. Ten volumes:

1. Musser, Charles. *The Emergence of Cinema: The American Screen to 1907*. 1994.
2. Bowser, Eileen. *The Transformation of Cinema, 1907–1915*. 1994.
3. Koszarski, Richard. *An Evening's Entertainment: The Age of the Silent Feature Picture, 1915–1928*. 1994.
4. Crafton, Donald. *The Talkies: American Cinema's Transition to Sound, 1926–1931*. 1999.

5. Balio, Tina. *Grand Design: Hollywood as a Modern Business Enterprise, 1930–1939.* 1996.
6. Schatz, Thomas. *Boom and Bust: American Cinema in the 1940s.* 1999.
7. Lev, Peter. *The Fifties: Transforming the Screen, 1950–1959.* 2006.
8. Paul Monaco. *The Sixties: 1960–1969.* 2003.
9. David A. Cook. *Lost Illusions: American Cinema in the Shadow of Watergate and Vietnam, 1970–1979.* 2002.
10. Prince, Stephen. *A New Pot of Gold: Hollywood under the Electronic Rainbow, 1980–1989.* 2002.

Friedman, Lester D. and Murray Pomerance, general editors. *Screen Decades: American Culture, American Cinema.* New Brunswick, NJ: Rutgers University Press, 2005–2007. This series includes:

Hark, Ina Rae, editor. *American Cinema of the 1930s: Themes and Variations.* New Brunswick, NJ: Rutgers University Press, 2007.

Dixon, Winston Wheeler, editor. *American Cinema of the 1940s: Themes and Variations.* New Brunswick, NJ: Rutgers University Press, 2005.

Pomerance, Murray, editor. *American Cinema of the 1950s: Themes and Variations.* New Brunswick, NJ: Rutgers University Press, 2005.

Grant, Barry Keith, editor. *American Cinema of the 1960s: Themes and Variations.* New Brunswick, NJ: Rutgers University Press, 2008.

Friedman, Lester D., editor. *American Cinema of the 1970s: Themes and Variations.* New Brunswick, NJ: Rutgers University Press, 2007.

Prince, Stephen, editor. *American Cinema of the 1980s: Themes and Variations.* New Brunswick, NJ: Rutgers University Press, 2007.

Journals
The American Historical Review
Cineaste
Film and History
Film Comment
Film Quarterly
The Historical Journal of Film, Radio and Television
Journal of American History
Literature/Film Quarterly

IDENTIFYING YOUR SOURCES

1. **What do you know, and what do you need to know:**
    *   Specifically about your topic and the film(s) related to it? More generally about the topic;
    *   More generally about the films: consider time period, genre.
2. **Identify and access** sources needed to address research questions.
    *   **Journal articles**: Use JSTOR and other databases, browse recent issues.
    *   **Books**: Search your library catalog, online book vendors for most recent titles. Rollins (see above) contains bibliographies for many topics in American history.
    *   **Online resources**: Peruse list provided in this section, search online for others.
    *   **Films**: For American history, check Rollins (see above) and other sources that identify films relevant to your topic of interest. Search online. DVD rental service such as Netflix or Blockbuster is immensely helpful for getting virtually anything available on DVD.
3. **Take charge** of your project, but consult with your reference librarians and your instructor early and as needed through the research process.

APPENDIX A

A Quick and Easy Guide to Citation

I recently read a student paper, written on an interesting topic and quite well organized, but when I started reading some very sophisticated analysis that I thought might have been a bit beyond the average undergraduate, I did a little checking and quickly found that the words indeed had been pulled from a Web site. Plagiarism, or the appropriation of the words and ideas of others without proper attribution, is dishonest and unprofessional. It assumes various forms, but this particular example seemed especially foolish to me, because discussing the opinions of film reviewers was completely appropriate to the paper topic. Quoting, discussing, and citing opinions as examples of the film's critical reception would have made the paper better than if the writer actually had ignored the critics and provided only his own assessment.

Writing a history paper involves extensive research using a variety of sources, including primary documents and secondary sources. Students have a lot of different habits with respect to documenting their research, and it may be that instances of plagiarism do result from carelessness, bad habits, or simply losing track of sources along the way. But it is still unacceptable. There is no one way to keep track of sources, but you will need a system, and developing that system is in itself a worthwhile, skill-building exercise.

Because of the variety of sources that historians use, both primary and secondary, they do not use the parenthetical citations you often find in other disciplines. Identifying a document and providing information as to where you found it can take up a bit of space, and you don't want your reader to forget what you were writing about. We therefore use footnotes or endnotes, marking the text itself only with a small superscript Arabic number at the end of the paragraph, like this.[1]

The superscript number corresponds to a numbered list, either at the bottom of the page (footnote) or at the end of the work (endnote), where you provide the full information on each reference. Make sure you know which of the two your instructor requires or prefers. A typical reference includes the author's name, the title of the work, publishing information, and page number. For example:

[1] Robert Sklar, *Movie-Made America: A Cultural History of American Movies* (New York: Vintage Books, 1994), 246.

Note that, unlike in the bibliography, the first name of the author goes first, the publishing information goes in parentheses, and items are separated by commas, not periods. The last number is the page number; we no longer use "p." or "pp." to indicate that (as in p. 5 or pp. 5–10). If you needed to cite Sklar further on in your paper, you would not need to repeat all the information. Scholars

---

[1] This is where a footnote would go. Again, make sure the numeral is Arabic, not Roman, which is sometimes the default setting for notes in Microsoft Word.

used to use terms like op. cit. and ibid., but that could get cumbersome and confusing. Now you simply pare subsequent references down to the essentials:

² Sklar, *Movie-Made America,* 294–295.

For the full reference, the reader can go back to the first reference, or get the full citation in the bibliography, which would look like this:

Sklar, Robert. *Movie-Made America: A Cultural History of American Movies.*
    New York: Vintage Books, 1994.

Note that, different from a footnote or endnote, in a bibliography entry the last name goes first and author, title, and publishing information are separated by periods. Format each entry as a single-spaced paragraph, using the hanging indent feature, and double space between entries.

    Quoting from a book is easy. Slightly more complex is quoting from a journal article, which you more than likely these days could find online. In the following citation, note that the journal article's title is placed in quotation marks, and that the film title and the journal title are both italicized, like book titles:

³ Thomas J. Knock, "'History with Lightning': The Forgotten Film *Wilson,*" *American Quarterly* 28(5) (1976) http://www.jstor.org (October 19, 2004), 539.

If you had found the article in a print version of the journal, you would not need to include the online reference, set off by < > marks, or the date accessed, noted in parentheses, though of course it is helpful in this case for your reader to know that the journal is accessible through JSTOR.

    You will no doubt have more questions as you document your sources carefully and conscientiously. *The Chicago Manual of Style,* a reference work of nearly 1,000 pages, available in print but also online, is a vital resource for history scholars, in which you can find anything you could ever possibly want to know about documentation. But the book requires a substantial investment, and as years pass between print editions, you are likely to find more up-to-date information online. For example, under "citation styles" in *online!* (www.bedfordstmartins.com/online), you can find most of the information you need. There are many other style guides you can find online, and your school may have its own version.

    A final note: Many of my students ask me how to quote a film. This is an interesting philosophical question in that it gets at the heart of how a movie is different from an article or a book. But whereas you could not cite numerically a specific scene of a movie you just saw at a movie theater or on videotape, you can cite a DVD more specifically, as in the following example:

⁴ 21."Fun and Games," *Joyeux Noël,* DVD, directed by Christian Carion (2005, Culver City, CA: Sony Pictures Classics Home Entertainment, 2006).

DVDs often used to include printed lists of scenes, but they rarely do anymore, so scenes, if named, are listed only in "scenes" off the main menu. Identifying the scene in this way is not essential, provided that your discussion is specific enough; but you should indicate the film's title, director, date, and studio. You also can quote from the bonus features, which often include interesting and helpful information about the production of the movie.

APPENDIX B

Films Discussed

Unless otherwise indicated, films are available on Region 1 DVD (United States, Canada, and some Caribbean islands).

DOCUMENTARY FILMS

Berlin: Symphony of a Great City. Germany: Walter Ruttmann, 1927.
The Civil War. USA: Ken Burns, 1990.
Cold War. USA: Jeremy Isaacs (producer), 1998. Unavailable on DVD (as of 2009).
Eyes on the Prize. USA: Henry Hampton, 1987.
Fahrenheit 9/11. USA: Michael Moore, 2004.
The Fog of War. USA: Errol Morris, 2004.
Harlan County USA. USA: Barbara Kopple, 1976.
Hearts and Minds. USA: Peter Davis, 1974.
Koyaanisqatsi. USA: Godfrey Reggio, 1982.
Night and Fog (*Nuit et Brouillard*). France: Alain Resnais, 1955.
The Plow That Broke the Plains. USA: Pare Lorentz, 1936.
The River. USA: Pare Lorentz, 1938.
Roger and Me. USA: Michael Moore, 1989.
Shoah. France: Claude Lanzmann, 1985.
The Sorrow and the Pity (*Le Chagrin et le pitié*). France: Marcel Ophüls, 1969.
The Thin Blue Line. USA: Errol Morris, 1988.
Triumph of the Will. Germany: Leni Riefenstahl, 1935.
Vietnam: A Television History. USA: Richard Ellison (producer), 1983.
The War. USA: Ken Burns, 2007.
The World at War. UK: Jeremy Isaacs (producer), 1974.
Why We Fight. USA: Frank Capra, 1943–1945.

NARRATIVE/FEATURE FILMS

The African Queen. USA: John Huston, 1951.
Alexander Nevsky. Soviet Union: Sergei Eisenstein and Dmitri Vasilyev, 1938.
All the President's Men. USA: Alan J. Pakula, 1976.
American History X. USA: Tony Kaye, 1998.
Amistad. USA: Steven Spielberg, 1997.
Annie Hall. USA: Woody Allen, 1977.
Apocalypto. USA: Mel Gibson, 2006.
The Apu Trilogy. India: Satyajit Ray, 1955–1959

> *Pather Panchali* ("Song of the Little Road"), 1955.
>
> *Aparajito* ("The Unvanquished"), 1956.
>
> *The World of Apu*, 1959.

Ararat. Canada/France: Atom Egoyan, 2002.

The Autobiography of Miss Jane Pittman. USA: John Korty, 1974.

The Aviator. USA: Martin Scorsese, 2004.

The Battle of Algiers. Algeria/Italy: Gillo Pontecorvo, 1966.

The Best Years of Our Lives. USA: William Wyler, 1946.

The Birth of a Nation. USA: D. W. Griffith, 1915.

Black and White in Color. Ivory Coast/France/West Germany/Switzerland: Jean-Jacques Annaud, 1976.

Black Girl (La Noire de . . .). France/Senegal: Ousmane Sembene, 1966

Bon voyage. France: Jean-Paul Rappenau, 2003.

The Bonfire of the Vanities. USA: Brian de Palma, 1990.

The Bounty. USA: Roger Donaldson, 1984.

Burnt By the Sun. Russia/France: Nikita Mikhalkov, 1994.

Cavalcade. USA: Frank Lloyd, 1933.

Casablanca. United States; Michael Curtiz, 1942

Citizen Kane. USA: Orson Welles, 1941.

City of God. Brazil: Fernando Meirelle and Kátia Lund, 2002.

Curse of the Golden Flower. China: Zhang Yimou, 2006.

The Day the Earth Stood Still. USA: Robert Wise, 1951.

Days of Heaven. USA: Terrence Malick, 1979.

Deliverance. USA: John Boorman, 1972.

Do the Right Thing. USA: Spike Lee, 1989.

Downfall. Germany: Oliver Hirschbiegel, 2004.

E.T.: The Extra-Terrestrial. USA: Steven Spielberg, 1982.

Evita. USA: Alan Parker, 1996.

Fanny and Alexander. Sweden/France/West Germany: Ingmar Bergman, 1982.

Flags of Our Fathers. USA: Clint Eastwood, 2006.

Forrest Gump. USA: Robert Zemeckis, 1994.

The Freshman. USA: Fred C. Newmeyer and Sam Taylor, 1925.

The Garden of the Finzi-Continis. Italy/West Germany: Vittorio De Sica, 1970.

Gentleman's Agreement. USA: Elia Kazan, 1947.

Glory. USA: E. Zwick, 1989.

The Godfather USA: Francis Ford Coppola, 1972.

The Godfather: Part II. USA: Francis Ford Coppola, 1974.

The Godfather: Part III. USA: Francis Ford Coppola, 1990.

Gone with the Wind. USA: Victor Fleming, 1939.

Good Bye Lenin! Germany: Wolfgang Becker, 2003.

The Graduate. USA: Mike Nichols, 1967.

Grand Canyon. Lawrence Kasdan, 1991.

The Grapes of Wrath. USA: John Ford, 1940.

The Great Ziegfeld. USA: Robert Z. Leonard, 1936

Hairspray. USA: John Waters, 1988.

Hairspray. USA: Adam Shankman, 2007.

Imitation of Life. USA: John M. Stahl, 1934.

Imitation of Life. USA: Douglas Sirk, 1959.

Indochine. France: Regis Wargnier, 1992.

JFK. USA: Oliver Stone, 1991.

Katyn. Poland: Andrzej Wajda, 2007.

The Lady Vanishes. UK: Alfred Hitchcock, 1938.

The Last King of Scotland. USA: Kevin Macdonald, 2006.

Like Water for Chocolate. Mexico: Alfonso Arau, 1992.

The Lives of Others. Germany: Florian Henckel von Donnersmarck, 2006.

Letters from Iwo Jima. USA: Clint Eastwood, 2006.

Life and Nothing But. France: Bertrand Tavernier, 1989.

The Long Walk Home. USA: Richard Pearce, 1990.

The Magnificent Ambersons. USA: Orson Welles, 1942.

Malcolm X. USA: Spike Lee, 1992.

The Marriage of Maria Braun. Germany: Rainer Werner Fassbinder, 1979.

Master and Commander: The Far Side of the World. USA: Peter Weir, 2003.

Matewan. USA: John Sayles, 1987.

Max Havelaar. Netherlands: Fons Rademakers, 1976. Region 1 DVD unavailable (2008).

My Man Godfrey. USA: Gregory La Cava, 1936.

Missing. USA: Costa-Gavras, 1982.

The Mission. UK: Roland Joffé, 1986.

Mississippi Burning. USA: Alan Parker, 1988.

Moolaadé. Senegal/France/Burkina Faso/Cameroon/Morocco/Tunisia: Ousmane Sembene, 2004.

The Motorcycle Diaries. Argentina/USA/Cuba/Germany/Mexico/UK/Chile/Peru/France: Walter Salles, 1984.

Mutiny on the Bounty. USA: Frank Lloyd, 1935.

Mutiny on the Bounty. USA: Lewis Milestone, 1962.

Nowhere in Africa. Germany: Caroline Link, 2001.

October (Ten Days That Shook the World). Soviet Union: Grigori Aleksandrov and Sergei Eisenstein, 1928.

The Official Story. Argentina: Luis Puenzo, 1985.

Pixote. Brazil: Hector Babenco, 1980.

The Queen. UK: Stephen Frears, 2006.

Quilombo. Brazil: Carlos Diegues, 1984.

Ragtime. USA: Milos Forman, 1981.

The Real Glory. USA: Henry Hathaway, 1939.

Rebel Without a Cause. USA: Nicholas Ray, 1955.

Reds. USA: Warren Beatty, 1981.

The Remains of the Day. UK/USA: James Ivory, 1993.

The Return of Martin Guerre. France: Daniel Vigne, 1982.

Schindler's List. United States: Steven Spielberg, 1993.

Saving Private Ryan. USA: Steven Spielberg, 1998.

The Searchers. USA: John Ford, 1956.

Seven Samurai. Japan: Akira Kurosawa, 1954.

Since You Went Away. USA: John Cromwell, 1944.

Stagecoach. USA: John Ford, 1939.

To Kill a Mockingbird. USA: Robert Mulligan, 1962.

The Tree of Wooden Clogs. Italy: Ermanno Olmi, 1978.

The Ugly American. USA: George Englund, 1963.

La Vie en rose (French title: *La Môme*). France: Olivier Dahan, 2007.

The Wild Bunch. USA: Sam Peckinpah, 1969.

Yankee Doodle Dandy. USA: Michael Curtiz, 1942.

Young Mr. Lincoln. USA: John Ford, 1939.

300. USA: Zack Snyder, 2006.

1900. Italy/France/West Germany: Bernardo Bertolucci, 1976.

INDEX

CPSIA information can be obtained
at www.ICGtesting.com
Printed in the USA
FFOW02n1626080118
44422480-44175FF